D0237064

RUSSIA

UKRAINE
MOLDOVA

TURKEY

CYPRUS

LIBYA

EGYPT

CHAD

SUDAN

CAR

CONGO-BRAZ
CONGO

ANGOLA

ZAMBIA

NAMIBIA

BOT

SOUTH
AFRICA

LESOTHO

SWAZ

ZIMB

MOZ

MALAWI

TANZANIA

SOMALIA

ETHIOPIA

DJIB

ERITREA

YEMEN

SAUDI
ARABIA

OMAN

UAE

QATAR

KUWAIT

IRAQ

IRAN

GEORGIA

ARM

AZER

TURKMEN

TAJIK

KIRGIZ

UZBEK

AFGH

PAKISTAN

INDIA

NEPAL

BHU

B'DESH

MYANMAR

SRI
LANKA

THAILAND

LAOS

CAMBODIA

VIETNAM

MALAYSIA

SING

BRUNEI

INDONESIA

HONG
KONG

MACAO

TAIWAN

PHILIPPINES

CHINA

MONGOLIA

KAZAKHSTAN

N. KOREA

S. KOREA

JAPAN

PAPUA
NEW GUINEA

AUSTRALIA

NEW ZEALAND

FIJI

SYRIA

LEB

ISR

JOR

TURKEY

UGAN

KENYA

MADAGASCAR

MAURITIUS

RUSSIA

The
Economist

Pocket
World in
Figures

2011 Edition

THE ECONOMIST IN ASSOCIATION WITH
PROFILE BOOKS LTD

Published by Profile Books Ltd,
3A Exmouth House, Pine Street, London EC1R OJH

This edition published by Profile Books in association with
The Economist, 2010

Material researched and compiled by
Andrea Burgess, Mark Doyle, Ian Emery, Andrew Gilbert,
Conrad Heine, Carol Howard, David McKelvey, Jane Shaw,
Roxana Willis, Christopher Wilson, Simon Wright

The greatest care has been taken in compiling this book. However,
no responsibility can be accepted by the publishers or compilers
for the accuracy of the information presented.

Typeset in Officina by MacGuru Ltd
info@macguru.org.uk

Printed in Italy by
Graphicom

A CIP catalogue record for this book is available
from the British Library

ISBN 978 1 84668 372 5

Contents

109 Part II   Country Profiles

Notes

This 2011 edition of *The Economist Pocket World in Figures*
includes new rankings on such diverse topics as internet use,
the minimum wage, forestation, car production, the Winter
Olympics, robberies and class sizes. The world rankings
consider 193 countries; all those with a population of at least
1m or a GDP of at least $1bn; they are listed on pages 250–54.
The country profiles cover 67 major countries. Also included
are profiles of the euro area and the world. The extent and
quality of the statistics available varies from country to
country. Every care has been taken to specify the broad
definitions on which the data are based and to indicate cases
where data quality or technical difficulties are such that
interpretation of the figures is likely to be seriously affected.
Nevertheless, figures from individual countries may differ
from standard international statistical definitions. The term
"country" can also refer to territories or economic entities.

Some country definitions

Macedonia is officially known as the Former Yugoslav Republic
of Macedonia. Data for Cyprus normally refer to Greek Cyprus
only. Data for China do not include Hong Kong or Macau. For
countries such as Morocco they exclude disputed areas.
Congo-Kinshasa refers to the Democratic Republic of Congo,
formerly known as Zaire. Congo-Brazzaville refers to the other
Congo. Data for the EU refer to the 27 members as at
January 1 2007, unless otherwise noted. Euro area data
normally refer to the 15 members that had adopted the euro
as at December 31 2008: Austria, Belgium, Cyprus, France,
Finland, Germany, Greece, Ireland, Italy, Luxembourg, Malta,
Netherlands, Portugal, Slovenia and Spain. For more
information about the EU and the euro area see page 248.

Statistical basis

The all-important factor in a book of this kind is to be able to
make reliable comparisons between countries. Although this
is never quite possible for the reasons stated above, the best
route, which this book takes, is to compare data for the same
year or period and to use actual, not estimated, figures
wherever possible. In some cases, only OECD members are
considered. Where a country's data is excessively out of date,
it is excluded. The research for this edition of *The Economist
Pocket World in Figures* was carried out in 2010 using the latest
available sources that present data on an internationally
comparable basis.

Data in the country profiles, unless otherwise indicated, refer to the year ending December 31 2008. Life expectancy , crude birth, death and fertility rates are based on 2005–10 averages; human development indices and energy data are for 2007; marriage and divorce, employment, health and education data refer to the latest year for which figures are available; internet hosts are as at January 2010.

Other definitions

Data shown in country profiles may not always be consistent with those shown in the world rankings because the definitions or years covered can differ.

Statistics for principal exports and principal imports are normally based on customs statistics. These are generally compiled on different definitions to the visible exports and imports figures shown in the balance of payments section.

Definitions of the statistics shown are given on the relevant page or in the glossary on pages 248–9. Figures may not add exactly to totals, or percentages to 100, because of rounding or, in the case of GDP, statistical adjustment. Sums of money have generally been converted to US dollars at the official exchange rate ruling at the time to which the figures refer.

Energy consumption data are not always reliable, particularly for the major oil producing countries; consumption per head data may therefore be higher than in reality. Energy exports can exceed production and imports can exceed consumption if transit operations distort trade data or oil is imported for refining and re-exported.

Abbreviations

bn	billion (one thousand million)	ha	hectare
EU	European Union	m	million
kg	kilogram	PPP	Purchasing power parity
km	kilometre	TOE	tonnes of oil equivalent
GDP	Gross domestic product	trn	trillion (one thousand billion)
GNI	Gross national income	...	not available

World
rankings

Countries: natural facts

Countries: *the largest[a]*
'000 sq km

1	Russia	17,075	31	Tanzania	945
2	Canada	9,971	32	Nigeria	924
3	China	9,561	33	Venezuela	912
4	United States	9,373	34	Namibia	824
5	Brazil	8,512	35	Pakistan	804
6	Australia	7,682	36	Mozambique	799
7	India	3,287	37	Turkey	779
8	Argentina	2,767	38	Chile	757
9	Kazakhstan	2,717	39	Zambia	753
10	Sudan	2,506	40	Myanmar	677
11	Algeria	2,382	41	Afghanistan	652
12	Congo	2,345	42	Somalia	638
13	Saudi Arabia	2,200	43	Central African Rep	622
14	Greenland	2,176	44	Ukraine	604
15	Mexico	1,973	45	Madagascar	587
16	Indonesia	1,904	46	Kenya	583
17	Libya	1,760	47	Botswana	581
18	Iran	1,648	48	France	544
19	Mongolia	1,565	49	Yemen	528
20	Peru	1,285	50	Thailand	513
21	Chad	1,284	51	Spain	505
22	Niger	1,267	52	Turkmenistan	488
23	Angola	1,247	53	Cameroon	475
24	Mali	1,240	54	Papua New Guinea	463
25	South Africa	1,226	55	Sweden	450
26	Colombia	1,142	56	Morocco	447
27	Ethiopia	1,134		Uzbekistan	447
28	Bolivia	1,099	58	Iraq	438
29	Mauritania	1,031	59	Paraguay	407
30	Egypt	1,000	60	Zimbabwe	391

Mountains: *the highest[b]*

	Name	Location	Height (m)
1	Everest	China-Nepal	8,848
2	K2 (Godwin Austen)	China-Jammu and Kashmir	8,611
3	Kangchenjunga	India-Nepal	8,586
4	Lhotse	China-Nepal	8,516
5	Makalu	China-Nepal	8,463
6	Cho Oyu	China-Nepal	8,201
7	Dhaulagiri	Nepal	8,167
8	Manaslu	Nepal	8,163
9	Nanga Parbat	Jammu and Kashmir	8,126
10	Annapurna I	Nepal	8,091
11	Gasherbrum I	China-Jammu and Kashmir	8,068
12	Broad Peak	China-Jammu and Kashmir	8,047
13	Gasherbrum II	China-Jammu and Kashmir	8,035
14	Xixabangma Feng	China	8,012

a Includes freshwater.
b Includes separate peaks which are part of the same massif.

Rivers: *the longest*

Name	Location	Length (km)
1 Nile	Africa	6,695
2 Amazon	South America	6,516
3 Yangtze	Asia	6,380
4 Mississippi-Missouri system	North America	5,959
5 Ob'-Irtysh	Asia	5,568
6 Yenisey-Angara-Selanga	Asia	5,550
7 Huang He (Yellow)	Asia	5,464
8 Congo	Africa	4,667
9 Rio de la Plata-Paraná	South America	4,500
10 Irtysh	Asia	4,440

Deserts: *the largest*

Name	Location	Area ('000 sq km)
1 Sahara	Northern Africa	8,600
2 Arabian	SW Asia	2,300
3 Gobi	Mongolia/China	1,166
4 Patagonian	Argentina	673
5 Great Victoria	W and S Australia	647
6 Great Basin	SW United States	492
7 Chihuahuan	N Mexico	450
8 Great Sandy	W Australia	400

Lakes: *the largest*

Name	Location	Area ('000 sq km)
1 Caspian Sea	Central Asia	371
2 Superior	Canada/US	82
3 Victoria	E Africa	69
4 Huron	Canada/US	60
5 Michigan	US	58
6 Tanganyika	E Africa	33
7 Baikal	Russia	31
Great Bear	Canada	31

Islands: *the largest*

Name	Location	Area ('000 sq km)
1 Greenland	North Atlantic Ocean	2,176
2 New Guinea	South-west Pacific Ocean	809
3 Borneo	Western Pacific Ocean	746
4 Madagascar	Indian Ocean	587
5 Baffin	North Atlantic Ocean	507
6 Sumatra	North-east Indian Ocean	474
7 Honshu	Sea of Japan-Pacific Ocean	227
8 Great Britain	Off coast of north-west Europe	218

Notes: Estimates of the lengths of rivers vary widely depending on eg, the path to take through a delta. The definition of a desert is normally a mean annual precipitation value equal to 250ml or less. Australia is defined as a continent rather than an island.

Population: size and growth

Largest populations
Millions, 2008

1	China	1,336.3	34	Poland	38.0
2	India	1,186.2	35	Algeria	34.4
3	United States	308.8	36	Canada	33.2
4	Indonesia	234.3	37	Uganda	31.9
5	Brazil	194.2	38	Morocco	31.6
6	Pakistan	167.0	39	Iraq	29.5
7	Bangladesh	161.3	40	Nepal	28.8
8	Nigeria	151.5	41	Afghanistan	28.2
9	Russia	141.8		Peru	28.2
10	Japan	127.9	43	Venezuela	28.1
11	Mexico	107.8	44	Uzbekistan	27.8
12	Philippines	89.7	45	Malaysia	27.0
13	Vietnam	88.5	46	Saudi Arabia	25.3
14	Ethiopia	85.2	47	Ghana	23.9
15	Germany	82.5		North Korea	23.9
16	Egypt	76.8	49	Yemen	23.1
17	Turkey	75.8	50	Taiwan	22.9
18	Iran	72.2	51	Mozambique	21.8
19	Congo-Kinshasa	64.7	52	Romania	21.3
20	Thailand	64.3	53	Australia	21.0
21	France	61.9	54	Syria	20.4
22	United Kingdom	61.0	55	Madagascar	20.2
23	Italy	58.9	56	Côte d'Ivoire	19.6
24	Myanmar	49.2	57	Sri Lanka	19.4
25	South Africa	48.8	58	Cameroon	18.9
26	South Korea	48.4	59	Angola	17.5
27	Colombia	46.7	60	Chile	16.8
28	Ukraine	45.9	61	Netherlands	16.5
29	Spain	44.6	62	Kazakhstan	15.5
30	Tanzania	41.5	63	Burkina Faso	15.2
31	Argentina	39.9	64	Cambodia	14.7
32	Sudan	39.4		Niger	14.7
33	Kenya	38.6	66	Malawi	14.3

Largest populations
Millions, 2050

1	India	1,614	15	Vietnam	112
2	China	1,417	16	Tanzania	109
3	United States	404	17	Japan	102
4	Pakistan	335	18	Iran	97
5	Nigeria	289		Turkey	97
6	Indonesia	288	20	Uganda	91
7	Bangladesh	222	21	Kenya	85
8	Brazil	219	22	Sudan	76
9	Ethiopia	174	23	Afghanistan	74
10	Congo-Kinshasa	148	24	Thailand	73
11	Philippines	146	25	United Kingdom	72
12	Egypt	130	26	Germany	71
13	Mexico	129	27	France	68
14	Russia	116	28	Iraq	64

Fastest growing populations
Average annual % change, 2005–10

1	Qatar	10.65	25	Kenya	2.64
2	Liberia	4.14	26	Senegal	2.62
3	Niger	3.86	27	Equatorial Guinea	2.60
4	Afghanistan	3.45	28	Ethiopia	2.59
5	Burkina Faso	3.39	29	Singapore	2.51
6	Timor-Leste	3.33	30	Guatemala	2.47
7	Uganda	3.27		Togo	2.47
8	Syria	3.26	32	Kuwait	2.44
9	West Bank and Gaza	3.18	33	Zambia	2.43
10	Benin	3.15	34	Kosovo	2.40
11	Eritrea	3.10		Mauritania	2.40
12	Jordan	3.02	36	Mali	2.37
13	Burundi	2.88		Papua New Guinea	2.37
	Tanzania	2.88	38	Mozambique	2.33
15	Yemen	2.86		Nigeria	2.33
16	United Arab Emirates	2.82	40	Macau	2.32
17	Malawi	2.78	41	Côte d'Ivoire	2.28
18	Chad	2.77	42	Somalia	2.27
19	Congo-Kinshasa	2.76	43	Cameroon	2.26
20	Gambia	2.75		Guinea	2.26
21	Madagascar	2.69	45	Guinea-Bissau	2.24
22	Angola	2.67	46	Sudan	2.20
	Rwanda	2.67	47	Iraq	2.17
	Sierra Leone	2.67	48	Pakistan	2.16

Slowest growing populations
Average annual % change, 2005–10

1	Georgia	-1.13	24	Armenia	0.17
2	Moldova	-1.00	25	Channel Islands	0.19
3	Lithuania	-0.97	26	Greece	0.22
4	Ukraine	-0.65	27	Denmark	0.24
5	Bulgaria	-0.64		Slovenia	0.24
6	Belarus	-0.47	29	Bermuda	0.25
7	Latvia	-0.46	30	Barbados	0.26
8	Romania	-0.42	31	Zimbabwe	0.27
9	Russia	-0.40	32	Uruguay	0.28
10	Hungary	-0.21	33	Portugal	0.35
11	Croatia	-0.15	34	Albania	0.37
12	Bosnia	-0.12		Austria	0.37
13	Estonia	-0.11		Malta	0.37
14	Germany	-0.09	37	Finland	0.38
15	Poland	-0.08		Trinidad & Tobago	0.38
16	Japan	-0.07	39	Martinique	0.39
	Virgin Islands (US)	-0.07		North Korea	0.39
18	Serbia	-0.06		South Korea	0.39
19	Cuba	0.02	42	Netherlands	0.41
20	Montenegro	0.03		Switzerland	0.41
21	Greenland	0.04	44	Czech Republic	0.42
22	Macedonia	0.08	45	Puerto Rico	0.43
23	Slovakia	0.10	46	El Salvador	0.44

Population: matters of breeding

Crude birth rates

Births per 1,000 population, 2005–10

Highest		Lowest	
1 Niger	54.1	1 Germany	8.1
2 Burkina Faso	47.8	2 Hong Kong	8.2
3 Afghanistan	46.6	Japan	8.2
4 Uganda	46.3	Singapore	8.2
5 Chad	45.8	5 Macau	8.3
6 Congo-Kinshasa	45.1	6 Malta	9.0
7 Somalia	44.2	Taiwan	9.0
8 Zambia	43.2	8 Austria	9.1
9 Angola	42.9	9 Bosnia	9.2
10 Mali	42.8	10 Italy	9.3
11 Tanzania	41.6	11 Channel Islands	9.4
12 Guinea-Bissau	41.4	12 Lithuania	9.5
13 Rwanda	41.0	South Korea	9.5
14 Malawi	40.5	14 Bulgaria	9.6
15 Sierra Leone	40.4	Croatia	9.6
16 Timor-Leste	40.2	Slovenia	9.6
17 Nigeria	40.1	17 Greece	9.7
18 Guinea	39.9	Switzerland	9.7
19 Benin	39.6	19 Poland	9.8
20 Mozambique	39.5	20 Hungary	9.9
21 Kenya	39.0	Portugal	9.9
22 Senegal	38.8	Ukraine	9.9
23 Ethiopia	38.6	23 Andorra	10.0
Liberia	38.6	Belarus	10.0
25 Equatorial Guinea	38.0	Romania	10.0
26 Eritrea	37.3	26 Latvia	10.1

Women[a] who use modern methods of contraception[b]

2007, highest, %		2007, lowest, %	
1 China	86.2	1 Somalia	1.2
2 Norway	82.2	2 Chad	1.7
3 United Kingdom	82.0	3 Guinea	4.0
4 Hong Kong	79.8	4 Angola	4.5
Thailand	79.8	5 Niger	5.0
6 Switzerland	77.5	6 Eritrea	5.1
7 France	76.5	7 Sudan	5.7
8 Finland	75.4	8 Congo-Kinshasa	5.8
9 Uruguay	75.0	9 Benin	5.9
10 South Korea	74.5	10 Sierra Leone	6.0
11 Belgium	72.9	11 Equatorial Guinea	6.1
12 Virgin Islands (US)	72.6	Guinea-Bissau	6.1
13 New Zealand	72.3	13 Mali	6.3
14 Puerto Rico	72.2	14 Timor-Leste	7.0
15 Canada	72.0	15 Côte d'Ivoire	8.0
Denmark	72.0	Mauritania	8.0
17 Cuba	71.6	17 Burundi	8.5

a Married women aged 15–49.
b Excludes traditional methods of contraception, such as the rhythm method.

Fertility rates, 2010–15
Average number of children per woman

Highest			Lowest		
1	Niger	7.15	1	Macau	0.95
2	Afghanistan	6.63	2	China	1.02
3	Timor-Leste	6.53		Hong Kong	1.02
4	Somalia	6.40	4	Taiwan	1.10
5	Uganda	6.38	5	Bosnia	1.21
6	Chad	6.20	6	South Korea	1.22
7	Congo-Kinshasa	6.07	7	Malta	1.26
8	Burkina Faso	5.95	8	Japan	1.27
9	Zambia	5.87		Poland	1.27
10	Angola	5.79		Singapore	1.27
11	Guinea-Bissau	5.73	11	Belarus	1.28
12	Malawi	5.59		Slovakia	1.28
13	Tanzania	5.58	13	Ukraine	1.31
14	Benin	5.49	14	Germany	1.32
	Mali	5.49		Romania	1.32
16	Guinea	5.45	16	Lithuania	1.34
17	Rwanda	5.43	17	Hungary	1.35
18	Ethiopia	5.38	18	Slovenia	1.36
19	Equatorial Guinea	5.36	19	Russia	1.37
20	Nigeria	5.32	20	Austria	1.38
21	Yemen	5.30		Greece	1.38
22	Sierra Leone	5.22		Italy	1.38
23	Liberia	5.15		Portugal	1.38
24	Mozambique	5.11	24	Bulgaria	1.40
25	Gambia	5.10		Latvia	1.40
26	West Bank and Gaza	5.09	26	Czech Republic	1.41

Sex ratio, males per 100 females, 2010

Highest			Lowest		
1	Qatar	306.9	1	Ukraine	85.5
2	United Arab Emirates	203.6	2	Estonia	85.6
3	Kuwait	146.1		Latvia	85.6
4	Bahrain	134.4	4	Russia	85.8
5	Oman	129.0	5	Netherlands Antilles	86.4
6	Saudi Arabia	120.7	6	Belarus	86.8
7	Greenland	113.0	7	Armenia	87.3
8	Bhutan	111.4	8	Lithuania	88.1
9	Andorra	110.0	9	Martinique	88.4
10	China	107.9	10	Georgia	88.7
11	Afghanistan	107.4	11	El Salvador	89.1
12	Faroe Islands	107.0	12	Lesotho	89.6
13	India	106.8	13	Hong Kong	90.0
	Libya	106.8		Virgin Islands (US)	90.0
15	Brunei	106.5	15	Hungary	90.4
16	Pakistan	106.1		Moldova	90.4
17	Iceland	105.9	17	Kazakhstan	90.8
18	Jordan	105.2	18	Macau	91.1
19	Timor-Leste	103.7	19	Cape Verde	91.7
			20	Guadeloupe	91.9

Population: age

Median age[a]

Highest, 2009			Lowest, 2009		
1	Japan	44.7	1	Niger	15.0
2	Germany	44.3	2	Uganda	15.6
3	Italy	43.3	3	Congo-Kinshasa	16.6
4	Bermuda	42.2	4	Burkina Faso	16.7
	Channel Islands	42.0	5	Malawi	16.8
	Finland	42.0		Zambia	16.0
7	Hong Kong	41.9	7	Afghanistan	16.9
	Switzerland	41.9	8	Chad	17.1
9	Austria	41.8	9	Angola	17.4
10	Bulgaria	41.7		Timor-Leste	17.4
	Slovenia	41.7	11	Tanzania	17.5
12	Croatia	41.6	12	Mali	17.6
	Greece	41.6		Somalia	17.6
14	Belgium	41.3		West Bank and Gaza	17.6
15	Portugal	41.0	15	Yemen	17.8
16	Sweden	40.9	16	Mozambique	17.9
17	Denmark	40.8	17	Ethiopia	18.0
	Netherlands	40.8		Senegal	18.0
19	Singapore	40.6	19	Sierra Leone	18.2
20	Spain	40.2	20	Benin	18.4
21	Andorra	40.1		Kenya	18.4
	France	40.1		Madagascar	18.4
23	Latvia	40.0	23	Guinea	18.5
24	Canada	39.9		Liberia	18.5
	United Kingdom	39.9	25	Nigeria	18.6
26	Hungary	39.8	26	Guinea-Bissau	18.7
	Lithuania	39.8		Rwanda	18.7
28	Czech Republic	39.6	28	Gambia	18.8
	Estonia	39.6		Guatemala	18.8
30	Ukraine	39.5	30	Zimbabwe	19.0
31	Bosnia	39.3	31	Eritrea	19.1
	Luxembourg	39.3	32	Cameroon	19.2
33	Malta	39.0	33	Equatorial Guinea	19.3
34	Norway	38.9		Iraq	19.3
35	Aruba	38.7		Swaziland	19.3
	Martinique	38.7	36	Central African Rep	19.5
37	Romania	38.5		Congo-Brazzaville	19.5
	Virgin Islands (US)	38.5		Côte d'Ivoire	19.5
39	Netherlands Antilles	38.4	39	Lesotho	19.8
40	Cuba	38.3		Togo	19.8
	Macau	38.3	41	Papua New Guinea	20.0
42	Belarus	38.2	42	Mauritania	20.1
	Poland	38.2	43	Burundi	20.3
44	Russia	38.1		Sudan	20.3
45	South Korea	37.9	45	Ghana	20.6
46	Australia	37.8		Laos	20.6
	Barbados	37.8	47	Tajikistan	20.7
48	Georgia	37.6	48	Honduras	20.9
	Serbia	37.6	49	Namibia	21.1

a Age at which there are an equal number of people above and below.

Largest population aged 0–14
% of total, 2010

1	Niger	50.1	19	Ethiopia	43.2
2	Uganda	48.7	20	Benin	42.9
3	Burkina Faso	46.4	21	Kenya	42.8
	Congo-Kinshasa	46.4	22	Guinea	42.6
5	Zambia	46.2		Guinea-Bissau	42.6
6	Afghanistan	45.9	24	Liberia	42.5
	Malawi	45.9		Madagascar	42.5
8	Chad	45.6	26	Nigeria	42.4
9	Somalia	44.9		Rwanda	42.4
10	Angola	44.7	28	Gambia	42.1
	Tanzania	44.7	29	Eritrea	41.5
	Timor-Leste	44.7		Guatemala	41.5
13	West Bank and Gaza	44.5	31	Cameroon	40.8
14	Mali	44.1	32	Equatorial Guinea	40.7
15	Mozambique	43.9		Iraq	40.7
16	Sierra Leone	43.5	34	Côte d'Ivoire	40.4
17	Senegal	43.3	35	Central African Rep	40.3
	Yemen	43.3	36	Congo-Brazzaville	40.2

Largest population aged 60 and over
% of total, 2010

1	Japan	30.5		Hungary	22.4
2	Italy	26.7		Slovenia	22.4
3	Germany	26.0		Spain	22.4
4	Sweden	25.0	22	Czech Republic	22.2
5	Finland	24.7	23	Malta	21.9
6	Bulgaria	24.5		Netherlands	21.9
7	Greece	24.3	25	Lithuania	21.5
8	Portugal	23.6	26	Norway	21.1
9	Croatia	23.5	27	Virgin Islands (US)	21.0
10	Belgium	23.4	28	Ukraine	20.9
	Denmark	23.4	29	Bermuda	20.4
12	Switzerland	23.3	30	Faroe Islands	20.3
13	France	23.2		Romania	20.3
14	Austria	23.1	32	Canada	20.0
15	United Kingdom	22.7	33	Serbia	19.7
16	Estonia	22.6	34	Puerto Rico	19.6
17	Latvia	22.5	35	Australia	19.5
18	Channel Islands	22.4	36	Poland	19.4

Largest population aged 80 and over
% of total, 2010

1	Japan	6.3	9	Austria	4.8
2	Italy	6.0	10	United Kingdom	4.7
3	France	5.5	11	Finland	4.6
4	Sweden	5.3	12	Portugal	4.5
5	Germany	5.1	13	Norway	4.5
6	Belgium	5.0	14	Denmark	4.2
	Spain	5.0		Estonia	4.2
	Switzerland	5.0	16	Slovenia	4.1

City living

Biggest cities[a]
Population m, 2010

1	Tokyo, Japan		36.7	49	Philadelphia, US	5.6
2	Delhi, India		22.1	50	Toronto, Canada	5.4
3	São Paulo, Brazil		20.3	51	Dongguan, China	5.3
4	Mumbai, India		20.0	52	Khartoum, Sudan	5.2
5	Mexico City, Mexico		19.5		Shenyang, China	5.2
6	New York, US		19.4	54	Barcelona, Spain	5.1
7	Shanghai, China		16.6	55	Chengdu, China	5.0
8	Kolkata, India		15.6		Chittagong, Bangladesh	5.0
9	Dhaka, Bangladesh		14.7		Dallas, US	5.0
10	Buenos Aires, Argentina	13.1		Foshan, China	5.0
	Karachi, Pakistan		13.1		Pune, India	5.0
12	Los Angeles, US		12.8	60	Riyadh, Saudi Arabia	4.9
13	Beijing, China		12.4	61	Luanda, Angola	4.8
14	Rio de Janeiro, Brazil		12.0		Singapore	4.8
15	Manila, Philippines		11.6	63	Atlanta, US	4.7
16	Osaka, Japan		11.4		Xian, China	4.7
17	Cairo, Egypt		11.0	65	Boston, US	4.6
18	Istanbul, Turkey		10.6		Houston, US	4.6
	Lagos, Nigeria		10.6		St Petersburg, Russia	4.6
	Moscow, Russia		10.6	68	Nanjing, China	4.5
21	Paris, France		10.5		Washington, DC, US	4.5
22	Seoul, South Korea		9.8	70	Alexandria, Egypt	4.4
23	Chongqing, China		9.4		Guadalajara, Mexico	4.4
24	Chicago, US		9.2		Sydney, Australia	4.4
	Jakarta, Indonesia		9.2	73	Harbin, China	4.3
26	Shenzhen, China		9.0		Yangon, Myanmar	4.3
27	Guangzhou, China		8.9	75	Detroit, US	4.2
	Lima, Peru		8.9		Surat, India	4.2
29	Kinshasa, Congo-Kinshasa	8.8	77	Abidjan, Côte d'Ivoire	4.1
30	London, United Kingdom	8.6		Pôrto Alegre, Brazil	4.1
31	Bogotá, Colombia		8.5	79	Ankara, Turkey	3.9
32	Tianjin, China		7.9		Brasília, Brazil	3.9
33	Wuhan, China		7.7		Hangzhou, China	3.9
34	Chennai, India		7.6		Melbourne, Australia	3.9
35	Bangalore, India		7.2		Monterrey, Mexico	3.9
	Tehran, Iran		7.2		Recife, Brazil	3.9
37	Hong Kong		7.1		Salvador, Brazil	3.9
	Lahore, Pakistan		7.1	86	Montréal, Canada	3.8
39	Bangkok, Thailand		7.0	87	Fortaleza, Brazil	3.7
40	Hyderabad, India		6.8		Johannesburg, S. Africa	3.7
	Taipei, Taiwan		6.8		Kabul, Afghanistan	3.7
42	Ho Chi Minh City, Vietnam	6.2		Phoenix, US	3.7
43	Santiago, Chile		6.0	91	Changchun, China	3.6
44	Baghdad, Iraq		5.9		Medellín, Colombia	3.6
	Belo Horizonte, Brazil		5.9	93	Curitiba, Brazil	3.5
	Madrid, Spain		5.9		Nairobi, Kenya	3.5
47	Ahmadabad, India		5.7		San Francisco, US	3.5
	Miami, US		5.7		Shantou, China	3.5

a Urban agglomerations. Data may change from year-to-year based on reassessments of agglomeration boundaries.

Fastest growing cities[b]

Total growth, 2010–15, %

1	Yamoussoukro, Côte d'Ivoire	43.8
2	Ouagadougou, Burkina Faso	38.5
3	Lilongwe, Malawi	28.9
4	Blantyre, Malawi	28.8
5	Abuja, Nigeria	28.4
6	Huambo, Angola	26.1
7	Luanda, Angola	26.0
8	Jinjiang, China	25.9
9	Sana'a, Yemen	25.3
10	Hanoi, Vietnam	24.9
	Kathmandu, Nepal	24.9
12	Vientiane, Laos	24.5
13	Niamey, Niger	24.3
14	Kampala, Uganda	24.1
15	Dar es Salaam, Tanzania	24.0
16	Kananga, Congo-Kins.	23.8
17	Kabul, Afghanistan	23.7
18	Mbuji-Mayi, Congo-Kins.	23.5
19	Kisangani, Congo-Kins.	23.3
20	Lubumbashi, Congon-Kins.	23.1
21	Bamako, Mali	22.8
22	Lomé, Togo	22.1
	Nairobi, Kenya	22.1
24	Kinshasa, Congo-Kins.	21.9
25	Mombasa, Kenya	21.3
26	Conakry, Guinea	21.2
	Kigali, Rwanda	21.2
	Matola, Mozambique	21.2
29	Yinchuan, China	20.7
30	Klang, Malaysia	20.6
31	Maputo, Mozambique	20.5
32	Cotonou, Benin	20.3
	Lufeng, China	20.3
34	Hohhot, China	20.1
35	Xiamen, China	19.7
36	Mogadishu, Somalia	19.6
	Zhongshan, China	19.6
38	Xuzhou, China	19.5
39	Huaibei, China	19.2
	Zunyi, China	19.2
41	Handan, China	19.1
	Yangzhou, China	19.1
43	Antananarivo, Madagascar	19.0
	Danang, Vietnam	19.0
45	Dongying, China	18.4
46	Huludao, China	18.3

Slowest growing cities[b]

Total growth, 2010–15, %

1	Monrovia, Liberia	-12.0
2	Dnipropetrovsk, Ukraine	-3.0
3	Saratov, Russia	-2.4
4	Donetsk, Ukraine	-2.1
5	Zaporizhzhya, Ukraine	-1.8
6	Havana, Cuba	-1.4
7	Volgograd, Russia	-1.1
8	Nizhniy Novgorod, Russia	-0.9
	Omsk, Russia	-0.9
10	Perm, Russia	-0.8
	Samara, Russia	-0.8
12	Rostov-on-Don, Russia	-0.6
13	Busan, South Korea	-0.5
	Kharkiv, Ukraine	-0.5
	Ufa, Russia	-0.5
16	Voronezh, Russia	-0.4
17	St Petersburg, Russia	-0.3
18	Cracow, Poland	-0.1
	Seoul, South Korea	-0.1
20	Kyoto, Japan	0.0
	Novosibirsk, Russia	0.0
22	Chelyabinsk, Russia	0.1
	Odessa, Ukraine	0.1
24	Osaka, Japan	0.2
	Prague, Czech Republic	0.2
26	Budapest, Hungary	0.3
	Hiroshima, Japan	0.3
28	Milan, Italy	0.4
	Rome, Italy	0.4
30	Montevideo, Uruguay	0.5
	Warsaw, Poland	0.5
32	Bucharest, Romania	0.6
	Daegu, South Korea	0.6
	Fukuoka, Japan	0.6
35	London, UK	0.7
	Naples, Italy	0.7
	San Juan, Puerto Rico	0.7
38	Athens, Greece	0.8
	Nagoya, Japan	0.8
	Turin, Italy	0.8
	Yerevan, Armenia	0.8
42	Moscow, Russia	0.9
	Pyongyang, N. Korea	0.9
44	Tokyo, Japan	1.0

b With populations over 750,000.

Urban population

Highest, %, 2010			*Lowest, %, 2010*	
1 Bermuda	100.0		1 Burundi	11.0
Cayman Islands	100.0		2 Papua New Guinea	12.5
Hong Kong	100.0		3 Uganda	13.3
Macau	100.0		4 Trinidad & Tobago	13.9
Singapore	100.0		5 Sri Lanka	14.3
6 Puerto Rico	98.8		6 Ethiopia	16.7
7 Guadeloupe	98.4		7 Niger	17.1
Kuwait	98.4		8 Nepal	18.6
9 Belgium	97.4		9 Rwanda	18.9
10 Qatar	95.8		10 Malawi	19.8
11 Virgin Islands (US)	95.3		11 Cambodia	20.1
12 Malta	94.7		12 Swaziland	21.4
13 Réunion	94.0		13 Eritrea	21.6
14 Iceland	93.4		14 Kenya	22.2
Venezuela	93.4		15 Afghanistan	22.6
16 Guam	93.2		16 Burkina Faso	25.7
Netherlands Antilles	93.2		17 Tajikistan	26.3
18 Uruguay	92.5		18 Tanzania	26.4
19 Argentina	92.4		19 Lesotho	26.9
20 Israel	91.9		20 Chad	27.6
21 Australia	89.1		21 St Lucia	28.0
22 Chile	89.0		22 Bangladesh	28.1
23 Bahrain	88.6		Timor-Leste	28.1
24 Andorra	88.0		24 Guinea-Bissau	30.0
25 Lebanon	87.2		India	30.0
26 Denmark	86.9		26 Madagascar	30.2
27 Brazil	86.5		27 Vietnam	30.4
28 New Zealand	86.2		28 Channel Islands	31.4
29 Gabon	86.0		29 Yemen	31.8
30 France	85.3		30 Laos	33.2

Quality of living index[a]

New York = 100, 2009				
1 Vienna, Austria	108.6		17 Berlin, Germany	105.0
2 Zurich, Switzerland	108.0		18 Melbourne, Australia	104.8
3 Geneva, Switzerland	107.9		19 Luxembourg	104.6
4 Auckland, New Zealand	107.4		20 Stockholm, Sweden	104.5
Vancouver, Canada	107.4		21 Montreal, Canada	104.2
6 Dusseldorf, Germany	107.2		Perth, Australia	104.2
7 Frankfurt, Germany	107.0		23 Hamburg, Germany	104.1
Munich, Germany	107.0		24 Nuremberg, Germany	103.9
9 Bern, Switzerland	106.5		Oslo, Norway	103.9
10 Sydney, Australia	106.3		26 Canberra, Australia	103.6
11 Copenhagen, Denmark	106.2		Dublin, Ireland	103.6
12 Wellington, N. Zealand	105.9		28 Calgary, Canada	103.5
13 Amsterdam, Neths.	105.7		Singapore	103.5
14 Ottawa, Canada	105.5		30 Stuttgart, Germany	103.3
15 Brussels, Belgium	105.4		31 Honolulu, US	103.1
16 Toronto, Canada	105.3			

a Based on 39 factors, ranging from political stability to natural environment.

Refugees[a] and asylum seekers

Refugees[a], country of origin
'000, 2008

1	Afghanistan	2,833.1		11	Eritrea	186.4
2	Iraq	1,903.5		12	Serbia	186.0
3	Somalia	561.2		13	Myanmar	184.4
4	Sudan	419.2		14	China	175.2
5	Colombia	373.5		15	Angola	171.4
6	Congo-Kinshasa	368.0		16	Sri Lanka	137.8
7	West Bank and Gaza	340.0		17	Central African Rep	125.1
8	Vietnam	328.2		18	Bhutan	105.0
9	Burundi	281.6		19	Russia	103.1
10	Turkey	214.4		20	Croatia	97.0

Countries with largest refugee[a] populations
'000, 2008

1	Pakistan	1,780.9		11	United States	279.6
2	Syria	1,105.7		12	Saudi Arabia	240.6
3	Iran	980.1		13	Venezuela	201.2
4	Germany	582.7		14	India	184.6
5	Jordan	500.4		15	Sudan	181.6
6	Chad	330.5		16	Canada	173.7
7	Tanzania	321.9		17	Uganda	162.1
8	Kenya	320.6		18	France	160.0
9	China	301.0		19	Congo-Kinshasa	155.2
10	United Kingdom	292.1		20	Yemen	140.2

Origin of asylum applications to industrialised countries
'000, 2008

1	Iraq	40.4		11	Iran	10.8
2	Somalia	21.8		12	Sri Lanka	9.6
3	Russia	20.4		13	Turkey	7.4
4	Afghanistan	18.4		14	Haiti	7.1
5	China	17.4		15	Bangladesh	6.2
6	Serbia	14.9		16	Zimbabwe	5.6
7	Nigeria	13.7		17	Georgia	5.5
8	Pakistan	13.2		18	Congo-Kinshasa	5.2
9	Eritrea	12.3		19	India	4.8
10	Mexico	12.2			Syria	4.8

Asylum applications in industrialised countries
'000, 2008

1	United States	49.6		10	Norway	14.4
2	Canada	36.9		11	Netherlands	13.4
3	France	35.4		12	Turkey	13.0
4	United Kingdom	31.3		13	Austria	12.8
5	Italy	30.3		14	Belgium	12.2
6	Sweden	24.4		15	Poland	7.2
7	Germany	22.1		16	Australia	4.8
8	Greece	19.9		17	Spain	4.5
9	Switzerland	16.6		18	Finland	4.0

a   According to UNHCR. Includes people in "refugee-like situations".

The world economy

Biggest economies
GDP, $bn, 2008

1	United States	14,093	24	Norway	452
2	Japan	4,911	25	Austria	414
3	China	4,327	26	Taiwan	391
4	Germany	3,649	27	Greece	356
5	France[a]	2,857	28	Iran	347
6	United Kingdom	2,674	29	Denmark	341
7	Italy	2,303	30	Argentina	328
8	Russia	1,679	31	Venezuela	314
9	Spain	1,604	32	United Arab Emirates	287
10	Brazil	1,575	33	South Africa	276
11	Canada	1,501	34	Finland	273
12	India	1,159	35	Thailand	272
13	Mexico	1,088	36	Ireland	268
14	Australia	1,015	37	Colombia	244
15	South Korea	929	38	Portugal	243
16	Netherlands	871	39	Malaysia	222
17	Turkey	735	40	Czech Republic	215
18	Poland	528		Hong Kong	215
19	Indonesia	511	42	Nigeria	207
20	Belgium	504	43	Israel	202
21	Switzerland	492	44	Romania	200
22	Sweden	479	45	Singapore	182
23	Saudi Arabia	469	46	Ukraine	180

Biggest economies by purchasing power
GDP PPP, $bn, 2008

1	United States	14,093	23	Argentina	571
2	China	7,909	24	Thailand	545
3	Japan	4,358	25	South Africa	493
4	India	3,359	26	Egypt	442
5	Germany	2,905	27	Pakistan	422
6	Russia	2,260	28	Colombia	396
7	United Kingdom	2,178	29	Malaysia	384
8	France	2,122	30	Belgium	377
9	Brazil	1,978	31	Venezuela	358
10	Italy	1,872	32	Sweden	341
11	Mexico	1,549	33	Ukraine	337
12	Spain	1,443	34	Greece	330
13	South Korea	1,344	35	Switzerland	324
14	Canada	1,302	36	Nigeria	317
15	Turkey	992		Philippines	317
16	Indonesia	908	38	Austria	316
17	Australia	831	39	Hong Kong	307
18	Iran	804	40	Romania	289
19	Taiwan	741	41	Norway	280
20	Netherlands	674	42	Algeria	276
21	Poland	659	43	Czech Republic	257
22	Saudi Arabia	591	44	Portugal	247

Note: For a list of 193 countries with their GDPs, see pages 250–254.
a Includes overseas departments.

Regional GDP

$bn, 2009		*% annual growth 2004–09*	
World	57,937	World	3.4
Advanced economies	40,056	Advanced economies	1.1
G7	30,991	G7	0.8
Euro area (16)	12,517	Euro area (16)	0.8
Asia[a]	7,793	Asia[a]	8.8
Latin America	3,975	Latin America	3.7
Eastern Europe[b]	3,250	Eastern Europe[b]	4.0
Middle East & N. Africa	1,978	Middle East & N. Africa	4.8
Sub-Saharan Africa	885	Sub-Saharan Africa	5.4

Regional purchasing power

GDP, % of total, 2009		*$ per head, 2009*	
World	100.0	World	10,360
Advanced economies	53.9	Advanced economies	37,116
G7	41.0	G7	38,772
Euro area (16)	15.2	Euro area (16)	31,970
Asia[a]	22.5	Asia[a]	4,456
Latin America	8.5	Latin America	10,654
Eastern Europe[b]	7.8	Eastern Europe[b]	11,877
Middle East & N. Africa	5.0	Middle East & N. Africa	8,546
Sub-Saharan Africa	2.4	Sub-Saharan Africa	2,179

Regional population

% of total (6.9bn), 2009		*No. of countries[c], 2009*	
Advanced economies	15.0	Advanced economies	33
G7	10.9	G7	7
Euro area (16)	4.8	Euro area (16)	16
Asia[a]	52.5	Asia[a]	26
Latin America	8.3	Latin America	32
Eastern Europe[b]	6.8	Eastern Europe[b]	27
Middle East & N. Africa	6.0	Middle East & N. Africa	20
Sub-Saharan Africa	11.4	Sub-Saharan Africa	44

Regional international trade

Exports of goods & services		*Current account balances*	
% of total, 2009		*$bn, 2009*	
Advanced economies	65.9	Advanced economies	-147
G7	36.3	G7	-291
Euro area (16)	28.8	Euro area (16)	-44
Asia[a]	14.4	Asia[a]	319
Latin America	5.1	Latin America	-19
Eastern Europe[b]	7.1	Eastern Europe[b]	5
Middle East & N. Africa	5.8	Middle East & N. Africa	35
Sub-Saharan Africa	1.8	Sub-Saharan Africa	-18

a Excludes Hong Kong, Japan, Singapore, South Korea and Taiwan.
b Includes, Russia, other CIS, Georgia, Mongolia and Turkey.
c IMF definition.

Living standards

Highest GDP per head
$, 2008

1	Luxembourg	109,900	36	Greenland	30,890
2	Bermuda	100,190	37	Hong Kong	30,860
3	Norway	94,760	38	New Zealand	30,440
4	Qatar	88,990	39	Guadeloupe[a]	28,340
5	Channel Islands[a]	77,130	40	Bahrain	28,240
6	Switzerland	64,330	41	Equatorial Guinea	28,100
7	United Arab Emirates	63,970	42	Martinique[a]	27,900
8	Denmark	62,120	43	Israel	27,650
9	Ireland	60,460	44	Slovenia	27,020
10	Kuwait	54,260	45	Aruba	25,830
11	Netherlands	52,960	46	Puerto Rico	24,650
12	Iceland	52,480	47	Portugal	22,920
13	Cayman Islands	52,020	48	Réunion[a]	22,650
14	Sweden	51,950	49	Bahamas	22,100
15	Finland	51,320	50	Czech Republic	20,670
16	Faroe Islands	50,500	51	Malta	20,030
17	Austria	49,600	52	Netherlands Antilles	19,510
18	Australia	47,370	53	South Korea	19,120
19	Belgium	47,090	54	Saudi Arabia	19,020
20	United States	46,350	55	Slovakia	18,210
21	Canada	45,070	56	Trinidad & Tobago	18,110
22	France	44,510	57	French Guiana[a]	17,920
23	Germany	44,450	58	French Polynesia	17,780
24	Andorra	44,290	59	Estonia	17,450
25	United Kingdom	43,540	60	Taiwan	17,050
26	Macau	41,430	61	Croatia	15,640
27	British Virgin Islands	40,560	62	Hungary	15,410
28	Italy	38,490	63	Oman[a]	15,270
29	Japan	38,460	64	Latvia	14,910
30	New Caledonia	37,620	65	Libya	14,800
31	Singapore	37,600	66	Barbados	14,430
32	Brunei	37,050	67	Virgin Islands (US)[b]	14,360
33	Spain	35,220	68	Guam[c]	14,240
34	Greece	31,670	69	Lithuania	14,100
35	Cyprus	31,410	70	Antigua & Barbuda	14,050

Lowest GDP per head
$, 2008

1	Burundi	140	11	Niger	360
2	Congo-Kinshasa	180	12	Afghanistan	370
3	Liberia	220	13	Guinea	390
4	Guinea-Bissau	270	14	Mozambique	440
5	Malawi	290		Nepal	440
6	Somalia	300	16	Timor-Leste	450
7	Zimbabwe	310		Togo	450
8	Ethiopia	320		Uganda	450
9	Eritrea	340	19	Central African Republic	460
10	Sierra Leone	350		Rwanda	460

a 2007   b 2004   c Estimate.

Highest purchasing power
GDP per head in PPP (USA = 100), 2008

1	Qatar[a]	262.6	36	Italy	67.5
2	Luxembourg	170.3	37	Bahamas[a]	64.3
3	Bermuda[ab]	150.8		Taiwan[a]	64.3
4	Macau	128.3	39	Greece	63.3
5	Norway	126.7	40	Israel	60.2
6	United Arab Emirates[c]	122.1	41	Slovenia	60.1
7	Brunei[c]	109.6	42	South Korea	59.7
8	Channel Islands[c]	107.4	43	New Zealand	58.8
9	Singapore	106.4	44	Cyprus	58.1
10	Kuwait[c]	104.1	45	Trinidad & Tobago	54.3
11	Faroe Islands[a]	104.0	46	Czech Republic	53.2
12	United States	100.0	47	Saudi Arabia	51.8
13	Andorra[a]	96.9	48	Guadeloupe[c]	50.2
14	Hong Kong	94.8		Portugal	50.2
15	Cayman Islands[ab]	94.5	50	Martinique[c]	49.4
16	Switzerland	91.5	51	Oman[c]	49.0
17	Ireland	90.3	52	Slovakia	47.8
18	Netherlands	88.4	53	Aruba[ab]	47.0
19	Canada	84.3	54	Malta[c]	45.6
20	Australia	83.7	55	Antigua & Barbuda	45.2
21	British Virgin Islands[ab]	83.1	56	Estonia	44.6
22	Austria	81.8	57	Hungary	42.7
23	Sweden	79.7	58	Réunion[c]	41.2
24	Iceland	79.6	59	Barbados[a]	39.9
25	Denmark	79.5	60	French Polynesia[ab]	38.8
26	Finland	78.1	61	Lithuania	38.3
27	United Kingdom	76.5	62	Croatia	38.1
28	Greenland[ac]	76.4	63	Poland	37.3
29	Germany	76.3	64	Puerto Rico[a]	37.1
30	Belgium	76.0	65	Latvia	35.3
31	Bahrain	75.3	66	Libya	35.0
32	Japan	73.6	67	Netherlands Antilles[ab]	34.5
33	Equatorial Guinea	73.1	68	Russia	34.4
34	France	71.3	69	Guam[ad]	32.4
35	Spain	68.3		New Caledonia[ae]	32.4

Lowest purchasing power
GDP per head in PPP (USA = 100), 2008

1	Zimbabwe[a]	0.4	10	Malawi	1.7
2	Congo-Kinshasa	0.7		Sierra Leone	1.7
3	Burundi	0.8		Timor-Leste	1.7
	Liberia	0.8	13	Mozambique	1.8
5	Guinea-Bissau	1.2		Togo	1.8
6	Somalia[a]	1.3	15	Ethiopia	1.9
7	Eritrea	1.4	16	Rwanda	2.2
8	Niger	1.5	17	Guinea	2.3
9	Central African Rep	1.6		Madagascar	2.3

Note: for definition of purchasing power parity see page 249.
a Estimate. b 2004 c 2007 d 2005 e 2003

The quality of life

Human development index[a]
Highest, 2007

1	Norway	97.1	31	Qatar	91.0
2	Australia	97.0	32	Portugal	90.9
3	Iceland	96.9	33	Barbados	90.3
4	Canada	96.6		Czech Republic	90.3
5	Ireland	96.5		United Arab Emirates	90.3
6	Netherlands	96.4	36	Malta	90.2
7	Sweden	96.3	37	Bahrain	89.5
8	France	96.1	38	Estonia	88.3
9	Japan	96.0	39	Poland	88.0
	Luxembourg	96.0		Slovakia	88.0
	Switzerland	96.0	41	Hungary	87.9
12	Finland	95.9	42	Chile	87.8
13	United States	95.6	43	Croatia	87.1
14	Austria	95.5	44	Lithuania	87.0
	Denmark	95.5	45	Antigua & Barbuda	86.8
	Spain	95.5	46	Argentina	86.6
17	Belgium	95.3		Latvia	86.6
18	Italy	95.1	48	Uruguay	86.5
19	New Zealand	95.0	49	Cuba	86.3
20	Germany	94.7	50	Bahamas	85.6
	United Kingdom	94.7	51	Costa Rica	85.4
22	Hong Kong	94.4		Mexico	85.4
	Singapore	94.4	53	Libya	84.7
24	Greece	94.2	54	Oman	84.6
25	South Korea	93.7	55	Venezuela	84.4
26	Israel	93.5	56	Saudi Arabia	84.3
27	Slovenia	92.9	57	Bulgaria	84.0
28	Brunei	92.0		Panama	84.0
29	Kuwait	91.6	59	Romania	83.7
30	Cyprus	91.4		Trinidad & Tobago	83.7

Human development index[a]
Lowest, 2007

1	Niger	34.0	10	Guinea-Bissau	39.6
2	Afghanistan	35.2	11	Mozambique	40.2
3	Sierra Leone	36.5	12	Ethiopia	41.4
4	Central African Rep	36.9	13	Guinea	43.5
5	Mali	37.1	14	Liberia	44.2
6	Burkina Faso	38.9	15	Gambia, The	45.6
	Congo-Kinshasa	38.9	16	Rwanda	46.0
8	Chad	39.2	17	Senegal	46.4
9	Burundi	39.4	18	Eritrea	47.2

a GDP or GDP per head is often taken as a measure of how developed a country is, but its usefulness is limited as it refers only to economic welfare. In 1990 the UN Development Programme published its first estimate of a Human Development Index, which combined statistics on two other indicators – adult literacy and life expectancy – with income levels to give a better, though still far from perfect, indicator of human development. In 1991 average years of schooling was combined with adult literacy to give a knowledge variable. The HDI is shown here scaled from 0 to 100; countries scoring over 80 are considered to have high human development, those scoring from 50 to 79 medium and those under 50 low.

Economic freedom index[a]
2010

1	Hong Kong	89.7		20	Macau	72.5
2	Singapore	86.1		21	Sweden	72.4
3	Australia	82.6		22	Austria	71.6
4	New Zealand	82.1		23	Germany	71.1
5	Ireland	81.3		24	Cyprus	70.9
6	Switzerland	81.1		25	St Lucia	70.5
7	Canada	80.4		26	Georgia	70.4
8	United States	78.0			Taiwan	70.4
9	Denmark	77.9		28	Botswana	70.3
10	Chile	77.2			Lithuania	70.3
11	United Kingdom	76.5		30	Belgium	70.1
12	Bahrain	76.3		31	El Salvador	69.9
	Mauritius	76.3			South Korea	69.9
14	Luxembourg	75.4		33	Czech Republic	69.8
15	Netherlands	75.0			Uruguay	69.8
16	Estonia	74.7		35	Slovakia	69.7
17	Finland	73.8		36	Spain	69.6
18	Iceland	73.7		37	Norway	69.4
19	Japan	72.9		38	Armenia	69.2

Gender-related development index[b]
2007

1	Australia	96.6		20	Germany	93.9
2	Norway	96.1		21	Greece	93.6
3	Canada	95.9		22	Hong Kong	93.4
	Iceland	95.9		23	Austria	93.0
5	France	95.6		24	Slovenia	92.7
6	Sweden	95.6		25	South Korea	92.6
7	Finland	95.4		26	Israel	92.1
	Netherlands	95.4		27	Cyprus	91.1
9	Spain	94.9		28	Portugal	90.7
10	Belgium	94.8		29	Brunei	90.6
	Ireland	94.8		30	Barbados	90.0
12	Denmark	94.7			Czech Republic	90.0
13	Switzerland	94.6		32	Bahrain	89.5
14	Italy	94.5			Malta	89.5
	Japan	94.5		34	Kuwait	89.2
16	Luxembourg	94.3		35	Qatar	89.1
	New Zealand	94.3		36	Estonia	88.2
	United Kingdom	94.3		37	Hungary	87.9
19	United States	94.2		38	United Arab Emirates	87.8

a Ranks countries on the basis of indicators of how government intervention can restrict the economic relations between individuals, published by the Heritage Foundation. The ranking includes data on labour and business freedom as well as trade policy, taxation, monetary policy, the banking system, foreign-investment rules, property rights, the amount of economic output consumed by the government, regulation policy, the size of the black market and the extent of wage and price controls. Countries are scored from 80–100 (free) to 0–49.9 (repressed).
b Combines similar data to the HDI (and also published by the UNDP) to give an indicator of the disparities in human development between men and women in individual countries. The lower the index, the greater the disparity.

Economic growth

Highest economic growth
Average annual % increase in real GDP, 1998–2008

1	Equatorial Guinea	21.1		Russia		6.8
2	Turkmenistan	14.9	29	Albania		6.6
3	Azerbaijan	14.6		Laos		6.6
4	Myanmar	11.7		Maldives		6.6
5	Angola[a]	10.9	32	Georgia		6.5
6	Armenia	10.3		Tanzania		6.5
	Qatar	10.3	34	Jordan		6.4
8	China	9.8		Mongolia		6.4
9	Cambodia[a]	9.5	36	Estonia		6.2
10	Kazakhstan	8.7	37	Bahrain		6.1
11	Mozambique	8.3		Lithuania		6.1
12	Bhutan[a]	8.1		Ukraine		6.1
	Sierra Leone	8.1		Uzbekistan		6.1
	Tajikistan[a]	8.1	41	Panama		5.9
15	Nigeria	7.9	42	Bangladesh		5.8
16	Rwanda	7.8		Belize		5.8
17	Trinidad & Tobago	7.6	44	Kuwait[a]		5.7
18	Belarus	7.5		Singapore		5.7
	Uganda	7.5	46	Bosnia		5.5
20	Ethiopia	7.3		Botswana		5.5
21	Vietnam	7.2		Burkina Faso		5.5
22	India	7.1		Ireland		5.5
23	Cape Verde	7.0		Malaysia		5.5
	Chad	7.0	51	Dominican Republic		5.4
	Sudan	7.0		South Korea		5.4
26	United Arab Emirates	6.9	53	Bulgaria		5.3
27	Latvia	6.8		Ghana		5.3

Lowest economic growth
Average annual % change in real GDP, 1998–2008

1	Eritrea[a]	-1.0	20	Fiji[a]		2.0
2	Côte d'Ivoire[a]	0.2		France		2.0
3	Gabon[a]	0.6		Switzerland		2.0
4	Haiti	0.7	23	Belgium		2.2
5	Dominica	1.0		Burundi[a]		2.2
6	Central African Rep[a]	1.1	25	Norway		2.3
7	Italy	1.2	26	Austria		2.4
	Japan	1.2		Netherlands		2.4
9	Jamaica	1.3		Paraguay		2.4
10	Germany	1.5	29	Swaziland		2.5
	Portugal	1.5	30	Papua New Guinea		2.6
	Togo	1.5		United Kingdom		2.6
13	Bahamas	1.7		United States		2.6
	Denmark	1.7	33	Congo-Kinshasa		2.7
15	Barbados	1.8	34	El Salvador		2.8
	Guyana	1.8		Sweden		2.8
	St Lucia	1.8	36	Argentina		2.9
	Uruguay	1.8		Canada		2.9
19	Brunei	1.9				

a Estimate.

Highest economic growth
Average annual % increase in real GDP, 1988–98

1	Equatorial Guinea	26.1		10	United Arab Emirates	6.6
2	China	9.6		11	Belize	6.5
3	Singapore	7.8		12	Ireland	6.4
4	Vietnam	7.7		13	South Korea	6.2
5	Chile	7.5		14	Uganda	6.1
6	Malaysia	7.4		15	Mali	5.9
7	Taiwan	6.8			Mauritius	5.9
8	Laos	6.7		17	Panama	5.8
	Maldives	6.7			Thailand	5.8

Lowest economic growth
Average annual % change in real GDP, 1988–98

1	Sierra Leone	-6.6			Mongolia	-0.3
2	Bulgaria	-5.7		12	Haiti	-0.2
3	Congo-Kinshasa	-5.3		13	Lebanon	-0.1
4	Romania	-2.9		14	Central African Rep	0.2
5	Rwanda	-1.4			Guinea-Bissau	0.2
6	Zambia	-1.2		16	Angola	0.3
7	Burundi	-1.0		17	Barbados	0.7
8	Albania	-0.5		18	Libya	0.8
9	Cameroon	-0.3			Suriname	0.8
	Hungary	-0.3		20	Niger	1.1

Highest services growth
Average annual % increase in real terms, 2000–08

1	Turkmenistan	17.1			Kazakhstan	10.6
2	Afghanistan	15.4		11	Sudan	10.5
3	Nigeria	14.4		12	Burundi	10.4
4	Armenia	13.4		13	Cambodia	10.2
5	Angola	12.4		14	Uganda	10.0
6	Congo-Kinshasa	11.5		15	Georgia	9.7
7	Moldova	11.3		16	United Arab Emirates	9.6
8	China	10.7		17	Ethiopia	9.5
9	Azerbaijan	10.6			India	9.5

Lowest services growth
Average annual % change in real terms, 2000–08

1	Zimbabwe	-10.0		11	Japan	1.6
2	Guinea	-4.2		12	Denmark	1.7
3	Central African Rep	-2.5			Portugal	1.7
4	Togo	-0.7			Switzerland	1.7
5	Eritrea	0.1		15	Finland	1.8
6	Côte d'Ivoire	0.7		16	Austria	2.1
7	Haiti	0.8			France	2.1
8	Guinea-Bissau	1.0		18	Belgium	2.2
9	Germany	1.2			Jamaica	2.2
10	Italy	1.3				

Note: Rankings of highest and lowest industrial growth 2000–08 can be found on page 46 and highest and lowest agricultural growth 2000–08 on page 49.

Trading places

Biggest exporters
% of total world exports (goods, services and income), 2008

1	Euro area (15)	16.99	22	Taiwan	1.36
2	United States	11.28	23	India	1.33
3	Germany	9.17	24	Austria	1.25
4	China	7.29	25	Australia	1.18
5	United Kingdom	5.46	26	Norway	1.16
6	Japan	4.82	27	Brazil	1.05
7	Netherlands	3.36		Malaysia	1.05
8	France	3.35	29	United Arab Emirates	1.04
9	Italy	3.34	30	Hong Kong	1.00
10	Canada	2.60	31	Denmark	0.98
11	Russia	2.53		Poland	0.98
12	Belgium	2.51	33	Thailand	0.94
13	South Korea	2.32	34	Turkey	0.80
14	Spain	2.26	35	Czech Republic	0.77
15	Switzerland	1.76	36	Indonesia	0.69
16	Ireland	1.50	37	Finland	0.66
	Saudi Arabia	1.50	38	Hungary	0.62
18	Sweden	1.45	39	Kuwait	0.49
19	Mexico	1.38	40	Iran	0.48
	Singapore	1.38	41	South Africa	0.46
21	Luxembourg	1.37		Venezuela	0.46

Most trade dependent
Trade[a] as % of GDP, 2008

1	Aruba	174.9
2	Equatorial Guinea	110.8
3	United Arab Emirates	104.5
4	Singapore	103.2
5	Vietnam	100.6
6	Bahrain	100.3
7	Slovakia	94.3
8	Malaysia	93.2
9	Guyana	91.3
10	Qatar	86.0
11	Iraq	85.9
12	Belgium	84.1
13	Liberia	82.3
14	Oman	81.8
15	Czech Republic	81.4
16	Belarus	80.2
17	Mongolia	78.3
18	Lesotho	78.2
19	Congo-Brazzaville	77.8
20	Hungary	77.5
21	Netherlands Antilles	76.3
22	Kyrgyzstan	74.8

Least trade dependent
Trade[a] as % of GDP, 2008

1	North Korea	7.4
2	United States	12.4
3	Bermuda	12.5
4	Brazil	14.1
5	Central African Rep	14.5
6	Japan	16.6
7	Rwanda	17.0
8	Burkina Faso	17.9
9	Colombia	18.3
10	Euro area	19.0
11	Haiti	19.3
12	Greece	19.7
13	Eritrea	20.0
	United Kingdom	20.0
15	Pakistan	20.8
16	Burundi	20.9
17	Cuba	21.3
18	India	21.4
19	Sudan	21.5
20	Nepal	21.8
21	Sierra Leone	22.4
22	Ethiopia	22.6

Notes: The figures are drawn wherever possible from balance of payment statistics so have differing definitions from trade statistics taken from customs or similar sources. For Hong Kong and Singapore, domestic exports and retained imports only are used. Euro area data exclude intra-euro area trade.

a Average of imports plus exports of goods.

Biggest traders of goods[a]
% of world, 2009

Exports			Imports		
1	China	9.6	1	United States	12.7
2	Germany	9.0	2	China	8.0
3	United States	8.5	3	Germany	7.4
4	Japan	4.7	4	France	4.4
5	Netherlands	4.0		Japan	4.4
6	France	3.8	6	United Kingdom	3.8
7	Italy	3.2	7	Netherlands	3.5
8	Belgium	3.0	8	Italy	3.2
9	South Korea	2.9	9	Belgium	2.8
10	United Kingdom	2.8	10	Canada	2.6
11	Canada	2.5		South Korea	2.6
12	Russia	2.4	12	Spain	2.3
13	Mexico	1.8	13	India	1.9
14	Spain	1.7		Mexico	1.9
15	Taiwan	1.6	15	Russia	1.5
16	Saudi Arabia[b]	1.5	16	Taiwan	1.4
17	Switzerland	1.4	17	Australia	1.3
	United Arab Emirates[b]	1.4	18	Poland	1.2
19	Malaysia	1.3		Switzerland	1.2
20	Australia	1.2			
	Brazil	1.2			
	India	1.2			
	Thailand	1.2			

Biggest earners from services and income
% of world exports of services and income, 2008

1	Euro area (15)	21.02	22	Austria	1.43
2	United States	17.42	23	South Korea	1.31
3	United Kingdom	10.48	24	Norway	1.25
4	Germany	8.08	25	Australia	1.10
5	Japan	4.80	26	Greece	0.78
6	Luxembourg	3.89	27	Taiwan	0.77
7	Netherlands	3.18	28	Finland	0.74
8	China	3.17	29	Poland	0.61
9	Spain	3.10	30	Portugal	0.59
10	Ireland	2.99	31	Brazil	0.57
11	Italy	2.93	32	Malaysia	0.56
12	Hong Kong	2.83		Turkey	0.56
13	Belgium	2.69	34	Thailand	0.54
14	France	2.20	35	Hungary	0.47
15	Switzerland	2.16	36	Israel	0.43
16	Sweden	1.95	37	Saudi Arabia	0.41
17	Singapore	1.87	38	Czech Republic	0.40
18	Canada	1.79	39	Egypt	0.37
19	India	1.58	40	Kuwait	0.35
20	Russia	1.47	41	Mexico	0.34
21	Denmark	1.46	42	Ukraine	0.31

a Individual countries only.
b Estimate.

Balance of payments: current account

Largest surpluses
$m, 2008

1	China	426,107	26	Finland	7,955
2	Germany	243,880	27	Denmark	7,549
3	Japan	156,630	28	Brunei	7,183
4	Saudi Arabia	134,046	29	Argentina	7,078
5	Russia	102,401	30	Switzerland	6,902
6	Norway	88,341	31	Kazakhstan	6,596
7	Kuwait	64,742	32	Angola	6,408
8	Netherlands	42,571	33	Macau	5,807
9	Sweden	40,317	34	Oman	5,469
10	Nigeria	39,357	35	Philippines	3,897
11	Malaysia	38,914	36	Uzbekistan	3,562
12	Venezuela	37,392	37	Turkmenistan	3,560
13	Libya	35,702	38	Luxembourg	3,176
14	Algeria	34,500	39	Gabon	3,103
15	Qatar	33,138	40	Bahrain	2,257
16	Hong Kong	30,532	41	Israel	2,120
17	Canada	27,281	42	Timor-Leste	2,021
18	Singapore	27,181	43	Bolivia	2,015
19	Taiwan	25,024	44	Equatorial Guinea	1,830
20	Iran	23,987	45	Bermuda	1,239
21	United Arab Emirates	22,200	46	Ecuador	1,120
22	Azerbaijan	16,454	47	Bangladesh	1,032
23	Austria	13,154	48	Papua New Guinea	805
24	Iraq	13,070	49	Cuba[a]	528
25	Trinidad & Tobago	8,775	50	Botswana	502

Largest deficits
$m, 2008

1	United States	-706,070	22	New Zealand	-11,237
2	Euro area (15)	-201,200	23	Hungary	-10,939
3	Spain	-154,129	24	Vietnam	-10,706
4	Italy	-78,144	25	Serbia	-8,855
5	France	-64,230	26	Colombia	-6,713
6	Greece	-51,313	27	Czech Republic	-6,631
7	Australia	-47,786	28	South Korea	-6,406
8	United Kingdom	-44,680	29	Iceland	-6,319
9	Turkey	-41,289	30	Croatia	-6,267
10	India	-36,088	31	Slovakia	-6,185
11	Portugal	-29,599	32	Morocco	-5,659
12	Brazil	-28,192	33	Lithuania	-5,627
13	Poland	-26,909	34	Belarus	-5,209
14	Romania	-23,719	35	Latvia	-4,492
15	South Africa	-20,981	36	Dominican Republic	-4,437
16	Mexico	-15,820	37	Cyprus	-4,349
17	Pakistan	-15,402	38	Peru	-4,180
18	Ireland	-14,222	39	Sri Lanka	-3,876
19	Ukraine	-12,763	40	Ghana	-3,543
20	Bulgaria	-12,577	41	Chile	-3,440
21	Belgium	-12,101	42	Slovenia	-3,329

Note: Euro area data exclude intra-euro area trade. a 2006

Largest surpluses as % of GDP
%, 2008

1	Timor-Leste	405.9	26	Bahrain	10.3
2	Brunei	49.4	27	Equatorial Guinea	9.9
3	Kuwait	43.7	28	China	9.8
4	Libya	38.3		Papua New Guinea	9.8
5	Trinidad & Tobago	36.3	30	Sweden	8.4
6	Azerbaijan	35.7	31	United Arab Emirates	7.7
7	Qatar	29.1	32	Angola	7.5
8	Saudi Arabia	28.6	33	Iran	6.9
9	Macau	26.6	34	Germany	6.7
10	Turkmenistan	23.2	35	Taiwan	6.4
11	Gabon	21.3	36	Russia	6.1
12	Algeria	20.7	37	Luxembourg	5.9
13	Norway	19.6	38	Kazakhstan	4.9
14	Bermuda	19.3		Netherlands	4.9
15	Nigeria	19.0	40	Guinea-Bissau	4.7
16	Malaysia	17.5	41	Botswana	3.7
17	Iraq	15.1	42	Austria	3.2
	Lesotho	15.1		Japan	3.2
19	Singapore	14.9	44	Nepal	3.0
20	Hong Kong	14.2	45	Finland	2.9
21	Uzbekistan	12.8	46	Philippines	2.3
22	Bolivia	12.1	47	Argentina	2.2
23	Venezuela	11.9		Denmark	2.2
24	Suriname	11.6	49	Côte d'Ivoire	2.1
25	Oman	10.4			

Largest deficits as % of GDP
%, 2008

1	Liberia	-172.2	21	Guyana	-16.6
2	Maldives	-51.6		Kosovo	-16.6
3	Iceland	-37.9	23	Albania	-16.1
4	Antigua & Barbuda	-31.5	24	Congo-Kinshasa	-15.8
5	Montenegro	-30.1	25	Netherlands Antilles[a]	-15.5
6	St Lucia	-29.3	26	Sierra Leone	-15.4
7	Burundi	-26.3	27	Bahamas	-15.0
8	Georgia	-25.3	28	Bosnia	-14.9
9	Bulgaria	-25.2	29	Honduras	-14.8
10	Zimbabwe	-23.2	30	Greece	-14.4
11	Nicaragua	-22.9		Senegal	-14.4
12	Ghana	-21.3	32	New Caledonia	-14.1
13	Jamaica	-20.8	33	Chad	-13.7
14	Madagascar	-20.5		Mongolia	-13.7
15	Mauritania	-19.5	35	Kyrgyzstan	-13.4
16	Fiji	-17.8	36	Latvia	-13.3
17	Serbia	-17.7		Niger	-13.3
18	Cyprus	-17.5	38	Cape Verde	-12.9
19	Moldova	-17.4	39	Macedonia	-12.7
20	Laos	-17.0			

a 2007

Workers' remittances
Inflows, $m, 2008

1	India	51,581	16	Lebanon	7,180
2	China	48,524	17	Pakistan	7,039
3	Mexico	26,304	18	Morocco	6,891
4	Philippines	18,643	19	Indonesia	6,795
5	France	15,908	20	Russia	6,033
6	Spain	11,776	21	Ukraine	5,769
7	Germany	11,064	22	Serbia and Mont.	5,538
8	Poland	10,727	23	Brazil	5,089
9	Nigeria	9,980	24	Colombia	4,884
10	Romania	9,380	25	Australia	4,638
11	Belgium	9,280	26	Guatemala	4,451
12	Bangladesh	8,995	27	Portugal	4,057
13	Egypt	8,694	28	El Salvador	3,804
14	United Kingdom	7,836	29	Jordan	3,794
15	Vietnam	7,200	30	Dominican Republic	3,487

Official reserves[a]
$m, end-2009

1	China	2,452,910	16	Switzerland	134,442
2	Japan	1,048,989	17	France	131,784
3	Euro area	661,090	18	Italy	131,498
4	Russia	438,929	19	Libya	104,051
5	Saudi Arabia	415,039	20	Mexico	99,888
6	United States	404,101	21	Malaysia	96,704
7	Taiwan	348,200	22	Iran	84,257
8	India	284,683	23	Poland	79,522
9	South Korea	270,438	24	Denmark	76,618
10	Hong Kong	255,813	25	Turkey	74,934
11	Brazil	238,539	26	United Kingdom	66,553
12	Singapore	187,803	27	Indonesia	66,119
13	Germany	179,533	28	Israel	60,611
14	Algeria	155,109	29	Canada	54,250
15	Thailand	138,419	30	Norway	48,859

Official gold reserves
Market prices, $m, end-2009

1	Euro area	377,537	14	United Kingdom	10,853
2	United States	284,381	15	Lebanon	10,027
3	Germany	119,114	16	Spain	9,842
4	Italy	85,728	17	Austria	9,788
5	France	85,151	18	Belgium	7,961
6	China	36,866	19	Algeria	6,068
7	Switzerland	36,366	20	Philippines	5,423
8	Japan	26,753	21	Libya	5,024
9	Russia	22,280	22	Saudi Arabia	4,998
10	Netherlands	21,413	23	Sweden	4,396
11	India	19,501	24	South Africa	4,361
12	Portugal	13,376	25	Turkey	4,060
13	Venezuela	12,615	26	Greece	3,931

a Foreign exchange, SDRs, IMF position and gold at market prices.

Exchange rates

The Economist's Big Mac index

		Big Mac prices in local currency	in $	Implied PPP[a] of the $	Actual $ exchange rate	Under (–)/ over (+) valuation against $, %

Countries with the most under-valued currencies, January 2010

1	China	12.50	1.83	3.49	6.83	-49
	Argentina	7.00	1.84	1.96	3.80	-49
3	Hong Kong	14.80	1.91	4.13	7.76	-47
4	Malaysia	7.05	2.08	1.97	3.39	-42
5	Thailand	70.00	2.11	19.55	33.14	-41
6	Philippines	101.52	2.21	28.36	45.92	-38
7	Indonesia	20,900.00	2.24	5,837.99	9,320.00	-37
8	Russia	70.00	2.34	19.55	29.93	-35
9	Taiwan	75.00	2.36	20.95	31.84	-34
	Egypt	13.00	2.38	3.63	5.47	-34
11	South Africa	17.95	2.46	5.01	7.30	-31
12	Mexico	32.00	2.50	8.94	12.81	-30
13	Saudi Arabia	10.00	2.67	2.79	3.75	-26
14	Peru	8.06	2.81	2.25	2.87	-22
15	Poland	8.10	2.86	2.26	2.84	-20
16	South Korea	3,400.00	2.98	949.72	1,140.50	-17
17	United Arab Em.	11.00	2.99	3.07	3.67	-16
18	Chile	1,600.00	3.18	446.93	503.10	-11
	Singapore	4.45	3.19	1.24	1.40	-11
20	Japan	320.00	3.50	89.39	91.54	-2

Countries with the most over-valued currencies, January 2010

1	Norway	40.00	7.02	11.17	5.70	96
2	Switzerland	6.50	6.30	1.82	1.03	76
3	Denmark	30.94	5.99	8.64	5.16	67
4	Sweden	39.00	5.51	10.89	7.08	54
5	Euro area[b]	3.36	4.84	1.07[c]	1.44[c]	35
6	Brazil	8.20	4.76	2.29	1.72	33
7	Israel	14.90	3.99	4.16	3.73	12
8	Australia	4.35	3.98	1.22	1.09	11
	Canada	4.12	3.97	1.15	1.04	11
10	Hungary	720.00	3.86	201.12	186.65	8
11	Turkey	5.65	3.83	1.58	1.47	7
12	Czech Republic	67.64	3.71	18.89	18.21	4
13	United Kingdom	2.29	3.67	1.56[d]	1.60[d]	3
14	New Zealand	4.90	3.61	1.37	1.36	1

a Purchasing-power parity: local price in the 34 countries listed divided by United States price ($3.58, average of four cities).
b Weighted average of prices in euro area.
c Dollars per euro.
d Dollars per pound.

Public finance and tax

Government debt
As % of GDP, 2009

1	Japan	189.3	16	Ireland	65.8
2	Italy	123.6	17	Norway	59.9
3	Iceland	117.6	18	Spain	59.3
4	Greece	114.9	19	Poland	58.1
5	Belgium	101.2	20	Sweden	52.7
6	Hungary	85.2	21	Czech Republic	46.5
7	France	84.5	22	Denmark	45.3
8	United States	83.9	23	Switzerland	44.4
9	Portugal	83.8	24	Finland	43.7
10	Canada	82.8	25	Slovakia	36.7
11	Euro area	81.8	26	South Korea	33.2
12	Germany	77.4	27	New Zealand	27.0
13	Austria	72.9	28	Luxembourg	18.2
14	Netherlands	71.4	29	Australia	15.9
15	United Kingdom	71.0			

Government spending
As % of GDP, 2009

1	Denmark	57.7	16	Spain	46.3
2	Finland	56.2	17	Czech Republic	45.7
	Sweden	56.2	18	Ireland	45.0
4	Iceland	55.9	19	Norway	44.4
5	France	55.5	20	Poland	43.8
6	Belgium	54.0	21	Canada	43.6
7	Austria	52.7	22	Luxembourg	43.2
8	United Kingdom	52.1	23	New Zealand	42.4
9	Italy	51.7	24	Japan	41.6
10	Portugal	51.6	25	United States	41.5
11	Hungary	51.5	26	Slovakia	39.0
12	Greece	51.3	27	Australia	37.5
13	Euro area	50.7	28	Switzerland	33.9
14	Netherlands	50.3	29	South Korea	33.8
15	Germany	47.7			

Tax revenue
As % of GDP, 2008

1	Denmark	48.3	14	Portugal	36.5
2	Sweden	47.1	15	Germany	36.4
3	Belgium	44.3	16	Iceland	36.0
4	Italy	43.2	17	United Kingdom	35.7
5	France	43.1	18	Poland[a]	34.9
6	Austria	42.9	19	New Zealand	34.5
7	Finland	42.8	20	Spain	33.0
8	Norway	42.1	21	Canada	32.2
9	Hungary	40.1	22	Greece	31.3
10	Luxembourg	38.3	23	Australia[a]	30.8
11	Netherlands[a]	37.5	24	Switzerland	29.4
12	Slovenia	37.1	25	Slovakia	29.3
13	Czech Republic	36.6	26	Ireland	28.3

Note: Includes only OECD countries.   a 2007

Tax wedge[a]

As % of total labour costs, 2009

Married couple, one earner on average wage, two children

1	Hungary	43.7	15	United Kingdom	26.4
2	France	41.7	16	Portugal	26.3
	Greece	41.7	17	Japan	23.7
4	Belgium	38.8	18	Slovakia	22.7
5	Sweden	37.5	19	Czech Republic	20.5
6	Finland	37.0	20	Canada	18.3
7	Austria	36.6	21	South Korea	17.2
8	Italy	35.7		Switzerland	17.2
9	Germany	33.7	23	Mexico	15.3
10	Spain	32.3	24	Australia	14.1
11	Norway	30.6	25	United States	13.7
12	Netherlands	29.7	26	Ireland	11.7
13	Denmark	28.8	27	Luxembourg	11.2
14	Poland	28.4	28	Iceland	8.6

Single person on average wage[b], no children

1	Belgium	55.2	15	Norway	37.4
2	Hungary	53.4	16	Portugal	37.2
3	Germany	50.9	17	Luxembourg	34.0
4	France	49.2		Poland	34.0
5	Austria	47.9	19	United Kingdom	32.5
6	Italy	46.5	20	Canada	30.8
7	Sweden	43.2	21	United States	29.4
8	Finland	42.4	22	Switzerland	29.3
9	Czech Republic	41.9	23	Japan	29.2
10	Greece	41.5	24	Ireland	28.6
11	Denmark	39.4	25	Iceland	28.3
12	Spain	38.2	26	Australia	26.7
13	Netherlands	38.0	27	South Korea	19.7
14	Slovakia	37.6	28	New Zealand	18.4

Single person earning 67% of average wage, two children

1	France	36.8	16	Korea	16.4
2	Greece	36.0	17	Czech Republic	15.0
3	Belgium	33.7	18	Denmark	13.2
4	Sweden	32.8	19	Mexico	11.8
5	Germany	31.3	20	Switzerland	11.4
6	Hungary	30.1	21	Netherlands	11.3
7	Poland	28.4	22	United Kingdom	8.9
	Spain	28.4	23	Iceland	4.9
9	Austria	26.4	24	United States	4.2
10	Finland	25.4	25	Luxembourg	0.3
11	Italy	25.0	26	Australia	-7.5
12	Japan	21.5	27	Canada	-7.7
13	Slovak Republic	21.2	28	Ireland	-9.5
14	Norway	20.6	29	New Zealand	-16.5
	Portugal	20.6			

a Gap between labour costs and net take-home pay.
b Annual gross wage earnings of the average worker.

Inflation

Consumer price inflation

Highest, 2009, %

1	Zimbabwe[a]	24,411.0
2	Venezuela	28.6
3	Myanmar[b]	26.8
4	Ghana	19.3
5	Yemen[b]	19.0
6	Congo-Kinshasa[b]	17.3
7	Ukraine	15.9
8	Qatar[b]	15.0
9	Sudan[b]	14.3
10	Angola	13.7
11	Pakistan	13.6
12	Iran	13.5
13	Zambia	13.4
14	Uganda	13.1
15	Belarus	12.9
16	Nigeria	12.4
17	Tanzania	12.1
18	Iceland	12.0
19	Egypt	11.8
20	Russia	11.7
21	Burundi	11.0
22	India	10.9
	Nepal[b]	10.9

Lowest, 2009, %

1	Ireland	-4.5
2	Aruba	-2.1
3	Guinea-Bissau	-1.7
4	Japan	-1.4
5	Belize	-1.1
	Senegal	-1.1
7	Taiwan	-0.9
8	Portugal	-0.8
	Thailand	-0.8
10	Cambodia	-0.7
	China	-0.7
	Jordan	-0.7
13	United Kingdom	-0.6
14	Switzerland	-0.5
15	Spain	-0.4
	United States	-0.4
17	Macedonia	-0.3
	Sweden	-0.3
19	Belgium	-0.1
	Estonia	-0.1
	Moldova	-0.1
	Suriname	-0.1

Highest average annual consumer price inflation, 2004–09, %

1	Zimbabwe[c]	2,176.3
2	Myanmar[d]	22.4
3	Venezuela	21.5
4	Ethiopia	18.1
5	Congo-Kinshasa[d]	17.1
6	Azerbaijan	17.0
7	Iraq	16.2
8	Ukraine	15.2
9	Angola	14.9
10	Ghana	14.5
11	Kenya	13.8
12	Jamaica	12.8
13	Zambia	12.7
14	Sri Lanka	12.5
15	Qatar[d]	12.3
	Yemen[d]	12.3
17	Burundi	11.7
18	Pakistan	11.6
19	Madagascar	11.5
20	Mongolia	11.4
	Russia	11.4
22	Costa Rica	11.2
23	Nigeria	11.0

Lowest average annual consumer price inflation, 2004–09, %

1	Japan	0.0
	Montenegro	0.0
3	Switzerland	1.0
4	Sweden	1.4
5	Taiwan	1.5
6	France	1.6
	Netherlands	1.6
8	Germany	1.7
9	Canada	1.8
10	Finland	1.8
11	Austria	1.9
	Portugal	1.9
13	Denmark	2.0
	Hong Kong	2.0
	Italy	2.0
	Singapore	2.0
17	Antigua & Barbuda	2.1
	Belgium	2.1
	Ireland	2.1
	Norway	2.1
21	Morocco	2.2
22	Israel	2.3
	Luxembourg	2.3

a 2007   b 2008   c 2004–07   d 2004-2008

Commodity prices

2009, % change on a year earlier			2000–09, % change	
1	Copper	156.8	1 Lead	420.6
2	Lead	151.0	2 Copper	298.4
3	Zinc	130.2	3 Gold	296.3
4	Sugar	109.0	4 Cocoa	283.9
5	Oil[a]	100.7	5 Tin	204.8
6	Rubber	94.0	6 Sugar	202.7
7	Nickel	92.2	7 Rice	180.2
8	Hides	77.5	8 Oil[a]	159.4
9	Tin	64.5	9 Palm oil	156.5
10	Tea	58.9	10 Rubber	149.8
11	Aluminium	55.4	11 Soya oil	147.3
12	Palm Oil	49.3	12 Zinc	122.2
13	Cotton	41.5	13 Nickel	119.2
14	Cocoa	34.3	14 Wheat	110.2
15	Gold	26.9	15 Soyabeans	108.4
16	Soya oil	22.8	16 Corn	100.3
17	Coffee	21.4	17 Soya meal	85.7
18	Timber	18.7	18 Lamb	74.1
19	Wool (Aus)	15.1	19 Coconut oil	70.5
20	Soyabeans	9.8	20 Tea	68.5
21	Beef (Aus)	7.8	21 Coffee	67.3
22	Soya meal	5.7	22 Beef (Aus)	50.4
23	Corn	5.2	23 Aluminium	44.9
24	Coconut oil	4.0	24 Cotton	34.3
25	Lamb	3.8	25 Wool (Aus)	26.3
26	Rice	3.5	26 Beef (US)	16.4

The Economist's house-price indicators

Q4 2009[b], % change on a year earlier			1997–2009[b], % change	
1	Hong Kong	27.7	1 South Africa	417
2	Singapore	24.5	2 Australia	197
3	Australia	13.6	3 United Kingdom	180
4	China	10.7	4 Spain	166
5	United Kingdom	9.0	5 Sweden	159
6	South Africa	6.6	6 Belgium	149
7	Switzerland	6.2	7 Ireland	142
8	Sweden	5.8	8 France	133
9	New Zealand	1.1	9 New Zealand	105
10	Canada	0.9	10 Italy	96
11	Germany	-0.4	11 Denmark	91
12	Netherlands	-2.0	12 Netherlands	86
13	United States	-2.5	13 Canada	68
14	Belgium	-3.0	14 United States	63
15	Japan	-4.0	15 Switzerland	31
16	Italy	-4.1	16 Singapore	9
17	France	-4.3	17 Hong Kong	-16
18	Spain	-6.3	18 Japan	-36
19	Denmark	-13.1		
20	Ireland	-18.5		

a West Texas Intermediate.   b Or latest.

Debt

Highest foreign debt[a]
$bn, 2008

1	Russia	402.5	24	Qatar	57.9
2	South Korea	382.3	25	Venezuela	50.2
3	China	378.2	26	Pakistan	49.3
4	Turkey	277.3	27	Colombia	46.9
5	Brazil	255.6	28	Latvia	42.1
6	India	230.6	29	South Africa	41.9
7	Poland	218.0	30	Bulgaria	38.0
8	Mexico	204.0	31	Kuwait	36.7
9	Indonesia	150.9	32	Egypt	32.6
10	United Arab Emirates	134.7	33	Lithuania	31.7
11	Argentina	128.3	34	Serbia	30.9
12	Kazakhstan	107.6	35	Peru	28.6
13	Romania	104.9	36	Vietnam	26.2
14	Ukraine	92.5	37	Singapore	25.5
15	Taiwan	90.4	38	Lebanon	24.4
16	Israel	86.1	39	Bangladesh	23.6
17	Czech Republic	80.8	40	Morocco	20.8
18	Saudi Arabia	78.8		Tunisia	20.8
19	Hong Kong	77.3	42	Sudan	19.6
20	Malaysia	66.2	43	Ecuador	16.9
21	Philippines	64.9	44	Guatemala	15.9
22	Thailand	64.8	45	Sri Lanka	15.2
23	Chile	64.3	46	Angola	15.1

Highest foreign debt burden[a]
Foreign debt as % of GDP, 2008

1	Liberia	515.4	22	Moldova	57.0
2	Zimbabwe	380.2	23	Kyrgyzstan	56.9
3	Guinea-Bissau	274.1	24	Togo	56.1
4	Latvia	127.3	25	Côte d'Ivoire	56.0
5	Burundi	124.7	26	Nicaragua	55.3
6	Congo-Kinshasa	118.2	27	Romania	54.7
7	Estonia	111.1	28	United Arab Emirates	52.9
8	Hungary	106.7	29	Ukraine	51.7
9	Laos	99.5	30	Panama	49.8
10	Kazakhstan	95.0	31	Macedonia	49.6
11	Lebanon	90.6	32	Central African Rep	48.7
12	Bulgaria	79.0	33	Slovakia	47.9
13	Guinea	73.2	34	Bahrain	47.2
14	Jamaica	69.7	35	El Salvador	46.6
15	Lithuania	69.3	36	Cambodia	46.0
16	Congo-Brazzaville	65.6	37	Bosnia	43.9
17	Serbia	63.5	38	Israel	42.6
18	Gambia	61.5	39	Poland	42.1
19	Eritrea	58.6	40	Chile	41.3
20	Tunisia	58.5		Guatemala	41.3
21	Qatar	57.7	42	South Korea	41.0

a Foreign debt is debt owed to non-residents and repayable in foreign currency; the figures shown include liabilities of government, public and private sectors. Developed countries have been excluded.

Highest foreign debt[a]

As % of exports of goods and services, 2008

1	Burundi	705	22	Uruguay	122
2	Eritrea	697	23	Brazil	121
3	Guinea-Bissau	496	24	Lithuania	120
4	Congo-Kinshasa	316		Pakistan	120
5	Liberia	306	26	Hungary	115
6	Zimbabwe	302	27	Serbia	111
7	Latvia	301	28	Burkina Faso	110
8	Sudan	296	29	Guatemala	109
9	Central African Rep	267	30	Colombia	108
10	Laos	261	31	Togo	106
11	Argentina	171	32	Poland	103
12	Turkey	170	33	Indonesia	102
13	Kazakhstan	164	34	El Salvador	98
14	Guinea	149	35	Armenia	97
	Romania	149		Qatar	97
16	Jamaica	148	37	Macedonia	96
17	Côte d'Ivoire	144		Moldova	96
18	Cuba	141		Sri Lanka	96
19	Estonia	134	40	Israel	94
20	Bulgaria	128	41	Lebanon	89
21	Ukraine	124	42	Tunisia	85

Highest debt service ratio[b]

Average, %, 2008

1	Liberia	131.3	23	Indonesia	13.4
2	Zimbabwe	47.7	24	Israel	13.0
3	Kazakhstan	41.8	25	Armenia	12.7
4	Latvia	37.7	26	Peru	12.5
5	Hungary	31.2	27	Guatemala	12.2
6	Lithuania	30.6	28	Mexico	12.1
7	Turkey	29.5	29	Russia	11.5
8	Burundi	28.1	30	Bolivia	11.3
9	Romania	25.3		Moldova	11.3
10	Poland	25.0	32	Cuba	10.9
11	Brazil	22.7	33	Argentina	10.7
12	Estonia	19.9	34	Costa Rica	10.5
13	Ukraine	19.4	35	Morocco	10.3
14	Chile	18.2	36	Czech Republic	10.2
15	Colombia	16.2	37	Namibia	10.0
16	Jordan	16.0	38	El Salvador	9.9
17	Philippines	15.5	39	Guinea	9.6
18	Bulgaria	14.7		Slovakia	9.6
19	Uruguay	14.6	41	South Korea	9.3
20	Jamaica	14.2		Sri Lanka	9.3
21	Lebanon	14.0	43	Côte d'Ivoire	9.2
22	Serbia	13.9		Panama	9.2

b Debt service is the sum of interest and principal repayments (amortisation) due on outstanding foreign debt. The debt service ratio is debt service expressed as a percentage of the country's exports of goods and services.

Aid

Largest recipients of bilateral and multilateral aid[a]
$m, 2008

1	Iraq	9,870	24	Zambia	1,086
2	Afghanistan	4,865	25	Lebanon	1,076
3	Ethiopia	3,327	26	Senegal	1,058
4	West Bank and Gaza	2,593	27	Serbia	1,047
5	Vietnam	2,552	28	Burkina Faso	998
6	Sudan	2,384	29	Colombia	972
7	Tanzania	2,331	30	Mali	964
8	India	2,108	31	Rwanda	931
9	Bangladesh	2,061	32	Malawi	913
10	Turkey	2,024	33	Haiti	912
11	Mozambique	1,994	34	Georgia	888
12	Uganda	1,657	35	Madagascar	841
13	Congo-Kinshasa	1,610	36	Somalia	758
14	Pakistan	1,539	37	Cambodia	743
15	China	1,489	38	Jordan	742
16	Kenya	1,360	39	Nicaragua	741
17	Egypt	1,348	40	Sri Lanka	730
18	Ghana	1,293	41	Botswana	716
19	Nigeria	1,290		Nepal	716
20	Liberia	1,250	43	Benin	641
21	Indonesia	1,225	44	Bolivia	628
22	Morocco	1,217	45	Ukraine	618
23	South Africa	1,125	46	Côte d'Ivoire	617

Largest recipients of bilateral and multilateral aid[a]
$ per head, 2008

1	West Bank and Gaza	675.2	23	Afghanistan	172.5
2	Cook Islands	562.0	24	Montenegro	171.5
3	Solomon Islands	439.8	25	Serbia	142.4
4	Cape Verde	437.1	26	Djibouti	142.2
5	Vanuatu	398.6	27	Congo-Brazzaville	139.5
6	Botswana	377.0	28	Seychelles	134.2
7	Anguilla	335.0	29	Nicaragua	130.4
8	Iraq	334.6	30	Bosnia & Herzegovina	128.0
9	Liberia	329.9	31	Jordan	125.6
10	Dominica	312.4	32	Bhutan	125.4
11	Grenada	300.4	33	Albania	122.8
12	São Tomé & Príncipe	293.9	34	St. Lucia	112.3
13	Kiribati	269.0	35	Macedonia	108.1
14	Lebanon	259.9	36	Armenia	98.3
15	Tonga	257.0	37	Namibia	98.0
16	Timor-Leste	252.3	38	Mauritania	97.1
17	St. Vincent & Gren.	243.6	39	Rwanda	95.7
18	Samoa	219.2	40	Mongolia	93.7
19	Guyana	217.8	41	Haiti	93.2
20	Georgia	203.6	42	Mozambique	91.5
21	Suriname	195.2	43	Antigua & Barbuda	91.3
22	Maldives	175.0	44	Croatia	89.7

a Israel also receives aid, but does not disclose amounts.

Largest bilateral and multilateral donors[a]
$m, 2008

1	United States	26,842	15	Belgium	2,386
2	Germany	13,981	16	Switzerland	2,038
3	United Kingdom	11,500	17	Austria	1,714
4	France	10,908	18	Ireland	1,328
5	Japan	9,579	19	Finland	1,166
6	Netherlands	6,993	20	South Korea	802
7	Spain	6,867	21	Turkey	780
8	Saudi Arabia	5,564	22	Greece	703
9	Italy	4,861	23	Portugal	620
10	Canada	4,785	24	Taiwan	435
11	Sweden	4,732	25	Luxembourg	415
12	Norway	3,963	26	Poland	372
13	Australia	2,954	27	New Zealand	348
14	Denmark	2,803	28	Kuwait	283

Largest bilateral and multilateral donors[a]
% of GDP, 2008

1	Saudi Arabia	1.19		Germany	0.38
2	Sweden	0.99	16	Canada	0.32
3	Norway	0.88	17	Australia	0.29
4	Denmark	0.82		Iceland	0.29
5	Netherlands	0.80	19	New Zealand	0.27
6	Luxembourg	0.77	20	Portugal	0.25
7	Ireland	0.50	21	Italy	0.21
8	Belgium	0.47	22	Greece	0.20
9	Finland	0.43		Japan	0.20
	Spain	0.43	24	Kuwait	0.19
	United Kingdom	0.43		United States	0.19
12	Austria	0.41	26	Czech Republic	0.12
	Switzerland	0.41	27	Taiwan	0.11
14	France	0.38		Turkey	0.11

Resource flow donors[b]
% of GNI, 2008

1	Austria	2.82	12	Belgium	0.89
2	Ireland	2.71	13	Norway	0.88
3	Switzerland	2.68	14	Portugal	0.67
4	Spain	1.96	15	Japan	0.63
5	Canada	1.63	16	Australia	0.43
6	United Kingdom	1.57	17	New Zealand	0.38
7	Denmark	1.50	18	Greece	0.35
8	France	1.44	19	Italy	0.25
9	Sweden	1.22	20	United States	0.10
10	Luxembourg	0.99	21	Finland	-0.08
11	Germany	0.91	22	Netherlands	-1.61

a China also provides aid, but does not disclose amounts.
b Including other official flows eg, export credits, private grants and flows.

Industry and services

Largest industrial output
$bn, 2008

1	United States[a]	3,073	23	Iran[a]	127
2	China	2,104	24	Thailand	120
3	Japan[a]	1,282		United Arab Emirates[a]	120
4	Germany	1,101	26	Switzerland[a]	119
5	United Kingdom	634	27	Belgium	117
6	Russia	625	28	Argentina	106
7	Italy	622	29	Algeria	103
8	France	584	30	Taiwan	97
9	Spain	463	31	South Africa	93
10	Brazil	440	32	Colombia	89
11	Mexico	404		Denmark	89
12	South Korea	345		Ireland[a]	89
13	India	334		Malaysia[a]	89
14	Saudi Arabia	329	36	Finland	88
15	Australia	295	37	Czech Republic	81
16	Indonesia	246	38	Chile	74
17	Netherlands	222	39	Libya	73
18	Norway	209	40	Greece	70
19	Turkey	203	41	Nigeria[a]	67
20	Poland	163		Ukraine	67
21	Sweden	134	43	Egypt	61
22	Austria	128			

Highest growth in industrial output
Average annual % increase in real terms, 2000–08

1	Chad	50.7	11	Trinidad & Tobago	11.4
2	Turkmenistan	27.3	12	Georgia	11.3
3	Azerbaijan	24.2	13	Kazakhstan	10.6
4	Afghanistan	17.5		Sudan	10.6
5	Armenia	15.1	15	Uganda	10.2
6	Angola	13.9	16	Mozambique	10.1
7	Cambodia	13.3	17	Vietnam	10.0
8	Belarus	12.6	18	Tanzania	9.6
9	Laos	11.9	19	Congo-Kinshasa	9.5
10	China	11.7	20	Ethiopia	9.2

Lowest growth in industrial output
Average annual % change in real terms, 2000–08

1	Zimbabwe	-10.0	11	Lithuania	0.3
2	Burundi	-6.2	12	Denmark	0.4
3	Hong Kong	-2.6		Italy	0.4
4	Côte d'Ivoire	-0.7	14	Moldova	0.6
5	Oman	-0.5	15	Central African Rep	0.7
6	Cameroon	-0.4	16	Eritrea	0.8
7	Portugal	-0.3		Kyrgyzstan	0.8
8	Taiwan	-0.2	18	Haiti	0.9
9	Norway	0.1	19	France	1.0
10	United Kingdom	0.2			

a 2006

Largest manufacturing output
$bn, 2008

1	China	1,850	21	Taiwan	100
2	United States	1,831	22	Poland	93
3	Japan	1,011		Sweden	93
4	Germany	855	24	Austria	84
5	Italy	424	25	Belgium	80
6	United Kingdom	360	26	Argentina	76
7	France	341	27	Finland	61
8	Russia	293		Ireland	61
9	Brazil	281	29	Malaysia	57
10	South Korea	257	30	Czech Republic	56
11	Spain	242	31	South Africa	52
12	Canada	210	32	Denmark	50
13	Mexico	203		Venezuela	50
14	India	202	34	Romania	48
15	Indonesia	140	35	Norway	43
16	Turkey	132	36	Puerto Rico	40
17	Netherlands	127	37	Colombia	39
18	Australia	110		Saudi Arabia	39
19	Thailand	106	39	Philippines	38
20	Switzerland	101		Ukraine	38

Largest services output
$bn, 2008

1	United States[a]	10,562		Indonesia	191
2	Japan[a]	3,036	28	Argentina	190
3	Germany	2,517	29	Portugal	180
4	France	2,215	30	Finland	177
5	United Kingdom	2,022	31	South Africa	174
6	China	1,734	32	Ireland[a]	168
7	Italy	1,635	33	Romania	135
8	Spain	1,096	34	Colombia	134
9	Brazil	1,029	35	Singapore	131
10	Russia	970	36	Iran[a]	130
11	Australia	694	37	Czech Republic	129
12	Mexico	643		Saudi Arabia	129
13	Netherlands	635	39	Thailand	120
14	India	622	40	Hungary	102
15	South Korea	560	41	Ukraine	99
16	Turkey	468	42	Chile	89
17	Belgium	383		Philippines	89
18	Poland	341	44	Pakistan	87
19	Sweden	338	45	Egypt	80
20	Switzerland[a]	302	46	Malaysia[a]	79
21	Taiwan	285	47	United Arab Emirates[a]	75
22	Austria	278	48	Peru	73
23	Greece	274	49	Kazakhstan	68
24	Denmark	248	50	Slovakia	58
25	Norway	238	51	Algeria	52
26	Hong Kong[a]	191	52	Serbia	50

a 2006

Agriculture

Largest agricultural output
$bn, 2008

1	China	489		Germany	32
2	India	202		Thailand	32
3	United States	183	18	Iran	29
4	Brazil	106	19	Australia	26
5	Russia	84	20	Philippines	25
6	Indonesia	74	21	Poland	24
7	Turkey	64		South Korea[a]	24
8	Japan[a]	63	23	Colombia	21
9	France	57		Egypt	21
10	Nigeria	54	25	Vietnam	20
11	Italy	46	26	Malaysia	19
12	Spain[a]	44	27	United Kingdom	18
13	Mexico	41	28	Bangladesh	15
14	Pakistan[a]	33		Ukraine	15
15	Argentina	32			

Most economically dependent on agriculture
% of GDP from agriculture, 2008

1	Liberia	61.3	14	Papua New Guinea	33.6
2	Guinea-Bissau	55.5	15	Ghana	33.5
3	Central African Rep	52.9	16	Burkina Faso[b]	33.3
4	Sierra Leone	50.2	17	Nigeria[a]	32.7
5	Tanzania[b]	45.3	18	Afghanistan	31.6
6	Ethiopia	44.5	19	Kyrgyzstan	29.8
7	Congo-Kinshasa	40.2	20	Mozambique	28.6
8	Rwanda	37.4	21	Gambia, The	28.5
9	Mali[a]	36.5	22	Guyana	28.1
10	Laos	34.7	23	Kenya	27.0
11	Cambodia	34.6	24	Sudan	25.8
12	Malawi	34.3	25	Madagascar	25.2
13	Nepal	33.7	26	Côte d'Ivoire	25.0

Least economically dependent on agriculture
% of GDP from agriculture, 2007

1	Macau	0.0	14	Japan[a]	1.4
2	Hong Kong[a]	0.1	15	Sweden	1.6
	Singapore	0.1		Taiwan	1.6
4	Trinidad & Tobago	0.3	17	Ireland[a]	1.7
5	Luxembourg	0.4		Netherlands	1.7
6	Brunei[b]	0.7	19	United Arab Emirates[a]	1.8
	United Kingdom	0.7	20	Austria	1.9
8	Belgium	0.8		Botswana	1.9
9	Germany	0.9		Libya	1.9
10	Norway	1.2	23	Equatorial Guinea	2.0
	Switzerland[a]	1.2		France	2.0
12	Denmark	1.3		Italy	2.0
	United States[a]	1.3	26	Cyprus	2.1

Highest growth in agriculture
Average annual % increase in real terms, 2000–08

1	Angola	13.6	10	Ethiopia	6.8
2	Guinea	9.9	11	Uzbekistan	6.6
3	Eritrea	9.3	12	Burkina Faso	6.2
4	Jordan	8.5	13	Iran	5.9
5	Tajikistan	8.3	14	Paraguay	5.8
6	Mozambique	7.8	15	Cambodia	5.6
7	Romania	7.5		Chile	5.6
8	Armenia	7.3		Mongolia	5.6
9	Nigeria	7.0	18	Belarus	5.5

Lowest growth in agriculture
Average annual % change in real terms, 2000–08

1	Turkmenistan	-13.3	9	Hong Kong	-3.3
2	Trinidad & Tobago	-9.2	10	Estonia	-2.9
3	Zimbabwe	-8.5	11	Belgium	-2.7
4	Greece	-4.3	12	Slovenia	-1.8
5	Bulgaria	-3.8	13	Moldova	-1.6
6	Lesotho	-3.6	14	Burundi	-1.5
7	Denmark	-3.5	15	Spain	-1.3
8	Ireland	-3.4	16	Mauritius	-1.2

Biggest producers
'000 tonnes, 2008

Cereals

1	China	481,009	6	Indonesia	76,575
2	United States	403,772	7	France	70,094
3	India	266,582	8	Canada	56,031
4	Russia	106,392	9	Ukraine	52,714
5	Brazil	79,682	10	Germany	50,105

Meat

1	China	74,539	6	Russia	6,136
2	United States	43,171	7	Mexico	5,631
3	Brazil	22,832	8	Spain	5,572
4	Germany	7,687	9	France	5,471
5	India	6,796	10	Canada	4,494

Fruit

1	China	107,838	6	Mexico	16,122
2	India	62,672	7	Indonesia	15,918
3	Brazil	38,988	8	Spain	15,835
4	United States	28,203	9	Philippines	15,421
5	Italy	17,653	10	Iran	13,604

Vegetables

1	China	457,730	5	Iran	16,173
2	India	78,886	6	Russia	14,058
3	United States	36,432	7	Egypt	13,751
4	Turkey	27,136	8	Italy	13,687

Commodities

Wheat

Top 10 producers, 2008–09 '000 tonnes		Top 10 consumers, 2008–09 '000 tonnes	
1 EU27	151,200	1 EU27	124,750
2 China	112,500	2 China	104,620
3 India	78,600	3 India	72,600
4 United States	68,000	4 Russia	39,800
5 Russia	63,800	5 United States	34,310
6 Canada	28,600	6 Pakistan	23,070
7 Ukraine	25,900	7 Turkey	17,830
8 Pakistan	21,500	8 Egypt	16,440
9 Australia	20,900	9 Iran	15,770
10 Turkey	17,000	10 Ukraine	12,830

Rice[a]

Top 10 producers, 2008–09 '000 tonnes		Top 10 consumers, 2008–09 '000 tonnes	
1 China	134,330	1 China	133,000
2 India	99,150	2 India	91,050
3 Indonesia	38,300	3 Indonesia	37,090
4 Bangladesh	31,000	4 Bangladesh	31,000
5 Vietnam	24,388	5 Vietnam	19,000
6 Thailand	19,850	6 Philippines	13,650
7 Philippines	10,753	7 Myanmar	9,550
8 Myanmar	10,150	8 Thailand	9,500
9 Brazil	8,569	9 Brazil	8,529
10 Japan	8,029	10 Japan	8,326

Sugar[b]

Top 10 producers, 2008 '000 tonnes		Top 10 consumers, 2008 '000 tonnes	
1 Brazil	32,290	1 India	22,550
2 India	25,936	2 EU27	20,471
3 EU27	16,376	3 China	14,725
4 China	15,405	4 Brazil	11,856
5 Thailand	7,774	5 United States	9,807
6 United States	6,956	6 Russia	6,180
7 Mexico	5,940	7 Mexico	5,031
8 Pakistan	4,997	8 Indonesia	4,605
9 Australia	4,619	9 Pakistan	4,538
10 Russia	3,789	10 Egypt	2,700

Coarse grains[c]

Top 5 producers, 2008–09 '000 tonnes		Top 5 consumers, 2008–09 '000 tonnes	
1 United States	326,200	1 United States	275,900
2 China	174,100	2 China	163,700
3 EU27	162,300	3 EU27	151,500
4 Brazil	53,600	4 Brazil	49,100
5 Russia	41,900	5 Mexico	42,900

Tea

Top 10 producers, 2008		*Top 10 consumers, 2008*	
'000 tonnes		*'000 tonnes*	
1 China	1,200	1 China	872
2 India	981	2 India	798
3 Kenya	346	3 Russia	178
4 Sri Lanka	319	4 Japan	134
5 Vietnam	166	Turkey	134
6 Turkey	155	6 United Kingdom	130
7 Indonesia	137	7 United States	117
8 Japan	93	8 Egypt	104
9 Argentina	72	9 Pakistan	99
10 Bangladesh	59	10 Iran	71

Coffee

Top 10 producers, 2008–09		*Top 10 consumers, 2008*	
'000 tonnes		*'000 tonnes*	
1 Brazil	2,760	1 United States	1,299
2 Vietnam	1,110	2 Brazil	1,052
3 Indonesia	561	3 Germany	572
4 Colombia	520	4 Japan	424
5 Mexico	279	5 Italy	354
6 India	262	6 France	309
7 Ethiopia	261	7 Russia	223
8 Peru	232	8 Spain	209
9 Guatemala	227	9 Indonesia	200
10 Honduras	207	10 Canada	193

Cocoa

Top 10 producers, 2007–08		*Top 10 consumers, 2007–08*	
'000 tonnes		*'000 tonnes*	
1 Côte d'Ivoire	1,382	1 United States	750
2 Ghana	729	2 Germany	317
3 Indonesia	485	3 France	235
4 Nigeria	220	4 United Kingdom	225
5 Cameroon	185	5 Russia	200
6 Brazil	171	6 Japan	166
7 Ecuador	111	7 Brazil	143
Togo	111	8 Italy	106
9 Papua New Guinea	52	9 Spain	105
10 Dominican Republic	41	10 Poland	73

a Milled.
b Raw.
c Includes: maize (corn), barley, sorghum, oats, rye, millet, triticale and other.

Copper

Top 10 producers[a], 2008
'000 tonnes

1	Chile	5,330
2	United States	1,330
3	Peru	1,268
4	China	931
5	Australia	886
6	Russia	785
7	Indonesia	650
8	Canada	607
9	Zambia	568
10	Poland	429

Top 10 consumers[b], 2008
'000 tonnes

1	China	5,134
2	United States	2,021
3	Germany	1,398
4	Japan	1,184
5	South Korea	815
6	Russia	717
7	Italy	635
8	Taiwan	582
9	India	515
10	Brazil	382

Lead

Top 10 producers[a], 2008
'000 tonnes

1	China	1,546
2	Australia	650
3	United States	413
4	Peru	345
5	Mexico	141
6	Canada	99
7	India	86
8	Bolivia	82
9	Sweden	65
10	Russia	60

Top 10 consumers[b], 2008
'000 tonnes

1	China	3,135
2	United States	1,470
3	Germany	375
4	South Korea	315
5	Japan	261
6	Italy	254
7	Spain	228
8	United Kingdom	222
9	Mexico	217
10	India	212

Zinc

Top 10 producers[a], 2008
'000 tonnes

1	China	3,151
2	Peru	1,581
3	Australia	1,519
4	United States	778
5	Canada	716
6	India	616
7	Mexico	454
8	Ireland	398
9	Kazakhstan	387
10	Bolivia	379

Top 10 consumers[c], 2008
'000 tonnes

1	China	4,016
2	United States	1,000
3	Japan	564
4	Germany	527
5	South Korea	488
6	India	439
7	Belgium	372
8	Italy	279
9	Spain	276
10	Brazil	271

Tin

Top 5 producers[a], 2008
'000 tonnes

1	China	121.2
2	Indonesia	96.0
3	Peru	39.0
4	Bolivia	17.3
5	Brazil	13.0

Top 5 consumers[b], 2008
'000 tonnes

1	China	127.7
2	Japan	32.2
3	United States	26.0
4	Germany	20.5
5	South Korea	16.3

Nickel

Top 10 producers[a], 2008		*Top 10 consumers[b], 2008*	
'000 tonnes		*'000 tonnes*	
1 Russia	286.8	1 China	305.2
2 Canada	259.6	2 Japan	185.3
3 Australia	200.0	3 United States	117.0
4 Indonesia	192.6	4 Germany	89.9
5 New Caledonia	102.6	5 South Korea	75.8
6 Philippines	83.9	6 Taiwan	68.9
7 China	71.5	7 Italy	67.9
8 Cuba	67.3	8 Belgium	46.7
9 Colombia	41.6	9 South Africa	44.1
10 Brazil	35.8	10 Finland	41.0

Aluminium

Top 10 producers[d], 2008		*Top 10 consumers[e], 2008*	
'000 tonnes		*'000 tonnes*	
1 China	13,177	1 China	12,413
2 Russia	3,800	2 United States	4,906
3 Canada	3,119	3 Japan	2,250
4 United States	2,659	4 Germany	1,950
5 Australia	1,974	5 India	1,284
6 Brazil	1,661	6 Russia	1,020
7 Norway	1,359	7 South Korea	964
8 India	1,308	8 Italy	951
9 United Arab Emirates	892	9 Brazil	932
10 Bahrain	872	10 Canada	714

Precious metals

Gold [a]		*Silver* [a]	
Top 10 producers, 2008		*Top 10 producers, 2008*	
tonnes		*tonnes*	
1 China	282.0	1 Peru	3,686
2 United States	233.0	2 Mexico	3,241
3 South Africa	220.6	3 China	2,800
4 Australia	215.0	4 Australia	1,926
5 Russia	184.5	5 Chile	1,404
6 Peru	179.9	6 United States	1,233
7 Canada	96.5	7 Poland	1,216
8 Ghana	79.5	8 Bolivia	1,114
9 Uzbekistan	73.2	9 Canada	755
10 Papua New Guinea	66.2	10 Kazakhstan	682

Platinum		*Palladium*	
Top 3 producers, 2008		*Top 3 producers, 2008*	
tonnes		*tonnes*	
1 South Africa	128.0	1 Russia	103.8
2 Russia	23.0	2 South Africa	68.9
3 United States/Canada	9.2	3 United States/Canada	25.8

a Mine production. b Refined consumption. c Slab consumption.
d Primary refined production. e Primary refined consumption.

Rubber (natural and synthetic)

Top 10 producers, 2008		*Top 10 consumers, 2008*	
'000 tonnes		*'000 tonnes*	
1 Thailand	3,275	1 China	6,404
2 China	2,885	2 United States	2,775
3 Indonesia	2,799	3 Japan	2,016
4 United States	2,314	4 India	1,175
5 Japan	1,651	5 Brazil	839
6 Russia	1,139	6 Germany	833
7 Malaysia	1,111	7 South Korea	687
8 India	980	8 Malaysia	594
9 South Korea	970	9 Thailand	593
10 Germany	791	10 Indonesia	553

Raw wool

Top 10 producers[a], 2008		*Top 10 consumers[a], 2008*	
'000 tonnes		*'000 tonnes*	
1 Australia	251	1 China	395
2 China	185	2 India	86
3 New Zealand	146	3 Italy	78
4 Argentina	38	4 Turkey	46
5 India	37	5 Iran	41
6 Iran	33	6 Russia	22
7 Uruguay	30	7 New Zealand	19
8 United Kingdom	28	8 Morocco	17
9 South Africa	27	South Korea	17
10 Russia	24	10 United Kingdom	16

Cotton

Top 10 producers, 2008–09		*Top 10 consumers, 2008–09*	
'000 tonnes		*'000 tonnes*	
1 China	8,025	1 China	9,000
2 India	4,930	2 India	3,863
3 United States	2,790	3 Pakistan	2,400
4 Pakistan	1,960	4 Turkey	1,140
5 Brazil	1,214	5 Brazil	974
6 Uzbekistan	1,000	6 United States	781
7 Turkey	440	7 Bangladesh	740
8 Australia	329	8 Indonesia	435
9 Turkmenistan	297	9 Mexico	400
10 Greece	240	10 Thailand	368

Major oil seeds[b]

Top 5 producers, 2008–09		*Top 5 consumers, 2008–09*	
'000 tonnes		*'000 tonnes*	
1 United States	88,620	1 China	95,420
2 Brazil	59,720	2 United States	58,375
3 China	52,865	3 EU25	44,105
4 Argentina	35,605	4 Argentina	36,925
5 India	29,880	5 Brazil	36,869

Oil[c]

Top 10 producers, 2009
'000 barrels per day

1	Russia	10,032
2	Saudi Arabia[d]	9,713
3	United States	7,196
4	Iran[d]	4,216
5	China	3,790
6	Canada	3,212
7	Mexico	2,979
8	United Arab Emirates[d]	2,599
9	Iraq[d]	2,482
10	Kuwait[d]	2,481

Top 10 consumers, 2009
'000 barrels per day

1	United States	18,686
2	China	8,625
3	Japan	4,396
4	India	3,183
5	Russia	2,695
6	Saudi Arabia[d]	2,614
7	Germany	2,422
8	Brazil	2,405
9	South Korea	2,327
10	Canada	2,195

Natural gas

Top 10 producers, 2009
Billion cubic metres

1	United States	593.4
2	Russia	527.5
3	Canada	161.4
4	Iran[d]	131.2
5	Norway	103.5
6	Qatar[d]	89.3
7	China	85.2
8	Algeria[d]	81.4
9	Saudi Arabia[d]	77.5
10	Indonesia[d]	71.9

Top 10 consumers, 2009
Billion cubic metres

1	United States	646.6
2	Russia	389.7
3	Iran[d]	131.7
4	Canada	94.7
5	China	88.7
6	Japan	87.4
7	United Kingdom	86.5
8	Germany	78.0
9	Saudi Arabia[d]	77.5
10	Italy	71.6

Coal

Top 10 producers, 2009
Million tonnes oil equivalent

1	China	1,552.9
2	United States	539.9
3	Australia	228.0
4	India	211.5
5	Indonesia[d]	155.3
6	South Africa	140.9
7	Russia	140.7
8	Poland	56.4
9	Kazakhstan	51.8
10	Colombia	46.9

Top 10 consumers, 2009
Million tonnes oil equivalent

1	China	1,537.4
2	United States	498.0
3	India	245.8
4	Japan	108.8
5	South Africa	99.4
6	Russia	82.9
7	Germany	71.0
8	South Korea	68.6
9	Poland	53.9
10	Australia	50.8

Oil[c]

Top proved reserves, end 2009
% of world total

1	Saudi Arabia[d]	19.8		5	Kuwait[d]	7.6
2	Venezuela[d]	12.9		6	United Arab Emirates[d]	7.3
3	Iran[d]	10.3		7	Russia	5.6
4	Iraq[d]	8.6		8	Libya[d]	3.3

a Clean basis.   b Soybeans, sunflower seed, cottonseed, groundnuts and rapeseed.
c Includes crude oil, shale oil, oil sands and natural gas liquids.   d Opec members.

Energy

Largest producers
Million tonnes oil equivalent, 2007

1	China	1,814	16	United Arab Emirates	178
2	United States	1,665	17	United Kingdom	176
3	Russia	1,231	18	Algeria	164
4	Saudi Arabia	551	19	South Africa	160
5	Euro area	460	20	Kuwait	147
6	India	451	21	Germany	137
7	Canada	413	22	Kazakhstan	136
8	Indonesia	331	23	France	135
9	Iran	323	24	Iraq	105
10	Australia	289	25	Qatar	103
11	Mexico	251	26	Libya	102
12	Nigeria	232	27	Angola	95
13	Brazil	216	28	Malaysia	94
14	Norway	214	29	Japan	90
15	Venezuela	184	30	Colombia	88

Largest consumers
Million tonnes oil equivalent, 2007

1	United States	2,340	16	Italy	178
2	China	1,956	17	Saudi Arabia	150
3	Euro area	1,229	18	Spain	144
4	Russia	672	19	Ukraine	137
5	India	595	20	South Africa	134
6	Japan	514	21	Australia	124
7	Germany	331	22	Nigeria	107
8	Canada	269	23	Thailand	104
9	France	264	24	Turkey	100
10	Brazil	236	25	Poland	97
11	South Korea	222	26	Pakistan	83
12	United Kingdom	211	27	Netherlands	80
13	Indonesia	191	28	Argentina	73
14	Iran	185		Malaysia	73
15	Mexico	184	30	Egypt	67

Energy efficiency[a]

Most efficient			Least efficient		
GDP per unit of energy use, 2007			*GDP per unit of energy use, 2007*		
1	Hong Kong	20.1	1	Congo-Kinshasa	1.0
2	Peru	14.7	2	Uzbekistan	1.3
3	Panama	12.7	3	Turkmenistan	1.6
4	Colombia	12.3	4	Mozambique	1.8
5	Ireland	11.9	5	Togo	2.0
6	Botswana	11.6		Trinidad & Tobago	2.0
7	Uruguay	11.4		Zambia	2.0
8	Switzerland	11.0	8	Ukraine	2.2
9	Lebanon	10.5	9	Iceland	2.3
10	Gabon	10.3	10	Kazakhstan	2.4
11	United Kingdom	9.9	11	Tanzania	2.5

a 2005 PPP $ per kg of oil equivalent.

Net energy importers
% of commercial energy use, 2007

Highest			Lowest		
1	Hong Kong	100	1	Congo-Brazzaville	-891
	Malta	100	2	Angola	-793
	Netherlands Antilles	100	3	Norway	-696
	Singapore	100	4	Brunei	-630
5	Luxembourg	98	5	Gabon	-549
6	Cyprus	97	6	Kuwait	-482
	Moldova	97	7	Libya	-470
8	Jordan	96	8	Qatar	-364
9	Lebanon	95	9	Algeria	-346
	Morocco	95	10	Azerbaijan	-337
11	Ireland	91	11	Oman	-283
12	Jamaica	90	12	Saudi Arabia	-267

Largest consumption per head
Kg of oil equivalent, 2007

1	Qatar	19,504	12	Finland	6,895
2	Iceland	15,708	13	Saudi Arabia	6,223
3	United Arab Emirates	11,832	14	Australia	5,888
4	Bahrain	11,551	15	Singapore	5,831
5	Trinidad & Tobago	11,506	16	Norway	5,704
6	Netherlands Antilles	11,321	17	Oman	5,678
7	Kuwait	9,463	18	Sweden	5,512
8	Luxembourg	8,790	19	Belgium	5,366
9	Canada	8,169	20	Netherlands	4,909
10	United States	7,766	21	Russia	4,730
11	Brunei	7,190	22	South Korea	4,586

Sources of electricity
% of total, 2007

Oil			Gas		
1	Malta	100.0	1	Qatar	100.0
	Netherlands Antilles	100.0		Turkmenistan	100.0
	Yemen	100.0	3	Trinidad & Tobago	99.6
4	Cyprus	99.9	4	Belarus	99.0
5	Eritrea	99.3		Brunei	99.0

Hydropower			Nuclear power		
1	Paraguay	100.0	1	France	77.9
2	Mozambique	99.9	2	Lithuania	73.0
3	Congo-Kinshasa	99.7	3	Belgium	55.1
4	Nepal	99.6	4	Slovakia	55.0
5	Zambia	99.4	5	Ukraine	47.2

Coal		
1	Botswana	99.5
2	Mongolia	96.1
3	South Africa	94.7
4	Estonia	93.5
5	Poland	93.0

Workers of the world

Highest % of population in labour force
2008 or latest

1	Qatar	87.4
2	Cayman Islands	68.4
3	Laos	66.6
4	Macau	62.2
5	Switzerland	60.8
6	Bhutan	60.4
7	China	59.5
8	Bermuda	59.4
9	Canada	58.9
10	Thailand	57.7
11	Norway	57.6
12	Iceland	57.5
13	Sweden	55.7
14	Denmark	55.2
15	United Arab Emirates	54.9
16	Latvia	53.5
	New Zealand	53.5
18	Russia	53.4
19	Peru	53.1
20	Hong Kong	52.9

21	Netherlands	52.8
22	Australia	52.5
23	Brazil	52.4
	Cyprus	52.4
25	Kuwait	52.3
26	Japan	52.1
27	Estonia	51.8
28	Austria	51.7
	South Korea	51.7
30	United Kingdom	51.4
	United States	51.4
32	Finland	51.3
33	Indonesia	51.1
34	Germany	51.0
	Slovenia	51.0
36	Spain	50.4
37	Ireland	50.3
38	Czech Republic	50.2
39	Portugal	50.1
40	Slovakia	49.9

Most male workforce
Highest % men in workforce, 2008 or latest

1	Qatar	89.3
2	Yemen	88.2
3	Saudi Arabia	84.6
4	Algeria	83.0
5	Iran	82.3
6	West Bank and Gaza	81.8
7	Oman	81.6
8	Syria	80.6
9	United Arab Emirates	79.6
10	Pakistan	78.8
11	Bangladesh	77.7
12	Guatemala	77.4
13	Egypt	77.1
14	Bahrain	76.4
15	Kuwait	74.8
16	Tunisia	73.4
	Turkey	73.4
18	Morocco	72.8
19	Fiji	69.3
20	Nicaragua	69.2
21	India	68.4
22	Malta	66.5
23	Honduras	65.3
24	Malaysia	64.2
25	Sri Lanka	63.9

Most female workforce
Highest % women in workforce, 2008 or latest

1	Benin	53.1
2	Belarus	52.8
3	Martinique	52.3
4	Netherlands Antilles	51.1
5	Mongolia	51.0
	Tanzania	51.0
7	Laos	50.2
8	Armenia	49.8
9	Ghana	49.6
	Kazakhstan	49.6
	Madagascar	49.6
12	Estonia	49.5
	Portugal	49.5
14	Cambodia	49.4
	Moldova	49.4
16	Lithuania	49.3
17	Guadeloupe	49.1
18	Azerbaijan	48.9
	Latvia	48.9
	Russia	48.9
21	Barbados	48.7

Lowest % of population in labour force
2008 or latest

1	Yemen	22.7	21	Nicaragua	36.5
2	West Bank and Gaza	23.9		South Africa	36.5
3	Algeria	27.6	23	Morocco	36.8
4	Syria	29.3	24	Georgia	36.9
5	Tajikistan	30.1	25	Oman	37.3
6	Saudi Arabia	30.3	26	Sri Lanka	37.8
7	Sudan	30.5	27	Honduras	37.9
8	Egypt	31.0	28	India	39.1
9	Armenia	31.4	29	Mongolia	40.5
10	Iran	32.1	30	Fiji	41.1
11	Pakistan	32.2	31	El Salvador	41.2
12	Congo-Brazzaville	32.3	32	Malta	41.4
13	Turkey	32.8	33	Philippines	41.7
14	Tunisia	34.6	34	Croatia	42.2
15	Bangladesh	34.7	35	Italy	42.3
16	Botswana	35.0	36	Albania	42.4
	Guatemala	35.0	37	Hungary	42.5
18	Puerto Rico	35.9	38	Mexico	42.7
19	Moldova	36.1		Panama	42.7
20	Bosnia	36.2	40	Chile	43.3

Highest rate of unemployment
% of labour force[a], 2008 or latest

1	Macedonia	33.8	26	Slovakia	9.5
2	Bosnia	29.0	27	Turkey	9.4
3	Swaziland	28.2	28	Mali	8.8
4	Guinea-Bissau	26.3	29	Egypt	8.7
5	West Bank and Gaza	25.7	30	Afghanistan	8.5
6	Réunion	24.2	31	Croatia	8.4
7	South Africa	22.9		Indonesia	8.4
8	Guadeloupe	22.7		Syria	8.4
9	Martinique	21.2	34	Kyrgyzstan	8.2
10	Botswana	17.6	35	Barbados	8.1
11	Ethiopia	16.7	36	Bahamas	7.9
12	Tunisia	14.2		Brazil	7.9
13	Albania	13.8	38	Chile	7.8
	Algeria	13.8		Hungary	7.8
15	Serbia	13.6	40	Greece	7.7
16	Georgia	13.3	41	Portugal	7.6
17	Jordan	12.7		Uruguay	7.6
18	Netherlands Antilles	12.0	43	Germany	7.5
19	Colombia	11.7		Latvia	7.5
20	Puerto Rico	11.6	45	France	7.4
21	Spain	11.3		Philippines	7.4
22	Jamaica	10.6		Venezuela	7.4
23	Iran	10.5	48	Argentina	7.3
24	Dominican Republic	10.0		Kazakhstan	7.3
25	Morocco	9.6		Mauritius	7.3

a ILO definition.

The business world

Global competitiveness
2010

	Overall	Government	Infrastructure
1	Singapore	Hong Kong	United States
2	Hong Kong	Singapore	Sweden
3	United States	Switzerland	Switzerland
4	Switzerland	Australia	Canada
5	Australia	New Zealand	Denmark
6	Sweden	Taiwan	Finland
7	Canada	Norway	Norway
8	Taiwan	Qatar	Germany
9	Norway	Malaysia	Iceland
10	Malaysia	Canada	Austria
11	Luxembourg	Denmark	Singapore
12	Netherlands	Luxembourg	Netherlands
13	Denmark	Sweden	Japan
14	Austria	Chile	France
15	Qatar	Finland	United Kingdom
16	Germany	Israel	Israel
17	Israel	Netherlands	Taiwan
18	China	Thailand	Australia
19	Finland	Ireland	Belgium
20	New Zealand	Kazakhstan	South Korea
21	Ireland	South Africa	Luxembourg
22	United Kingdom	United States	New Zealand
23	South Korea	Indonesia	Hong Kong
24	France	Estonia	Ireland
25	Belgium	China	Malaysia
26	Thailand	South Korea	Czech Republic
27	Japan	Austria	Estonia
28	Chile	Germany	Spain
29	Czech Republic	United Kingdom	Portugal
30	Iceland	India	Lithuania
31	India	Philippines	China
32	Poland	Bulgaria	Italy
33	Kazakhstan	Czech Republic	Greece
34	Estonia	Lithuania	Slovenia
35	Indonesia	Peru	Hungary
36	Spain	Poland	Poland
37	Portugal	Japan	Qatar
38	Brazil	Colombia	Russia
39	Philippines	Jordan	Kazakhstan
40	Italy	Russia	Slovakia
41	Peru	Slovakia	Ukraine
42	Hungary	France	Croatia
43	Lithuania	Belgium	Romania
44	South Africa	Portugal	Chile

Notes: Overall competitiveness of 58 economies is calculated by combining four factors: economic performance, government efficiency, business efficiency and infrastructure. Column 1 is based on 246 criteria, using hard data and survey data. Column 2 measures government efficiency, looking at public finance, fiscal policy, institutional and societal frameworks and business legislation. Column 3 includes basic, technological and scientific infrastructure, health and environment, and education.

The business environment

		2010–14 score	2005–2009 score	2005–2009 ranking
1	Singapore	8.70	8.62	1
2	Switzerland	8.44	8.50	2
3	Finland	8.43	8.27	5
4	Canada	8.40	8.44	3
	Hong Kong	8.40	8.35	4
6	Australia	8.32	8.22	9
	Denmark	8.32	8.22	7
8	New Zealand	8.28	7.97	14
	Sweden	8.28	8.21	10
10	Netherlands	8.15	8.23	6
11	Norway	8.05	8.05	12
	Taiwan	8.05	7.61	19
13	United States	8.01	8.22	8
14	Germany	7.96	8.02	13
15	Chile	7.94	7.78	16
16	Belgium	7.85	7.82	15
17	Ireland	7.83	8.12	11
18	Qatar	7.82	7.28	22
19	France	7.73	7.58	20
20	Austria	7.69	7.73	17
21	United Kingdom	7.51	7.67	18
22	Spain	7.49	7.34	21
23	Israel	7.48	7.21	24
24	Malaysia	7.38	7.22	23
25	South Korea	7.37	6.87	31
26	Japan	7.35	7.07	29
27	United Arab Emirates	7.32	7.17	25
28	Poland	7.28	6.94	30
29	Czech Republic	7.27	7.15	26
	Estonia	7.27	7.11	28
31	Bahrain	7.13	7.14	27
32	Slovakia	6.99	6.84	32
33	Slovenia	6.97	6.84	33
34	Kuwait	6.96	6.54	38
35	Cyprus	6.90	6.81	34
	Mexico	6.90	6.66	36
37	Hungary	6.79	6.59	37
38	Thailand	6.77	6.28	43
39	Portugal	6.72	6.69	35
40	Brazil	6.62	6.37	41
41	Lithuania	6.55	6.38	40
42	Costa Rica	6.47	6.36	42
43	Italy	6.43	6.43	39
44	Saudi Arabia	6.40	5.99	49
45	Peru	6.38	6.17	44
46	China	6.36	5.83	54

Note: Scores reflect the opportunities for, and hindrances to, the conduct of business, measured by countries' rankings in ten categories including market potential, tax and labour-market policies, infrastructure, skills and the political environment. Scores reflect average and forecast average over given date range.

Business creativity and research

Innovation index[a]
2009

1	United States	5.77		13	Netherlands	4.79
2	Switzerland	5.56		14	Belgium	4.62
3	Finland	5.53		15	United Kingdom	4.60
4	Japan	5.51		16	Iceland	4.55
5	Sweden	5.39		17	Norway	4.53
6	Taiwan	5.28		18	France	4.50
7	Germany	5.11		19	Austria	4.46
8	Singapore	5.09		20	Australia	4.43
9	Israel	5.06		21	Luxembourg	4.31
10	Denmark	5.04		22	Ireland	4.29
11	South Korea	4.84		23	New Zealand	4.10
12	Canada	4.80		24	Malaysia	4.06

Technological readiness index[b]
2009

1	Sweden	6.15		13	United States	5.61
2	Netherlands	6.02		14	Iceland	5.57
3	Switzerland	6.01		15	South Korea	5.50
4	Denmark	5.92		16	Estonia	5.49
5	Luxembourg	5.91		17	United Arab Emirates	5.44
6	Singapore	5.90		18	Taiwan	5.43
7	Norway	5.81		19	Australia	5.39
8	United Kingdom	5.79			Austria	5.39
9	Hong Kong	5.68		21	Ireland	5.27
10	Finland	5.64		22	Belgium	5.26
11	Canada	5.63		23	France	5.24
	Germany	5.63			New Zealand	5.24

Brain drain[c]

Highest, 2009			Lowest, 2009		
1	Bosnia	1.9	1	Qatar	6.0
2	Guyana	1.9		United States	6.0
3	Serbia	1.9	3	Switzerland	5.8
4	Zimbabwe	1.9		United Arab Emirates	5.8
5	Nepal	2.0	5	Norway	5.4
6	Algeria	2.2		Singapore	5.4
7	Bulgaria	2.2	7	Bahrain	5.2
8	Bolivia	2.3		Chile	5.2
9	Kyrgyzstan	2.3		Hong Kong	5.2
10	Macedonia	2.3		Sweden	5.2
11	Burundi	2.4			
12	Chad	2.4			

a The innovation index is a measure of the adoption of new technology, and the interaction between the business and science sectors. It includes measures of the investment into research institutions and protection of intellectual property rights.
b The technological readiness index measures the ability of the economy to adopt new technologies. It includes measures of information and communication technology (ICT) usage, the regulatory framework with regard to ICT, and the availability of new technology to business.
c Scores: 1=talented people leave for other countries, 7=they always remain in home country.

Total expenditure on R&D

% of GDP, 2007		*$bn, 2007*	
1 Israel	4.68	1 United States	368.8
2 Sweden	3.64	2 Japan	148.4
3 Finland	3.47	3 Germany	83.8
4 Japan	3.40	4 France	53.9
5 South Korea	3.01	5 China	48.8
6 Switzerland	2.90	6 United Kingdom	42.7
7 United States	2.67	7 South Korea	28.6
8 Taiwan	2.62	8 Canada	27.0
9 Austria	2.56	9 Italy	21.1
10 Denmark	2.55	10 Sweden	16.5
11 Germany	2.53	11 Australia	15.8
12 Singapore	2.27	12 Spain	14.8
13 Australia	2.09	13 Brazil	14.7
14 France	2.08	14 Russia	14.5
15 Canada	1.89	15 Netherlands	13.2
16 Belgium	1.87	16 Switerland	10.5
17 United Kingdom	1.76	17 Taiwan	10.1
18 Netherlands	1.70	18 Austria	9.5
19 Luxembourg	1.63	19 Belgium	8.6
20 Norway	1.57	20 Finland	8.5
21 Czech Republic	1.54	21 Denmark	7.9
22 Slovenia	1.53	22 Israel	7.7
23 China	1.49	23 Norway	6.1
24 Ireland	1.31	24 India	4.8
25 Spain	1.20	25 Mexico	3.9

Patents

No. of patents granted to residents		*No. of patents in force*	
Total, average 2005–07		*Per 100,000 people, 2007*	
1 Japan	127,644	1 Luxembourg	5,605
2 United States	81,329	2 Ireland	3,233
3 South Korea	78,122	3 Hong Kong	2,856
4 Taiwan	36,722	4 Taiwan	1,389
5 China	25,909	5 South Korea	1,170
6 Russia	19,005	6 Sweden	1,150
7 Germany	13,839	7 Singapore	970
8 France	9,642	8 Japan	879
9 Italy	5,257	9 Belgium	839
10 United Kingdom	2,929	10 Finland	823
11 Ukraine	2,485	11 New Zealand	809
12 Spain	2,185	12 United Kingdom	637
13 Netherlands	1,802	13 France	633
14 Canada	1,636	14 Germany	599
15 Kazakhstan	1,412	15 United States	593
16 Sweden	1,252	16 Australia	463
17 Poland	1,250	17 Norway	380
18 Australia	1,088	18 Canada	371
19 Finland	1,009	19 Portugal	367
20 Austria	961	20 Spain	355
21 India	954	21 Slovenia	353

Business costs and FDI

Office occupancy costs

Rent, taxes and operating expenses, $ per sq. metre, November 2009

1	London (West End), UK	1,990	12	Rio de Janeiro, Brazil	942
2	Tokyo (Inner Central), Japan	1,848	13	Abu Dhabi, UAE	909
				Milan, Italy	909
3	Tokyo (Outer Central), Japan	1,497	15	Zurich, Switzerland	898
			16	São Paulo, Brazil	881
4	Hong Kong (Central, CBD)	1,481	17	Dublin, Ireland	875
5	Moscow, Russia	1,416	18	Geneva, Switzerland	850
6	Paris, France	1,319	19	Istanbul, Turkey	834
7	Mumbai (CBD), India	1,304	20	Frankfurt am Main, Germany	812
8	Dubai, UAE	1,172	21	Hong Kong (Citywide)	809
9	London (City), UK	1,163	22	Edinburgh, UK	775
10	New Delhi (CBD), India	957	23	Manchester, UK	767
11	Luxembourg City, Luxembourg	954	24	New York (Midtown), US	742
			25	Rome, Italy	740

Minimum wage

Minimum wage as a ratio of the median wage of full-time workers, 2008

1	France	0.63	11	United Kingdom	0.46
2	New Zealand	0.59	12	Poland	0.45
3	Greece	0.53		Spain	0.45
	Ireland	0.53	14	Netherlands	0.43
5	Australia	0.52		Slovakia	0.43
6	Belgium	0.51	16	Canada	0.42
7	Slovenia	0.50		Lithuania	0.42
8	Hungary	0.47	18	Luxembourg	0.40
	Portugal	0.47	19	South Korea	0.39
	Romania	0.47			

Foreign direct investment[a]

Inflows, $m, 2008			*Outflows, $m, 2008*		
1	United States	316,112	1	United States	311,796
2	France	117,510	2	France	220,046
3	China	108,312	3	Germany	156,457
4	United Kingdom	96,939	4	Japan	128,020
5	Russia	70,320	5	United Kingdom	111,411
6	Spain	65,539	6	Switzerland	86,295
7	Hong Kong	63,003	7	Canada	77,667
8	Belgium	59,680	8	Spain	77,317
9	Australia	46,774	9	Belgium	68,278
10	Brazil	45,058	10	Hong Kong	59,920
11	Canada	44,712	11	Netherlands	57,571
12	Sweden	43,655	12	Russia	52,390
13	India	41,554	13	China	52,150
14	Saudi Arabia	38,223	14	Italy	43,839
15	Germany	24,939	15	Sweden	37,351
16	Japan	24,426	16	Australia	35,938
17	Singapore	22,725	17	Denmark	28,868

Note: CBD is Central Business District.
a Investment in companies in a foreign country.

Business burdens and corruption

Number of days taken to register a new company
Lowest, 2010

1	New Zealand	1
2	Australia	2
3	Georgia	3
	Rwanda	3
	Singapore	3
6	Belgium	4
	Hungary	4
	Macedonia	4
9	Albania	5
	Canada	5
	Iceland	5
	Saudi Arabia	5

Highest, 2010

1	Suriname	694
2	Guinea-Bissau	213
3	Haiti	195
4	Congo-Kinshasa	149
5	Venezuela	141
6	Equatorial Guinea	136
7	Brazil	120
8	Brunei	116
9	Laos	100
10	Zimbabwe	96
11	Cambodia	85
12	Eritrea	84
13	Timor-Leste	83
14	Iraq	77

Corruption perceptions index[a]
2009, 10 = least corrupt

Lowest

1	New Zealand	9.4
2	Denmark	9.3
3	Singapore	9.2
	Sweden	9.2
5	Switzerland	9.0
6	Finland	8.9
	Netherlands	8.9
8	Australia	8.7
	Canada	8.7
	Iceland	8.7
11	Norway	8.6
12	Hong Kong	8.2
	Luxembourg	8.2
14	Germany	8.0
	Ireland	8.0

Highest

1	Somalia	1.1
2	Afghanistan	1.3
3	Myanmar	1.4
4	Iraq	1.5
	Sudan	1.5
6	Chad	1.6
7	Uzbekistan	1.7
8	Burundi	1.8
	Equatorial Guinea	1.8
	Guinea	1.8
	Haiti	1.8
	Iran	1.8
	Turkmenistan	1.8
14	Angola	1.9
	Congo-Brazzaville	1.9
	Congo-Kinshasa	1.9
	Guinea-Bissau	1.9
	Kyrgyzstan	1.9
	Venezuela	1.9

Business software piracy
% of software that is pirated, 2008

1	Georgia	95
2	Armenia	92
	Bangladesh	92
	Zimbabwe	92
5	Azerbaijan	90
	Moldova	90
	Sri Lanka	90
8	Yemen	89

9	Libya	87
10	Pakistan	86
	Venezuela	86
12	Indonesia	85
	Iraq	85
	Vietnam	85
15	Algeria	84
	Ukraine	84

a This index ranks countries based on how much corruption is perceived by business people, academics and risk analysts to exist among politicians and public officials.

Businesses and banks

Largest non-bank businesses
By market capitalisation, $bn
End December 2008

1	Exxon Mobil	United States	397.2
2	PetroChina	China	259.7
3	Microsoft	United States	251.7
4	BHP Billiton	Australia/United Kingdom	232.7
5	Wal-Mart Stores	United States	201.6
6	China Mobile	China	201.3
7	Procter & Gamble	United States	184.4
8	General Electric	United States	170.7
9	AT&T	United States	168.0
10	Royal Dutch Shell	United Kingdom/Netherlands	164.2
11	Johnson & Johnson	United States	162.2
12	Toyota Motor	Japan	156.7
13	Berkshire Hathaway	United States	149.6
14	Chevron	United States	148.3
15	Vodafone	United Kingdom	143.9
16	BP	United Kingdom	143.6
17	Nestlé	Switzerland	140.7
18	Cisco Systems	United States	132.2
19	Roche	Switzerland	132.1
20	Total	France	121.0
21	Pfizer	United States	119.5
22	Oracle	United States	117.6
23	Apple	United States	113.9
24	Novartis	Switzerland	113.0

End June 2010

1	Exxon Mobil	United States	291.9
2	PetroChina	China	267.1
3	Apple	United States	228.9
4	Microsoft	United States	201.7
5	China Mobile	China	201.4
6	Berkshire Hathaway	United States	197.4
7	Wal-Mart Stores	United States	178.3
8	Procter & Gamble	United States	172.7
9	Nestlé	Switzerland	166.6
10	Johnson & Johnson	United States	162.9
11	BHP Billiton	Australia/United Kingdom	161.7
12	IBM	United States	158.3
13	Royal Dutch Shell	United Kingdom/Netherlands	154.5
14	General Electric	United States	154.0
15	AT&T	United States	142.9
16	Petrobras	Brazil	142.7
17	Google	United States	141.7
18	Chevron	United States	136.3
19	Novartis	Switzerland	128.1
20	Vale	Brazil	123.5
21	Cisco Systems	United States	121.7
22	Roche	Switzerland	120.4
23	Toyota Motor	Japan	117.9
24	Coca-Cola	United States	115.6

Largest banks
By market capitalisation, $bn
End December 2008

1	Industrial and Commercial Bank of China	China	173.9
2	China Construction Bank	China	128.3
3	Wells Fargo	United States	124.7
4	JPMorgan Chase	United States	117.7
5	HSBC Holdings	United Kingdom	116.8
6	Bank of China	China	98.2
7	Mitsubishi UFJ Financial Group	Japan	89.2
8	Banco Santander	Spain	75.3
9	Bank of America	United States	70.6
10	Royal Bank of Canada	Canada	52.3
11	Commonwealth Bank of Australia	Australia	50.7
12	Sumitomo Mitsui	Japan	49.7
13	Itaú Unibanco	Brazil	46.2
14	Intesa Sanpaolo	Italy	45.2
15	BBVA	Spain	44.5

End June 2010

1	Industrial and Commercial Bank of China	China	210.5
2	China Construction Bank	China	189.1
3	HSBC Holdings	United Kingdom	157.9
4	JPMorgan Chase	United States	145.7
5	Bank of America	United States	144.2
6	Wells Fargo	United States	133.4
7	Bank of China	China	127.6
8	Citigroup	United States	109.0
9	Banco Santander	Spain	86.9
10	Itaú Unibanco	Brazil	74.1
11	Royal Bank of Canada	Canada	67.7
12	Mitsubishi UFJ Financial Group	Japan	64.4
13	BNP Paribas	France	63.8
14	Commonwealth Bank of Australia	Australia	61.6
15	Toronto-Dominion Bank	Canada	56.3

Central bank staff
Per 100,000 population, 2009

Highest			Lowest		
1	Cayman Islands	307.1	1	China	0.2
2	Bermuda	217.9	2	Somalia	0.6
3	Seychelles	128.9	3	Ethiopia	0.8
4	Netherlands Antilles	91.9		Pakistan	0.8
5	Barbados	87.2	5	India	1.8
6	Panama	81.3	6	Central African States	2.1
7	Bahamas	75.1	7	North Korea	2.3
8	Malta	74.3	8	Brazil	2.4
9	Suriname	68.1		Myanmar	2.4
10	Aruba	66.0	10	Indonesia	2.5
11	Belize	55.4	11	Mexico	2.6
12	Luxembourg	51.4	12	Eritrea	2.7

Stockmarkets

Largest market capitalisation

$bn, end 2009

1	United States	15,077	23	Singapore	311
2	China	5,008	24	Belgium	261
3	Japan	3,378	25	Malaysia	256
4	United Kingdom	2,796	26	Norway	227
5	Hong Kong	2,292	27	Turkey	226
6	France	1,972	28	Chile	209
7	Canada	1,681	29	Denmark	187
8	Germany	1,298	30	Israel	182
9	Spain	1,297	31	Indonesia	178
10	Australia	1,258	32	Thailand	138
11	India	1,179	33	Poland	135
12	Brazil	1,167	34	Colombia	133
13	Switzerland	1,071	35	United Arab Emirates	110
14	Russia	861	36	Luxembourg	106
15	South Korea	836	37	Portugal	99
16	South Africa	705	38	Kuwait	96
17	Taiwan	696	39	Finland	91
18	Netherlands	543	40	Egypt	90
19	Sweden	432	41	Qatar	88
20	Mexico	341	42	Philippines	80
21	Saudi Arabia	319	43	Peru	70
22	Italy	317	44	New Zealand	67

Largest gains in global stockmarkets

$ terms, % increase December 31 2008 to December 29 2009

1	Brazil (BVSP)	142.6	25	Pakistan (KSE)	50.5
2	Russia (RTS $ terms)	128.7	26	Austria (ATX)	49.9
3	China (SSEB $ terms)	125.8	27	Hong Kong (Hang Seng)	49.4
4	Indonesia (JSX)	114.0	28	Malaysia (KLSE)	47.0
5	Turkey (ISE)	97.7	29	Denmark (OMXCB)	46.2
6	Argentina (MERV)	94.5	30	United States (NAScomp)	45.1
7	Norway (OSEAX)	91.3	31	Netherlands (AEX)	43.8
8	India (BSE)	88.3	32	Czech Republic (PX)	40.7
9	Israel (TA-100)	88.2	33	United Kingdom	
10	Chile (IGPA)	86.9		(FTSE 100)	39.9
11	Taiwan (TWI)	78.2	34	Belgium (Bel 20)	38.8
12	Hungary (BUX)	77.7	35	Egypt (Case 30)	36.5
13	China (SSEA)	76.1	36	Spain (Madrid SE)	34.5
14	Thailand (SET)	72.8	37	Germany (DAX)[a]	31.1
15	Colombia (IGBC)	71.7	38	Euro area	
16	Australia (All Ord.)	69.5		(FTSE Euro 100)	29.6
17	Venezuela (IBC)	69.0	39	France (CAC 40)	29.1
18	Singapore (STI)	68.3	40	Greece (Athex Comp)	28.9
19	South Africa (JSE AS)	61.1	41	Euro area (DJ STOXX 50)	28.2
	Sweden (OMXS30)	61.1	42	Saudi Arabia (Tadawul)	27.6
20	South Korea (KOSPI)	60.8	43	Italy (FTSE/MIB)	26.0
21	Mexico (IPC)	59.1	44	United States (S&P 500)	24.7
22	Poland (WIG)	53.2	45	Switzerland (SMI)	22.7
24	Canada (S&P TSX)	51.8	46	Japan (Nikkei 225)	21.5

a Total return index.

Highest growth in value traded
$ terms, % increase, 2004-09

1	Vietnam	10,457.1
2	Morocco	1,654.1
3	Bangladesh	1,540.6
4	Mongolia	1,500.0
5	United Arab Emirates	1,376.7
6	Ecuador	1,266.7
7	Montenegro	1,212.0
8	China	1,096.9
9	Zambia[a]	928.6
10	Malawi[b]	900.0
11	Egypt	841.7
12	Colombia	785.6
13	Brazil	593.7
14	Papua New Guinea[c]	525.0
15	Zimbabwe[a]	497.1
16	West Bank and Gaza[b]	494.5
17	Tunisia	456.2
18	Cyprus	438.1
19	Hong Kong	429.1
20	Lebanon	428.9
21	Russia	421.7
22	Philippines	369.3
23	Indonesia	318.4
24	Kazakhstan	317.4
25	Nepal	271.0
26	Mauritius	247.4
27	Poland	236.6
28	Oman	226.5
29	Chile	224.1
30	Singapore	210.2
31	Ukraine	194.0
32	India	187.2
33	Croatia	187.0
34	Côte d'Ivoire	183.0
35	Peru	178.3
36	Nigeria	174.6
37	Jordan	156.1
38	South Korea	147.5
39	New Zealand	141.6
40	United States	141.5
41	Ghana[b]	127.3
42	Uzbekistan	125.0
43	South Africa	110.3
44	Bahrain	107.5

Highest growth in number of listed companies
% increase, 2004-09

1	Vietnam	623.1
2	Serbia	333.2
3	Montenegro	180.0
4	Mauritius	114.6
5	United Arab Emirates	90.0
6	Ukraine	85.8
7	Kuwait	83.2
8	Malawi[b]	75.0
9	Saudi Arabia	74.0
10	Croatia	70.3
11	Papua New Guinea[a]	66.7
12	Qatar	65.5
13	Uganda	60.0
14	El Salvador[a]	59.4
15	Poland	57.3
16	Malta	53.8
17	Morocco	50.0
18	Nepal	43.5
19	Jordan	41.7
20	Kyrgyzstan	33.3
21	Oman	32.3
22	Kazakhstan	30.2
23	Sweden	30.1
24	Ecuador	30.0
25	Russia	29.8
26	West Bank and Gaza[a]	29.6
27	Hong Kong	29.0
28	Australia	24.2
29	Estonia	23.1
30	China	22.8
31	Ghana	20.7
32	Indonesia	20.2
33	Zimbabwe	19.0
34	Kenya	17.0
35	Bahrain	16.7
	Tanzania[b]	16.7
37	Denmark	15.7
38	Zambia[a]	15.4
39	Thailand	15.3
40	Norway	14.5
41	Uruguay	14.3
42	Bulgaria	13.3
43	South Korea	13.0
44	Tunisia	11.4
45	Botswana	11.1
46	Bolivia	8.8
47	Italy	8.2

a 2004–07   b 2004–08   c 2004–06

Transport: roads and cars

Longest road networks
Km, 2008 or latest

1	United States	6,478,345	21	Saudi Arabia	235,486
2	China	3,680,623	22	Argentina	231,374
3	India	3,407,584	23	Vietnam	226,095
4	Brazil	1,837,000	24	Philippines	201,236
5	Canada	1,199,800	25	Romania	199,021
6	Japan	1,190,744	26	Nigeria	193,486
7	France	1,050,274	27	Iran	175,354
8	Russia	946,000	28	Ukraine	169,404
9	Australia	814,120	29	Colombia	164,339
10	Sweden	796,184	30	Hungary	159,780
11	Spain	667,989	31	Belgium	153,890
12	Italy	487,868	32	Czech Republic	128,848
13	Turkey	427,142	33	Netherlands	127,700
14	Indonesia	402,590	34	Algeria	109,517
15	United Kingdom	396,976	35	Egypt	108,761
16	Poland	386,906	36	Austria	107,620
17	South Africa	364,877	37	South Korea	105,435
18	Mexico	359,112	38	Malaysia	98,924
19	Pakistan	262,478	39	Ireland	97,560
20	Germany	260,184	40	Belarus	96,518

Densest road networks
Km of road per km² land area, 2008 or latest

1	Macau	21.3	21	Austria	1.3
2	Malta	7.1		Estonia	1.3
3	Singapore	5.1		Spain	1.3
4	Belgium	5.0	24	Lithuania	1.2
5	Bahrain	4.1		Poland	1.2
6	Japan	3.2	26	Latvia	1.1
7	Netherlands	3.1		South Korea	1.1
8	Luxembourg	2.0		Taiwan	1.1
9	France	1.9	29	India	1.0
	Hong Kong	1.9		Portugal	1.0
	Slovenia	1.9	31	Israel	0.9
12	Sweden	1.8		Mauritius	0.9
13	Denmark	1.7		Slovakia	0.9
	Hungary	1.7	34	Romania	0.8
	Switzerland	1.7	35	Azerbaijan	0.7
16	Czech Republic	1.6		Germany	0.7
	Italy	1.6		Philippines	0.7
	United Kingdom	1.6		United States	0.7
19	Cyprus	1.4		Vietnam	0.7
	Ireland	1.4	40	Albania	0.6

Most crowded road networks
Number of vehicles per km of road network, 2008 or latest

1	Qatar	250.5	26	Poland	45.3
2	Hong Kong	245.1	27	Austria	43.6
3	Singapore	220.5	28	Spain	41.4
4	Kuwait	209.4	29	Cyprus	41.1
5	Macau	204.7	30	Czech Republic	38.1
6	Taiwan	171.6	31	Slovakia	38.0
7	Germany	167.8	32	Finland	37.5
8	United Arab Emirates	166.0	33	Belgium	37.4
9	South Korea	156.0	34	United States	36.7
10	Thailand	145.4	35	Denmark	36.2
11	Israel	123.7		Ukraine	36.2
12	Malta	123.6	37	New Zealand	35.5
13	Bahrain	121.4	38	France	35.4
14	United Kingdom	87.4	39	Russia	35.0
15	Italy	83.5	40	Morocco	34.7
16	Mauritius	82.2	41	Kazakhstan	30.1
17	Malaysia	78.7	42	Norway	29.0
18	Jordan	75.2	43	Slovenia	28.8
19	Netherlands	68.3	44	Moldova	28.7
20	Luxembourg	67.7	45	Algeria	26.2
21	Portugal	67.3	46	Ireland	23.4
22	Japan	62.4	47	Mexico	23.3
23	Switzerland	61.0	48	Macedonia	23.1
24	Croatia	58.0		Turkey	23.1
25	Bulgaria	56.9	50	Lithuania	22.3

Most used road networks
'000 vehicle-km per year per km of road network, 2008 or latest

1	Hong Kong	5,407	21	Bulgaria	535
2	Singapore	4,509	22	France	521
3	Germany	2,456	23	New Zealand	433
4	Israel	2,364	24	Norway	375
5	Bahrain	1,885	25	Czech Republic	366
6	United Kingdom	1,262	26	Poland	357
7	South Korea	1,250	27	Ireland	348
8	Croatia	890	28	Romania	341
9	Netherlands	861	29	South Africa	338
10	Luxembourg	853	30	Spain	336
11	Switzerland	814	31	Morocco	309
12	Cyprus	750	32	Mexico	307
13	United States	740	33	Slovenia	296
14	Austria	665	34	Australia	272
15	Finland	656	35	Canada	264
16	Japan	652		Egypt	264
17	Belgium	651	37	Slovakia	258
18	Peru	632	38	China	228
19	Denmark	628	39	Pakistan	189
20	Ecuador	574	40	Iceland	174

Highest car ownership
Number of cars per 1,000 population, 2008 or latest

1	Iceland	669	26	Kuwait	431
2	Luxembourg	664	27	Czech Republic	423
3	New Zealand	656	28	Latvia	417
4	Italy	609	29	Portugal	415
5	Brunei	608	30	Poland	393
6	Malta	550	31	Estonia	388
7	Australia	540	32	Denmark	381
8	Guam	532	33	Lebanon	359
9	Switzerland	529	34	Croatia	341
10	Austria	511	35	Bahrain	307
11	Slovenia	510	36	Hungary	303
12	France	496	37	Qatar	284
	United Kingdom	496	38	Bulgaria	281
14	Germany	491	39	Slovakia	269
	Spain	491	40	Taiwan	255
16	Finland	487	41	Israel	249
17	Lithuania	486	42	South Korea	248
18	Belgium	474	43	New Caledonia	245
19	Sweden	468	44	Malaysia	237
20	Netherlands	467	45	Réunion	229
21	Norway	461	46	Oman	209
22	Cyprus	460	47	Belarus	193
23	Japan	446		Russia	193
24	Greece	439	49	Romania	166
25	Ireland	437	50	Macedonia	149

Lowest car ownership
Number of cars per 1,000 population, 2008 or latest

1	Bangladesh	1		Myanmar	4
	Chad	1		Niger	4
	Cuba	1	23	Benin	5
	Ethiopia	1		Gambia, The	5
	Malawi	1		Guinea	5
	Rwanda	1		Liberia	5
7	Central African Rep	2	27	Pakistan	6
	Congo-Kinshasa	2		Papua New Guinea	6
	Eritrea	2	29	Burkina Faso	7
	Laos	2		Equatorial Guinea	7
	Mali	2	31	Congo-Brazzaville	8
	Nepal	2		Maldives	8
	Vietnam	2		Philippines	8
14	Burundi	3	34	Cameroon	9
	Guinea-Bissau	3		Kenya	9
	Lesotho	3	36	Haiti	10
	Madagascar	3	37	Nigeria	12
	Mauritania	3	38	Honduras	13
19	Ghana	4	39	Angola	15
	Mozambique	4		India	15

Car production

Number of cars produced, '000, 2008

1	Japan	10,108		21	Ukraine	414
2	China	6,712		22	Hungary	342
3	Germany	5,527			Malaysia	342
4	South Korea	3,804		24	Thailand	318
5	United States	3,750		25	Indonesia	314
6	Brazil	2,427		26	Argentina	301
7	France	2,145		27	Australia	276
8	Spain	1,943		28	South Africa	272
9	India	1,767		29	Sweden	252
10	United Kingdom	1,447		30	Romania	231
11	Canada	1,343		31	Pakistan	196
12	Russia	1,309		32	Taiwan	184
13	Mexico	1,260		33	Slovenia	180
14	Czech Republic	933		34	Venezuela	140
15	Iran	901		35	Portugal	132
16	Poland	840		36	Austria	125
17	Belgium	680		37	Colombia	88
18	Italy	659		38	Egypt	72
19	Turkey	656		39	Netherlands	59
20	Slovakia	576		40	Morocco	36

Cars sold

New car registrations, '000, 2008

1	United States	7,009		21	Malaysia	372
2	China	5,700		22	Argentina	354
3	Japan	4,538		23	Turkey	321
4	Germany	3,090		24	Poland	320
5	Russia	2,695		25	Austria	294
6	Italy	2,160		26	Switzerland	288
7	United Kingdom	2,132		27	Romania	286
8	France	2,050		28	Greece	267
9	India	1,669		29	Sweden	254
10	Brazil	1,653		30	Saudi Arabia	240
11	Spain	1,161		31	Pakistan	215
12	South Korea	1,017		32	Portugal	213
13	Canada	875		33	Colombia	186
14	Australia	800		34	Thailand	185
15	Mexico	765		35	Taiwan	184
16	Belgium	536		36	Egypt	178
17	Netherlands	500		37	Indonesia	162
18	South Africa	490		38	Israel	158
19	Nigeria	455		39	Chile	157
20	Venezuela	433		40	Hungary	156

Transport: planes and trains

Most air travel
Million passenger-km[a] per year, 2009

1	United States	1,277,955	16	India	69,646
2	China	283,013	17	Brazil	66,308
3	United Kingdom	232,273	18	Thailand	57,102
4	Germany	219,926	19	Italy	51,650
5	France	154,464	20	Malaysia	44,677
6	Japan	140,750	21	Turkey	35,844
7	Canada	107,431	22	Qatar	34,592
8	Singapore	96,432	23	Mexico	34,354
9	Netherlands	93,964	24	Indonesia	34,308
10	Spain	88,861	25	South Africa	28,546
11	Hong Kong	87,548	26	Switzerland	28,189
12	United Arab Emirates	86,443	27	Saudi Arabia	27,667
13	South Korea	82,236	28	Portugal	23,178
14	Russia	81,478	29	Israel	18,890
15	Ireland	72,696	30	Philippines	18,737

Busiest airports
Total passengers, m, 2009

1	Atlanta, Hartsfield	87.7
2	London, Heathrow	66.0
3	Beijing, Capital	65.7
4	Chicago, O'Hare	64.5
5	Tokyo, Haneda	61.9
6	Paris, Charles de Gaulle	57.9
7	Los Angeles, Intl.	56.9
8	Dallas, Ft. Worth	56.2
9	Frankfurt, Main	51.1
10	Denver, Intl.	50.3
11	Madrid, Barajas	48.5
12	New York, JFK	45.9
13	Hong Kong, Intl.	45.5
14	Amsterdam, Schiphol	43.6
15	Dubai, Intl.	41.5

Total cargo, m tonnes, 2009

1	Memphis, Intl.	3.71
2	Hong Kong, Intl.	3.48
3	Shanghai, Pudong Intl.	2.65
4	Seoul, Incheon	2.37
5	Anchorage, Intl.	2.04
6	Louisville, Standiford Fd.	1.97
7	Dubai, Intl.	1.96
8	Frankfurt, Main	1.93
9	Tokyo, Narita	1.90
10	Paris, Charles de Gaulle	1.83
11	Singapore, Changi	1.68
12	Miami, Intl.	1.57
13	Los Angeles, Intl.	1.53
14	Beijing, Capital	1.45
15	Taipei, Taoyuan Intl.	1.42

Average daily aircraft movements, take-offs and landings, 2009

1	Atlanta, Hartsfield	2,655
2	Chicago, O'Hare	2,269
3	Dallas, Ft. Worth	1,755
4	Denver, Intl.	1,665
5	Houston, George Bush Intercont.	1,582
6	Los Angeles, Intl.	1,498
7	Paris, Charles de Gaulle	1,433
8	Las Vegas, McCarran Intl.	1,396
9	Charlotte/Douglas, Intl.	1,390
10	Beijing	1,344
11	Philadelphia, Intl.	1,293
12	London, Heathrow	1,273
13	Frankfurt, Main	1,268
14	Phoenix, Skyharbor Intl.	1,251
15	Madrid, Barajas	1,194
16	Detroit, Metro	1,182
17	Minneapolis, St Paul	1,180
18	New York, JFK	1,125
	Newark	1,125
20	Toronto, Pearson Intl.	1,116

a Air passenger–km data refer to the distance travelled by aircraft of national origin.

Longest railway networks
'000 km, 2008

1	United States	226.2	21	Czech Republic	9.5
2	Russia	85.2	22	Turkey	8.7
3	China	66.5	23	Hungary	7.8
4	India	63.3		Pakistan	7.8
5	Canada	58.3	25	Iran	7.6
6	France	33.8	26	Australia	6.8
7	Germany	33.7	27	Finland	5.9
8	Brazil	29.8	28	Austria	5.7
9	Mexico	26.7	29	Belarus	5.5
10	Argentina	25.0	30	Chile	5.4
11	South Africa	22.1	31	Cuba	5.1
12	Ukraine	21.7	32	Algeria	4.7
13	Japan	20.0	33	Thailand	4.4
14	Poland	19.8	34	Bulgaria	4.2
15	Italy	17.0		Uzbekistan	4.2
16	United Kingdom	16.2	36	Norway	4.1
17	Spain	15.0	37	Serbia	3.8
18	Kazakhstan	14.2	38	Belgium	3.6
19	Romania	10.8		Congo-Brazzaville	3.6
20	Sweden	9.9		Slovakia	3.6

Most rail passengers
Km per person per year, 2008

1	Switzerland	2,292	13	Sweden	773
2	Japan	1,995	14	Belarus	771
3	France	1,370	15	Italy	769
4	Denmark	1,329	16	Finland	731
5	Austria	1,245	17	India	719
6	Russia	1,096	18	Luxembourg	666
7	Ukraine	1,057	19	South Korea	645
8	Belgium	1,009	20	Czech Republic	634
9	Kazakhstan	965	21	China	589
10	Germany	933	22	Hungary	565
11	Netherlands	922	23	Norway	558
12	United Kingdom	842	24	Spain	499

Most rail freight
Million tonnes-km per year, 2008

1	China	2,523,917	13	Poland	29,940
2	United States	2,431,181	14	France	26,482
3	Russia	1,865,305	15	Uzbekistan	24,238
4	India	551,448	16	Japan	22,100
5	Brazil	267,700	17	Iran	20,540
6	Canada	262,312	18	Austria	20,202
7	Kazakhstan	197,302	19	Latvia	18,693
8	Ukraine	196,188	20	Italy	13,569
9	South Africa	113,342	21	Switzerland	12,460
10	Germany	93,948	22	Lithuania	11,888
11	Australia	62,063	23	Turkmenistan	11,547
12	Belarus	42,472	24	Czech Republic	11,249

Transport: shipping

Merchant fleets
Number of vessels, by country of domicile, 2009

1	Japan	3,720	11	Denmark	914
2	Germany	3,522	12	Singapore	876
3	China	3,499	13	Indonesia	821
4	Greece	3,064	14	Italy	820
5	Russia	2,073	15	Netherlands	758
6	Norway	2,027	16	Hong Kong	680
7	United States	1,782	17	Taiwan	631
8	South Korea	1,235	18	India	564
9	Turkey	1,163	19	Vietnam	456
10	United Kingdom	918	20	Malaysia	435

By country of domicile, deadweight tonnage, m, January 2009

1	Japan	173.3	11	Taiwan	29.8
2	Greece	169.4	12	Singapore	28.2
3	Germany	105.0	13	Italy	19.8
4	China	92.8	14	Russia	18.3
5	Norway	50.2	15	Canada	17.2
6	South Korea	46.6		India	17.2
7	United States	40.0	17	Turkey	15.5
8	Hong Kong	33.7	18	Saudi Arabia	14.9
9	Denmark	31.6	19	Iran	14.6
10	United Kingdom	30.9	20	Belgium	13.4

Maritime trading
% of value of world trade generated, January 2009

1	United States	10.7	14	Spain	2.1
2	Germany	8.2	15	Singapore	2.0
3	China	7.9	16	Mexico	1.9
4	Japan	4.8	17	India	1.5
5	France	4.0		Taiwan	1.5
6	Netherlands	3.7	19	Saudi Arabia	1.3
7	Italy	3.4	20	Australia	1.2
	United Kingdom	3.4		Malaysia	1.2
9	Belgium	2.9		Poland	1.2
10	Canada	2.7		Switzerland	1.2
11	Russia	2.6	24	Austria	1.1
	South Korea	2.6		Brazil	1.1
13	Hong Kong	2.3			

% of world fleet deadweight tonnage, by country of ownership, January 2009

1	Japan	15.7	10	Italy	1.8
2	Germany	9.5	11	Russia	1.7
3	China	8.4	12	Canada	1.6
4	South Korea	4.2		India	1.6
5	United States	3.6	14	Saudi Arabia	1.4
6	Hong Kong	3.1	15	Belgium	1.2
7	United Kingdom	2.8	16	Malaysia	1.1
8	Taiwan	2.7	17	Netherlands	0.8
9	Singapore	2.6	18	France	0.6

Note: Deadweight tonnage is the weight the ships can safely carry.

Tourism

Most tourist arrivals
Number of arrivals, '000, 2008

1	France	79,300	21	Portugal	11,696
2	United States	58,030	22	Macau	10,605
3	Spain	57,316	23	Netherlands	10,104
4	China	53,049	24	South Africa	9,592
5	Italy	42,734	25	Croatia	9,415
6	United Kingdom	30,142	26	Hungary	8,814
7	Ukraine	25,392	27	Switzerland	8,608
8	Turkey	24,994	28	Japan	8,351
9	Germany	24,886	29	Ireland	8,028
10	Mexico	22,637	30	Singapore	7,778
11	Malaysia	22,052	31	Belgium	7,165
12	Austria	21,935	32	Tunisia	7,049
13	Russia	20,090	33	South Korea	6,891
14	Greece	17,835	34	Czech Republic	6,649
15	Hong Kong	17,320	35	Indonesia	6,234
16	Canada	17,128	36	Bulgaria	5,780
17	Saudi Arabia	14,757	37	Australia	5,586
18	Thailand	14,584	38	Syria	5,430
19	Poland	12,960	39	India	5,367
20	Egypt	12,296	40	Brazil	5,050

Biggest tourist spenders
$m, 2008

1	United States	84,149	11	Spain	19,662
2	Germany	83,240	12	Netherlands	19,521
3	United Kingdom	76,760	13	Belgium	17,444
4	France	37,523	14	Hong Kong	15,985
5	Italy	27,956	15	Australia	14,394
6	China	27,762	16	Sweden	13,600
7	Japan	27,044	17	Norway	13,487
8	Canada	24,096	18	Singapore	12,822
9	Russia	22,038	19	United Arab Emirates	11,905
10	South Korea	21,027	20	Austria	10,755

Largest tourist receipts
$m, 2008

1	United States	110,090	13	Hong Kong	15,300
2	Spain	61,628	14	Malaysia	15,277
3	France	55,595	15	Canada	15,106
4	Italy	45,727	16	Switzerland	14,408
5	China	40,843	17	Macau	13,382
6	Germany	40,018	18	Netherlands	13,375
7	United Kingdom	36,028	19	Mexico	13,289
8	Australia	24,660	20	Sweden	12,490
9	Turkey	21,951	21	Belgium	12,396
10	Austria	21,791	22	Russia	11,943
11	Thailand	17,651	23	India	11,832
12	Greece	17,114	24	Poland	11,771

Education

Primary enrolment
Number enrolled as % of relevant age group

Highest		Lowest	
1 Sierra Leone	158	1 Eritrea	52
2 Madagascar	152	2 Papua New Guinea	55
3 Rwanda	151	3 Niger	62
4 Burundi	136	4 Côte d'Ivoire	74
5 Brazil	130	Sudan	74
6 Iran	128	6 Oman	75
7 Nepal	124	7 Central African Rep	77
Syria	124	8 Burkina Faso	79
9 Indonesia	121	9 Armenia	80
10 Belize	120	10 Chad	83
Colombia	120	11 Senegal	84
Guinea-Bissau	120	12 Pakistan	85
Malawi	120	Yemen	85
Uganda	120	14 Gambia, The	86
15 Zambia	119	15 Andorra	87

Highest secondary enrolment
Number enrolled as % of relevant age group

1	Australia	148		Iceland	110
2	Netherlands	120	13	Azerbaijan	106
	New Zealand	120	14	Bulgaria	105
4	Denmark	119	15	Sweden	103
	Spain	119	16	Greece	102
6	Latvia	115		Uzbekistan	102
7	France	113	18	Canada	101
	Ireland	113		Germany	101
	Norway	113		Japan	101
10	Finland	111		Portugal	101
11	Belgium	110			

Highest tertiary enrolment[a]
Number enrolled as % of relevant age group

1	Cuba	122	11	Norway	76
2	South Korea	96		Lithuania	76
3	Finland	94	13	Australia	75
4	Greece	91		Russia	75
5	Slovenia	85		Sweden	75
6	United States	82	16	Belarus	73
7	Denmark	80	17	Iceland	72
8	New Zealand	79	18	Latvia	69
	Ukraine	79	19	Argentina	68
10	Venezuela	78		Spain	68

Notes: Latest available year 2005–09. The gross enrolment ratios shown are the actual number enrolled as a percentage of the number of children in the official primary age group. They may exceed 100 when children outside the primary age group are receiving primary education.

a Tertiary education includes all levels of post-secondary education including courses leading to awards not equivalent to a university degree, courses leading to a first university degree and postgraduate courses.

Least literate
% adult population[a]

#	Country	Value	#	Country	Value
1	Mali	26.2		Côte d'Ivoire	54.6
2	Burkina Faso	28.7	17	Bangladesh	55.0
	Niger	28.7	18	Morocco	56.4
4	Chad	32.7	19	Mauritania	56.8
5	Ethiopia	35.9	20	Nepal	57.9
6	Guinea	38.0	21	Liberia	58.1
7	Sierra Leone	39.8	22	Papua New Guinea	59.6
8	Benin	40.8	23	Nigeria	60.1
9	Senegal	41.9	24	Yemen	60.9
10	Gambia, The	45.3	25	India	62.8
11	Guinea-Bissau	51.0	26	Togo	64.9
12	Bhutan	52.8	27	Eritrea	65.3
13	Pakistan	53.7	28	Ghana	65.8
14	Mozambique	54.0	29	Burundi	65.9
15	Central African Rep	54.6	30	Egypt	66.4

Class sizes
Pupils per teacher in primary schools

#	Country	Value	#	Country	Value
1	Malawi	93		Cambodia	49
2	Central African Rep	90	16	Eritrea	47
3	Rwanda	68		Kenya	47
4	Mozambique	64		Madagascar	47
5	Chad	62	19	Cameroon	46
	Guinea-Bissau	62		Nigeria	46
7	Zambia	61	21	Benin	45
8	Ethiopia	59	22	Guinea	44
9	Burundi	52		Sierra Leone	44
	Congo-Brazzaville	52	24	Côte d'Ivoire	42
	Tanzania	52	25	Timor-Leste	41
12	Mali	51	26	Congo-Kinshasa	39
13	Uganda	50		Niger	39
14	Burkina Faso	49		Togo	39

Education spending
% of GDP

Highest			Lowest		
1	Cuba	13.3	1	Bermuda	1.2
2	Lesotho	12.4	2	Central African Rep	1.3
3	Moldova	8.2		United Arab Emirates	1.3
4	Botswana	8.1	4	Zambia	1.4
	Maldives	8.1	5	Cambodia	1.6
6	Denmark	7.9	6	Guinea	1.7
	Swaziland	7.9	7	Congo-Kinshasa	1.8
8	Iceland	7.6	8	Azerbaijan	1.9
9	Burundi	7.2		Chad	1.9
10	Timor-Leste	7.1	10	Eritrea	2.0
	Tunisia	7.1		Gambia, The	2.0
12	Cyprus	7.0		Lebanon	2.0
	Kenya	7.0		Macau	2.0

a   Latest available year 2004–09.

Life expectancy

Highest life expectancy
Years, 2010–15

#	Country	Value	#	Country	Value
1	Japan	83.7	25	Luxembourg	80.3
2	Hong Kong	82.8		Malta	80.3
3	Andorra[a]	82.5	27	Cyprus	80.2
	Switzerland	82.5		Martinique	80.2
5	Iceland	82.3	29	Greece	80.1
6	Australia	82.2		United Kingdom	80.1
7	France	81.9	31	South Korea	80.0
8	Italy	81.6	32	United States	79.9
	Spain	81.6	33	Channel Islands	79.8
	Sweden	81.6		Guadeloupe	79.8
11	Israel	81.5	35	Virgin Islands (US)	79.7
12	Canada	81.4	36	Costa Rica	79.4
	Macau	81.4		Faroe Islands[a]	79.4
14	Norway	81.3		Portugal	79.4
15	New Zealand	81.0		Puerto Rico	79.4
	Singapore	81.0	40	Chile	79.1
17	Austria	80.8		Cuba	79.1
	Belgium	80.8		Slovenia	79.1
19	Netherlands	80.6	43	Denmark	79.0
20	Finland	80.5	44	Barbados	78.2
	Germany	80.5		Kuwait	78.2
	Ireland	80.5	46	United Arab Emirates	78.1
23	Bermuda[a]	80.4	47	Taiwan[a]	78.0
	Cayman Islands[a]	80.4	48	Brunei	77.7

Highest male life expectancy
Years, 2010–15

#	Country	Value	#	Country	Value
1	Iceland	80.8	10	Canada	79.2
2	Andorra[a]	80.3		Norway	79.2
3	Switzerland	80.2	12	New Zealand	79.1
4	Japan	80.1	13	France	78.6
5	Australia	80.0		Italy	78.6
6	Hong Kong	79.9		Spain	78.6
7	Sweden	79.6	16	Netherlands	78.5
8	Israel	79.4		Singapore	78.5
	Macau	79.4	18	Malta	78.4

Highest female life expectancy
Years, 2010–15

#	Country	Value	#	Country	Value
1	Japan	87.2		Iceland	83.9
2	Hong Kong	85.7	11	Bermuda[a]	83.7
3	France	85.1	12	Canada	83.6
4	Andorra[a]	84.8		Finland	83.6
5	Spain	84.7		Sweden	83.6
	Switzerland	84.7	15	Israel	83.4
7	Italy	84.6		Macau	83.4
8	Australia	84.4		Norway	83.4
9	Belgium	83.9		Singapore	83.4

a 2009 estimate.

Lowest life expectancy
Years, 2010–15

1	Afghanistan	45.5	26	Malawi	56.3
2	Lesotho	46.9	27	Kenya	56.9
3	Central African Rep	48.6	28	Senegal	57.1
4	Swaziland	48.7	29	Ethiopia	57.2
5	Congo-Kinshasa	48.8	30	Gambia, The	57.5
6	Sierra Leone	48.9	31	Ghana	58.0
7	Nigeria	49.1	32	Mauritania	58.2
8	Mozambique	49.2	33	Tanzania	58.3
9	Angola	49.3	34	Côte d'Ivoire	59.6
10	Zambia	49.4	35	Sudan	59.8
11	Guinea-Bissau	49.6	36	Guinea	60.1
12	Chad	50.0		Liberia	60.1
13	Mali	50.2	38	Eritrea	61.4
14	Zimbabwe	50.4	39	Haiti	62.1
15	Somalia	51.5	40	Namibia	62.2
16	Rwanda	52.0	41	Madagascar	62.3
17	Equatorial Guinea	52.1		Papua New Guinea	62.3
18	Burundi	52.4	43	Gabon	62.5
19	Cameroon	52.7	44	Timor-Leste	63.2
20	South Africa	52.9	45	Benin	63.3
21	Niger	53.8		Cambodia	63.3
22	Burkina Faso	54.5	47	Togo	64.0
	Congo-Brazzaville	54.5	48	Myanmar	64.5
24	Botswana	55.5	49	Yemen	64.9
25	Uganda	55.6	50	India	65.2

Lowest male life expectancy
Years, 2010–15

1	Afghanistan	45.5	11	Mozambique	48.8
2	Lesotho	46.9	12	Mali	49.5
3	Angola	47.2	13	Swaziland	49.7
	Central African Rep	47.2	14	Rwanda	50.0
	Congo-Kinshasa	47.2		Somalia	50.0
6	Sierra Leone	47.6	16	Zimbabwe	50.4
7	Guinea-Bissau	48.1	17	Burundi	50.7
8	Nigeria	48.6	18	Equatorial Guinea	50.9
9	Chad	48.7	19	South Africa	51.8
	Zambia	48.7	20	Cameroon	52.0

Lowest female life expectancy
Years, 2010–15

1	Afghanistan	45.5	10	Congo-Kinshasa	50.4
2	Lesotho	46.6	11	Mali	50.9
3	Swaziland	47.6	12	Guinea-Bissau	51.2
4	Mozambique	49.4	13	Chad	51.3
5	Nigeria	49.7	14	Angola	51.4
6	Zimbabwe	49.8	15	Somalia	53.0
7	Central African Rep	50.0	16	Equatorial Guinea	53.3
	Zambia	50.0	17	Cameroon	53.4
9	Sierra Leone	50.3	18	South Africa	53.8

Death rates and infant mortality

Highest death rates
Number of deaths per 1,000 population, 2010–15

1	Afghanistan	18.20		49	Denmark	10.40
2	Lesotho	16.30			Greece	10.40
3	Ukraine	16.10		51	Gambia, The	10.30
4	Congo-Kinshasa	15.80			Kenya	10.30
	Guinea-Bissau	15.80			North Korea	10.30
6	Central African Rep	15.70		54	Montenegro	10.20
7	Chad	15.50			Slovenia	10.20
8	Nigeria	15.30		56	Slovakia	10.10
9	Angola	15.20		57	Tanzania	10.00
10	Russia	15.10		58	Côte d'Ivoire	9.80
	South Africa	15.10			Japan	9.80
12	Mozambique	14.70			Senegal	9.80
13	Belarus	14.60			Sweden	9.80
	Bulgaria	14.60			United Kingdom	9.80
15	Sierra Leone	14.50		63	Belgium	9.70
	Somalia	14.50			Finland	9.70
	Zambia	14.50			Guinea	9.70
18	Mali	14.20			Macedonia	9.70
	Swaziland	14.20		67	Channel Islands	9.60
20	Latvia	13.90		68	Austria	9.50
21	Equatorial Guinea	13.80			Liberia	9.50
	Lithuania	13.80			Mauritania	9.50
23	Rwanda	13.50			Sudan	9.50
24	Hungary	13.40		72	Uruguay	9.20
25	Moldova	13.30		73	Thailand	9.10
26	Cameroon	13.20		74	Armenia	9.00
27	Niger	13.10			France	9.00
28	Estonia	13.00		76	Gabon	8.90
29	Burundi	12.90			Haiti	8.90
	Zimbabwe	12.90			Spain	8.90
31	Romania	12.60		79	Myanmar	8.80
32	Georgia	12.50			Netherlands	8.80
33	Congo-Brazzaville	12.30		81	Faroe Islands[a]	8.70
34	Botswana	12.10		82	Norway	8.50
35	Croatia	12.00			Switzerland	8.50
	Serbia	12.00		84	Malta	8.40
37	Burkina Faso	11.80			Namibia	8.40
38	Uganda	11.10		86	Trinidad & Tobago	8.30
39	Germany	11.00		87	Benin	8.20
40	Czech Republic	10.90			Madagascar	8.20
41	Kazakhstan	10.80			Martinique	8.20
42	Ethiopia	10.70			Puerto Rico	8.20
43	Malawi	10.60		91	Greenland[a]	8.10
44	Bosnia	10.50			Guadeloupe	8.10
	Ghana	10.50			India	8.10
	Italy	10.50			Luxembourg	8.10
	Poland	10.50		95	Mauritius	8.00
	Portugal	10.50				

Note: Both death and, in particular, infant mortality rates can be underestimated in certain countries where not all deaths are officially recorded.   a 2009 estimate.

Highest infant mortality
Number of deaths per 1,000 live births, 2010–15

1	Afghanistan	146.9		Côte d'Ivoire	75.9
2	Chad	123.3	24	Malawi	74.0
3	Congo-Kinshasa	109.4	25	Gambia, The	72.2
4	Angola	105.3	26	Ethiopia	70.9
5	Guinea-Bissau	104.5	27	Mauritania	68.8
6	Nigeria	103.2	28	Ghana	67.0
7	Somalia	101.2	29	Uganda	66.9
8	Mali	99.6	30	Togo	65.7
9	Sierra Leone	99.0	31	Myanmar	63.4
10	Central African Rep	97.3	32	Sudan	61.9
11	Rwanda	92.4	33	Haiti	60.9
12	Burundi	91.0	34	Lesotho	60.7
13	Equatorial Guinea	90.9	35	Pakistan	57.4
14	Guinea	88.0	36	Madagascar	57.3
15	Liberia	87.7	37	Kenya	57.2
16	Niger	81.4	38	Tajikistan	56.4
17	Cameroon	79.8	39	Timor-Leste	56.3
18	Zambia	78.4	40	Senegal	55.7
19	Congo-Brazzaville	77.5	41	Tanzania	55.2
20	Benin	77.1	42	Swaziland	53.2
21	Mozambique	76.9	43	Cambodia	52.8
22	Burkina Faso	75.9	44	India	49.5

Lowest death rates
No. deaths per 1,000 pop., 2010–15

1	United Arab Emirates	1.5
2	Kuwait	2.1
	Qatar	2.1
4	Bahrain	2.6
5	Oman	2.8
6	Brunei	3.0
7	Syria	3.3
	West Bank and Gaza	3.3
9	Belize	3.5
10	Saudi Arabia	3.6
11	Jordan	4.0
12	Libya	4.2
13	Costa Rica	4.3
14	British Virgin Is[a]	4.4
15	Malaysia	4.6
	Nicaragua	4.6
17	Cape Verde	4.7
	Macau	4.7
	Philippines	4.7

Lowest infant mortality
No. deaths per 1,000 live births, 2010–15

1	Bermuda[a]	2.5
2	Iceland	2.8
3	Sweden	2.9
4	Singapore	3.0
5	Finland	3.1
	Japan	3.1
7	Norway	3.3
8	Czech Republic	3.6
	Hong Kong	3.6
	Slovenia	3.6
11	Greece	3.7
12	Andorra[a]	3.8
	France	3.8
	Italy	3.8
	Spain	3.8
16	Switzerland	3.9
17	Belgium	4.0
	Germany	4.0
	Luxembourg	4.0
20	Australia	4.1
	Austria	4.1
	Portugal	4.1

a 2009 estimate.

Death and disease

Diabetes

% of population aged 20–79, 2010 estimate

1	Mauritius	17.0
2	Réunion	16.1
3	Bahrain	14.4
4	Netherlands Antilles	14.0
5	Saudi Arabia	13.6
6	French Polynesia	13.5
7	Qatar	13.3
8	Aruba	12.8
9	Singapore	12.7
	Virgin Islands (US)	12.7
11	Portugal	12.4
	Puerto Rico	12.4
13	United States	12.3
14	United Arab Emirates	12.2
15	Germany	12.0
16	Canada	11.6
17	Sri Lanka	11.5
18	Trinidad & Tobago	11.4
19	Switzerland	11.3

Cardiovascular disease

Deaths per 100,000 population, age standardised, 2004

1	Turkmenistan	832
2	Kazakhstan	792
3	Afghanistan	719
4	Armenia	674
5	Uzbekistan	663
6	Kyrgyzstan	653
7	Russia	645
8	Tajikistan	642
9	Moldova	634
10	Ukraine	633
11	Belarus	614
12	Somalia	601
13	Azerbaijan	593
14	Iraq	586
15	Yemen	544
16	Sudan	543
17	Bulgaria	529
18	Egypt	515
19	Albania	485

Cancer

Deaths per 100,000 population, age standardised, 2004

1	Mongolia	289
2	Bolivia	239
3	Hungary	204
4	Angola	190
5	Sierra Leone	184
6	Niger	182
7	Armenia	178
	Czech Republic	178
9	Poland	177
10	Côte d'Ivoire	170
11	Kazakhstan	168
12	Denmark	167
	Uruguay	167
14	Croatia	166
	Equatorial Guinea	166
	Mali	166
17	Slovakia	165
	Slovenia	165
19	Afghanistan	164
20	Peru	163
	Serbia	163
22	Estonia	162

Tuberculosis

Incidence per 100,000 population, 2008

1	Swaziland	1,227
2	South Africa	960
3	Zimbabwe	762
4	Namibia	747
5	Botswana	712
6	Lesotho	635
7	Sierra Leone	608
8	Timor-Leste	498
9	Cambodia	490
10	Zambia	468
11	Gabon	452
12	Togo	438
13	Mozambique	420
14	Côte d'Ivoire	410
15	Myanmar	404
16	Congo-Brazzaville	393
17	Somalia	388
18	Rwanda	387
19	Congo-Kinshasa	382
20	Ethiopia	368
21	Burundi	357
22	North Korea	344
23	Central African Rep	336

Note: Statistics are not available for all countries. The number of cases diagnosed and reported depends on the quality of medical practice and administration and can be under-reported in a number of countries.

Measles immunisation
*Lowest % of children aged
12–23 months, 2008*

1	Chad	23
2	Somalia	24
3	Laos	52
4	Lebanon	53
5	Papua New Guinea	54
6	Gabon	55
7	Haiti	58
8	Sierra Leone	60
9	Benin	61
10	Central African Rep	62
	Nigeria	62
	South Africa	62
	Yemen	62
14	Côte d'Ivoire	63
15	Guinea	64
	Liberia	64
17	Mauritania	65
18	Azerbaijan	66
	Ecuador	66
	Zimbabwe	66

DPT[a] immunisation
*Lowest % of children aged
12–23 months, 2008*

1	Chad	20
2	Somalia	31
3	Gabon	38
4	Venezuela	47
5	Papua New Guinea	52
6	Haiti	53
7	Central African Rep	54
	Nigeria	54
9	Sierra Leone	60
10	Laos	61
11	Iraq	62
	Zimbabwe	62
13	Guinea-Bissau	63
14	Liberia	64
	Uganda	64
16	Guinea	66
	India	66
	Niger	66
19	Benin	67
	South Africa	67

HIV/AIDS
*Prevalence among population
aged 15–49, %, 2007*

1	Swaziland	26.1
2	Botswana	23.9
3	Lesotho	23.2
4	South Africa	18.1
5	Namibia	15.3
	Zimbabwe	15.3
7	Zambia	15.2
8	Mozambique	12.5
9	Malawi	11.9
10	Central African Rep	6.3
11	Tanzania	6.2
12	Gabon	5.9
13	Uganda	5.4
14	Cameroon	5.1
15	Côte d'Ivoire	3.9
16	Chad	3.5
	Congo-Brazzaville	3.5
18	Equatorial Guinea	3.4
19	Togo	3.3
20	Nigeria	3.1
21	Bahamas	3.0
22	Rwanda	2.8
23	Suriname	2.4
24	Haiti	2.2

AIDS
*Estimated deaths per 100,000
pop., 2007*

1	Zimbabwe	1,049
2	Lesotho	896
3	Swaziland	876
4	South Africa	721
5	Botswana	585
6	Malawi	488
7	Zambia	470
8	Mozambique	379
9	Central African Rep	253
10	Uganda	249
11	Namibia	246
12	Tanzania	237
13	Cameroon	210
14	Côte d'Ivoire	197
15	Gabon	173
16	Congo-Brazzaville	170
17	Togo	138
18	Chad	130
19	Burundi	129
20	Nigeria	115
21	Bahamas	100
	Belize	100
23	Ghana	89
24	Ethiopia	81

a Diptheria, pertussis and tetanus

Health

Highest health spending
As % of GDP, 2007

1	United States	15.7
2	Burundi	13.9
3	Timor-Leste	13.6
4	France	11.0
5	Switzerland	10.8
6	Liberia	10.6
7	Cuba	10.4
	Germany	10.4
9	Moldova	10.3
	Rwanda	10.3
11	Austria	10.1
	Canada	10.1
13	Argentina	10.0
	Portugal	10.0
15	Malawi	9.9
	Serbia	9.9
17	Bosnia	9.8
	Denmark	9.8
	Malaysia	9.8
20	Greece	9.6
21	Belgium	9.4
22	Iceland	9.3
23	Sweden	9.1
24	New Zealand	9.0
25	Australia	8.9
	Jordan	8.9
	Montenegro	8.9
	Netherlands	8.9
	Norway	8.9
	Zimbabwe	8.9

Lowest health spending
As % of GDP, 2007

1	Myanmar	1.9
2	Equatorial Guinea	2.1
3	Indonesia	2.2
	Kuwait	2.2
5	Brunei	2.4
	Congo-Brazzaville	2.4
	Mauritania	2.4
	Oman	2.4
9	Angola	2.5
	Iraq	2.5
11	Turkmenistan	2.6
12	Libya	2.7
	Pakistan	2.7
	United Arab Emirates	2.7
15	Singapore	3.1
16	Papua New Guinea	3.2
17	Eritrea	3.3
18	Bangladesh	3.4
	Saudi Arabia	3.4
20	Sudan	3.5
21	Syria	3.6
22	Azerbaijan	3.7
	Bahrain	3.7
	Kazakhstan	3.7
	Thailand	3.7
26	Ethiopia	3.8
	Qatar	3.8
28	Philippines	3.9
	Yemen	3.9

Highest pop. per doctor
2008 or latest

1	Tanzania	125,000
2	Liberia	71,429
3	Sierra Leone	62,500
4	Malawi	52,632
	Niger	52,632
6	Bhutan	50,000
7	Ethiopia	45,455
8	Rwanda	41,667
9	Mozambique	37,037
10	Burundi	33,333
11	Somalia	28,571
12	Gambia, The	26,316
13	Chad	25,000
14	Guinea-Bissau	22,222
15	Eritrea	20,000
16	Togo	18,868
17	Zambia	18,182

Lowest pop. per doctor
2008 or latest

1	Cuba	156
2	Greece	187
3	Belarus	205
4	Georgia	220
5	Russia	232
6	Belgium	236
7	Uruguay	239
8	Lithuania	248
9	Switzerland	252
10	Netherlands	255
11	Norway	257
12	Kazakhstan	258
13	Austria	264
	Azerbaijan	264
15	Iceland	265
16	Spain	266
17	France	268

Most hospital beds
Beds per 1,000 pop., 2008 or latest

1	Japan	14.0		21	Luxembourg	6.3
2	Belarus	11.2		22	Moldova	6.1
3	Russia	9.7			Mongolia	6.1
4	Ukraine	8.7		24	Cuba	6.0
5	South Korea	8.6		25	Israel	5.8
6	Germany	8.3		26	Estonia	5.6
7	Czech Republic	8.1		27	Switzerland	5.5
	Lithuania	8.1		28	Serbia	5.4
9	Azerbaijan	7.9			Tajikistan	5.4
10	Austria	7.8		30	Belgium	5.3
	Malta	7.8			Croatia	5.3
12	Kazakhstan	7.7			Iceland	5.3
13	Barbados	7.6			Ireland	5.3
	Latvia	7.6		34	Poland	5.2
15	France	7.2		35	Kyrgyzstan	5.1
16	Hungary	7.1		36	Nepal	5.0
17	Finland	6.8		37	Greece	4.8
	Slovakia	6.8			Netherlands	4.8
19	Romania	6.5			Uzbekistan	4.8
20	Bulgaria	6.4		40	Slovenia	4.7

Obesity[a]

Men, % of total population

1	Lebanon	36.3
2	Qatar	34.6
3	United States	32.2
4	Panama	27.9
5	Kuwait	27.5
6	Saudi Arabia	26.4
7	Greece	26.0
8	Scotland	24.9
9	New Zealand	24.7
10	Mexico	24.4
11	England	24.1
12	Czech Republic	23.9
13	Austria	23.3
14	Canada	22.9
	Malta	22.9
16	Albania	22.8
17	Croatia	21.6
18	Wales	21.0
19	Lithuania	20.6
20	Germany	20.5
21	Chile	19.6
22	Argentina	19.5
23	Australia	19.3
24	Luxembourg	18.8
25	Slovakia	17.8

Women, % of total population

1	Qatar	45.3
2	Saudi Arabia	44.0
3	Lebanon	38.3
4	Panama	36.1
5	Albania	35.6
6	United States	35.5
7	Mexico	34.5
8	Egypt	33.1
9	United Arab Emirates	31.4
10	Kuwait	29.9
11	Turkey	29.4
12	Chile	29.3
13	Scotland	26.5
14	Jordan	26.3
15	New Zealand	26.0
16	Bosnia	25.0
17	England	24.9
18	Oman	23.8
19	Canada	23.2
20	Peru	23.0
21	Croatia	22.7
22	Czech Republic	22.3
23	Australia	22.2
24	Morocco	21.7
25	Russia	21.6

a Defined as body mass index of 30 or more – see page 248. Latest available years.

Marriage and divorce

Highest marriage rates
Number of marriages per 1,000 population, 2008 or latest available year

1	Virgin Islands (US)	35.8	26	Albania	7.1
2	British Virgin Is	19.6		South Korea	7.1
3	Mongolia	15.7	28	Turkmenistan	6.9
4	Bermuda	13.7	29	Moldova	6.8
	Tajikistan	13.7	30	Channel Islandsª	6.5
6	Iran	11.8	31	Lithuania	6.4
7	Jordan	10.2		Montenegro	6.4
8	Azerbaijan	9.5		Philippines	6.4
	Kazakhstan	9.5		Romania	6.4
	Lebanon	9.5		Turkey	6.4
11	Guam	9.4	36	Cyprus	6.3
12	Belarus	9.3		Hong Kong	6.3
13	Mauritius	9.2		Trinidad & Tobago	6.3
14	Algeria	9.0	39	Egypt	6.2
15	Cayman Islands	8.9	40	Bahamas	6.1
16	West Bank and Gaza	8.8		Malta	6.1
17	Fiji	8.6	42	Costa Rica	5.9
18	Jamaica	8.5		Puerto Rico	5.9
	Kyrgyzstan	8.5	44	Finland	5.8
20	Russia	7.9		Malaysia	5.8
21	United States	7.7		Netherlands Antilles	5.8
22	Macedonia	7.4		Tunisia	5.8
	Taiwan	7.4	48	China	5.7
24	Denmark	7.2		Georgia	5.7
	Indonesia	7.2		Ukraine	5.7

Lowest marriage rates
Number of marriages per 1,000 population

1	Colombia	1.7		France	3.9
2	Qatar	2.6		Macau	3.9
	Venezuela	2.6		South Africa	3.9
4	Peru	2.8	21	Bulgaria	4.0
	St Lucia	2.8	22	Hungary	4.1
6	Argentina	3.0	23	Belgium	4.2
7	Andorra	3.1		Dominican Republic	4.2
8	Slovenia	3.2		Netherlands	4.2
9	Chile	3.3		Suriname	4.2
10	Martinique	3.4	27	Canada	4.4
	Panama	3.4		French Polynesia	4.4
12	Guadeloupe	3.5		Guatemala	4.4
13	New Caledonia	3.6		Italy	4.4
	Réunion	3.6		Thailand	4.4
	United Arab Emirates	3.6	32	Luxembourg	4.5
16	Uruguay	3.8		Saudi Arabia	4.5
17	Brazil	3.9			

a Jersey only
Note: The data are based on latest available figures (no earlier than 2003) and hence will be affected by the population age structure at the time. Marriage rates refer to registered marriages only and, therefore, reflect the customs surrounding registry and efficiency of administration.

Highest divorce rates
Number of divorces per 1,000 population, 2008 or latest available year

1	Guam	11.9	27	Netherlands Antilles	2.6
2	South Korea	4.4	28	Bulgaria	2.5
3	Uruguay	4.3		Costa Rica	2.5
4	Moldova	4.2		Kazakhstan	2.5
5	Aruba	4.0		Norway	2.5
6	Russia	3.9	32	Finland	2.4
	Virgin Islands (US)	3.9		Latvia	2.4
8	Puerto Rico	3.8		Portugal	2.4
9	Belarus	3.7	35	Australia	2.3
10	Lithuania	3.5		Hungary	2.3
	Taiwan	3.5		Luxembourg	2.3
	Ukraine	3.5		Slovakia	2.3
13	Czech Republic	3.4	39	Austria	2.2
14	United States	3.3		France	2.2
15	Estonia	3.2		Trinidad & Tobago	2.2
16	Cuba	3.1	42	Canada	2.1
	Denmark	3.1		Cyprus	2.1
18	Belgium	3.0		Jordan	2.1
	Cayman Islands	3.0		Sweden	2.1
20	Germany	2.9	46	Japan	2.0
	United Kingdom	2.9		Kuwait	2.0
22	Bermuda	2.8		Réunion	2.0
	British Virgin Is	2.8	49	Dominican Republic	1.8
24	Hong Kong	2.7		Iceland	1.8
	New Zealand	2.7		Romania	1.8
	Switzerland	2.7			

Lowest divorce rates
Number of divorces per 1,000 population, 2008 or latest available year

1	Guatemala	0.1	19	Armenia	0.9
2	Vietnam	0.2		Ecuador	0.9
3	Bahamas	0.3		Indonesia	0.9
4	Bosnia	0.5		Panama	0.9
	Chile	0.5		Venezuela	0.9
	Georgia	0.5	24	Azerbaijan	1.0
7	Egypt	0.7		Mauritius	1.0
	Macedonia	0.7		Saudi Arabia	1.0
	Mexico	0.7		South Africa	1.0
	Mongolia	0.7		United Arab Emirates	1.0
	Montenegro	0.7	29	Spain	1.1
	St Lucia	0.7		Thailand	1.1
	Tajikistan	0.7		Tunisia	1.1
14	Brazil	0.8		West Bank and Gaza	1.1
	Ireland	0.8	33	Greece	1.2
	Italy	0.8		Macau	1.2
	Qatar	0.8		Serbia	1.2
	Turkey	0.8		Slovenia	1.2

Households and living costs

Number of households
Biggest, m, 2008

1	China	384.8	14	Pakistan	24.5
2	India	218.5	15	Italy	24.1
3	United States	117.3	16	Ukraine	20.0
4	Indonesia	65.6	17	Vietnam	19.5
5	Brazil	53.5	18	Iran	19.0
6	Russia	52.9	19	Philippines	18.6
7	Japan	50.1	20	Egypt	18.4
8	Germany	39.9	21	Thailand	18.0
9	Nigeria	30.5	22	Turkey	17.8
10	United Kingdom	27.0	23	Congo-Kinshasa	17.6
11	Mexico	26.9	24	South Korea	17.5
12	France	26.6	25	Spain	17.1
13	Bangladesh	26.5	26	Ethiopia	15.4

Households with single occupation
% of total, 2008

1	Sweden	46.9	15	Lithuania	32.0
2	Norway	39.5	16	Hungary	31.2
3	Denmark	38.9	17	Japan	30.5
	Finland	38.9	18	Poland	28.4
5	Germany	38.4	19	Italy	28.2
6	Netherlands	35.6	20	Belarus	27.2
7	Austria	35.4	21	Canada	27.0
	Slovakia	35.4	22	United States	26.9
9	Estonia	35.0	23	Bulgaria	24.9
10	United Kingdom	33.8	24	Australia	24.4
11	France	33.6	25	Russia	24.3
12	Belgium	32.8	26	Spain	24.1
	Czech Republic	32.8	27	Slovenia	23.9
14	Ukraine	32.6	28	Ireland	23.1

Highest cost of living[a]
February 2010, USA=100

1	France	150	13	Germany	116
2	Japan	146		Ireland	116
3	Norway	144		Spain	116
4	Denmark	138	16	New Caledonia	114
5	Finland	132	17	Hong Kong	110
6	Venezuela	125	18	Italy	109
7	Switzerland	124		Netherlands	109
8	Austria	121	20	Israel	107
9	Australia	120	21	Luxembourg	105
	Singapore	120	22	Sweden	104
11	Belgium	119	23	Czech Republic	100
12	United Kingdom	118	24	Canada	99

a The cost of living index shown is compiled by the Economist Intelligence Unit for use
  by companies in determining expatriate compensation: it is a comparison of the cost
  of maintaining a typical international lifestyle in the country rather than a
  comparison of the purchasing power of a citizen of the country. The index is based on
  typical urban prices an international executive and family will face abroad. The prices

Number of households
Smallest, m, 2008

1	British Virgin Is	0.005	14	Swaziland	0.210
2	Cayman Islands	0.010	15	Gabon	0.240
3	Bermuda	0.017	16	Cyprus	0.270
4	Antigua & Barbuda	0.021	17	Congo-Brazzaville	0.520
5	Aruba	0.029	18	Estonia	0.590
6	Guam	0.035	19	Macedonia	0.600
7	Cape Verde	0.120	20	United Arab Emirates	0.720
8	Iceland	0.130	21	Slovenia	0.730
	Malta	0.130	22	Albania	0.790
	Réunion	0.130	23	Latvia	0.810
11	Qatar	0.180	24	Jordan	1.100
12	Luxembourg	0.190		Uruguay	1.100
13	Bahrain	0.200			

Households with six or more occupants
% of total, 2008

1	Kuwait	60.3	16	Bolivia	26.3
2	Pakistan	58.4	17	Venezuela	24.6
3	United Arab Emirates	53.0	18	Peru	21.9
4	Saudi Arabia	47.5	19	Turkey	19.6
5	Algeria	46.0	20	South Africa	19.4
6	Turkmenistan	42.2	21	Vietnam	19.3
7	Jordan	41.7	22	Mexico	18.3
8	Morocco	39.7	23	Singapore	16.6
9	India	38.1	24	Ecuador	16.4
10	Nigeria	37.5	25	Colombia	15.9
11	Tunisia	36.0	26	Argentina	15.2
12	Philippines	32.9	27	Israel	12.9
13	Azerbaijan	28.3	28	Indonesia	12.7
14	Malaysia	28.0	29	Kazakhstan	10.4
15	Egypt	27.3	30	Chile	10.2

Lowest cost of living[a]
February 2010, USA=100

1	Pakistan	40		Costa Rica	60
2	India	48		Panama	60
	Iran	48	14	Kazakhstan	62
4	Nepal	51	15	Sri Lanka	63
5	Libya	52		Uzbekistan	63
	Philippines	52	17	Brunei	64
7	Paraguay	56		Cambodia	64
8	Algeria	57		Romania	64
9	Ukraine	58	20	Ecuador	65
10	Bangladesh	59		Vietnam	65
11	Argentina	60			

are for products of international comparable quality found in a supermarket or department store. Prices found in local markets and bazaars are not used unless the available merchandise is of the specified quality and the shopping area itself is safe for executive and family members. New York City prices are used as the base, so United States = 100.

Telephones and computers

Telephone
Telephone lines per 100 people, 2008

1	Bermuda	89.0	20	Guadeloupe	53.1
2	British Virgin Is	82.9	21	Slovenia	50.1
3	Cayman Islands	68.3	22	Ireland	49.7
4	Virgin Islands (US)	67.7	23	United States	49.6
5	Switzerland	64.1	24	Israel	45.7
6	Germany	62.5	25	Denmark	45.6
7	Taiwan	62.0	26	Spain	45.4
8	Iceland	61.3	27	Cyprus	45.1
9	Malta	59.2		Netherlands Antilles	45.1
10	Barbados	58.8	29	Australia	44.5
11	Hong Kong	58.7	30	Andorra	44.3
12	Montenegro	58.2		Netherlands	44.3
13	Sweden	57.8		South Korea	44.3
14	France	56.4	33	Faroe Islands	44.0
15	Canada	54.9	34	Antigua & Barbuda	43.9
16	Luxembourg	54.2	35	Martinique	42.6
	United Kingdom	54.2	36	Croatia	42.5
18	Réunion	53.9	37	Belgium	42.1
19	Greece	53.7	38	New Zealand	41.4

Mobile telephone
Subscribers per 100 people, 2008

1	United Arab Emirates	208.7		Hungary	122.1
2	Estonia	188.2	31	Ukraine	121.1
3	Bahrain	185.8	32	Ireland	120.7
4	Macau	177.2	33	Sweden	118.3
5	Hong Kong	165.9	34	Montenegro	118.1
6	Barbados	159.1	35	Switzerland	118.0
7	Antigua & Barbuda	157.7	36	Cyprus	117.9
8	Italy	151.6	37	Argentina	116.6
9	Lithuania	151.2	38	Oman	115.6
10	Luxembourg	147.1	39	Poland	115.3
11	Saudi Arabia	142.9	40	Panama	115.2
12	Maldives	142.8	41	Aruba	114.6
13	Russia	141.1	42	Romania	114.5
14	Portugal	139.6	43	El Salvador	113.3
15	Bulgaria	138.3	44	Trinidad & Tobago	112.9
16	Singapore	138.2	45	Spain	111.7
17	Czech Republic	133.5	46	Belgium	111.6
18	Croatia	133.0	47	Faroe Islands	110.6
19	Qatar	131.4	48	Taiwan	110.3
20	Austria	129.7	49	Norway	110.2
21	United Kingdom	129.3	50	Guatemala	109.2
22	Finland	128.8		New Zealand	109.2
23	Germany	128.3	52	Iceland	108.6
24	Israel	127.4		Netherlands Antilles	108.6
25	Denmark	125.7	54	Bahamas	106.0
26	Netherlands	124.8	55	Australia	105.0
27	Greece	123.9	56	Uruguay	104.7
28	Macedonia	122.6	57	Malaysia	102.6
29	Bermuda	122.1	58	Slovakia	102.2

Computer
Computers per 100 people, 2008

1	Israel[a]	122.1	26	Italy[a]	36.7
2	Switzerland	96.2	27	United Arab Emirates	33.1
3	Canada	94.2	28	Latvia	32.7
4	Netherlands	91.2	29	Georgia	27.2
5	Sweden	88.1	30	Serbia	25.8
6	United States	80.6	31	Hungary	25.6
7	United Kingdom	80.2	32	Estonia	25.5
8	Australia[a]	75.7	33	Mongolia	24.6
9	Singapore	74.3	34	Lithuania	24.2
10	Saudi Arabia	69.8	35	Namibia	23.9
11	Hong Kong	69.3	36	Malaysia	23.1
12	Japan	67.6	37	Romania	19.2
13	Germany	65.6	38	Portugal	18.2
14	France	65.2	39	Mauritius	17.6
15	Norway	62.9	40	Oman	16.9
16	Ireland	58.2		Poland	16.9
17	Slovakia	58.1	42	Qatar	15.7
18	South Korea	57.6	43	Mexico	14.4
19	Denmark	54.9	44	Russia	13.3
20	New Zealand	52.6	45	Trinidad & Tobago	13.2
21	Finland[a]	50.0	46	Ecuador	13.0
22	Slovenia	42.5	47	Moldova	11.4
23	Spain	39.3	48	Colombia	11.2
24	Belgium[a]	37.7	49	Bulgaria	11.0
25	Macedonia	36.8	50	Sudan	10.7

Broadband
Subscribers per 100 people, 2008

1	Sweden	41.1	21	Austria	20.7
2	Denmark	36.9		Singapore	20.7
3	Netherlands	35.3	23	Ireland	20.1
4	Switzerland	33.7	24	Spain	19.8
5	Norway	33.3	25	Italy	18.9
6	South Korea	31.8	26	Lithuania	17.6
7	Finland	30.5	27	Hungary	17.4
8	Canada	29.6	28	Czech Republic	16.9
9	France	28.4	29	Portugal	15.4
10	Hong Kong	28.1	30	Greece	13.4
	United Kingdom	28.1	31	Poland	12.6
12	Belgium	27.7	32	United Arab Emirates	12.4
13	Germany	27.5	33	Croatia	11.8
14	United States	24.1	34	Romania	11.7
15	Australia	24.0	35	Slovakia	11.2
16	Estonia	23.7	36	Bulgaria	11.1
17	Japan	23.6	37	Macedonia	8.9
18	Israel	23.0	38	Latvia	8.8
19	New Zealand	21.4	39	Chile	8.5
20	Slovenia	21.1	40	Qatar	8.1

a 2007

The internet and music

Internet hosts

	By country, April 2010			*Per 1,000 pop., April 2010*	
1	United States[a]	415,723,182	1	United States[a]	1,346.3
2	Japan	54,067,517	2	Iceland	1,078.2
3	Italy	22,804,359	3	Finland	826.7
4	Germany	21,462,183	4	Netherlands	768.2
5	Brazil	18,848,263	5	Denmark	749.1
6	China	15,309,629	6	Norway	707.7
7	France	15,006,654	7	Australia	625.1
8	Australia	13,126,248	8	New Zealand	588.2
9	Mexico	12,677,932	9	Estonia	558.5
10	Netherlands	12,675,126	10	Luxembourg	522.4
11	Poland	10,249,601	11	Sweden	464.9
12	Russia	10,147,891	12	Cayman Islands	437.7
13	Canada	7,797,974	13	Japan	422.7
14	United Kingdom	7,300,559	14	Belgium	416.6
15	Taiwan	6,227,753	15	Italy	387.2
16	Argentina	6,012,497	16	Austria	383.5
17	India	4,488,807	17	Czech Republic	337.3
18	Finland	4,381,255	18	Lithuania	331.7
19	Belgium	4,374,379	19	Andorra	304.4
20	Sweden	4,277,497	20	Ireland	299.1
21	Denmark	4,119,946	21	Portugal	293.7
22	Spain	3,794,613	22	Croatia	278.0
23	Czech Republic	3,440,693	23	Taiwan	272.0
24	Norway	3,326,219	24	Greenland	270.1
25	Austria	3,221,814	25	Poland	269.7
26	Portugal	3,142,618	26	Hungary	262.5
27	Turkey	3,028,064	27	Germany	260.1
28	Hungary	2,625,399	28	Bermuda	252.0

Music sales

	Total including downloads, $m, 2009			*$ per head, 2009*	
1	United States	7,939	1	Japan	42.7
2	Japan	5,459	2	Norway	39.1
3	United Kingdom	2,154	3	United Kingdom	35.3
4	Germany	2,148	4	Denmark	30.9
5	France	1,380	5	Switzerland	30.1
6	Australia	564	6	Austria	29.7
7	Canada	522	7	Australia	26.9
8	Netherlands	366	8	Iceland	26.4
9	Italy	338	9	Germany	26.0
10	Spain	319	10	United States	25.7
11	Brazil	290	11	Ireland	24.4
12	South Korea	285	12	France	22.3
13	Austria	250	13	Netherlands	22.2
14	Russia	232	14	Belgium	21.0
15	Switzerland	226	15	Finland	19.9
16	Belgium	220	16	Sweden	19.7
17	India	199	17	New Zealand	18.6
18	Mexico	191	18	Canada	15.7

a Includes all hosts ending ".com", ".net" and ".org", which exaggerates the numbers.

Internet

% of households with internet, 2008

1	South Korea	94.3		26	France	62.3
2	Iceland	87.7		27	Malta	59.0
3	Netherlands	86.1		28	Slovenia	58.9
4	Sweden	84.4		29	Slovakia	58.3
5	Norway	84.0		30	Estonia	58.1
6	Denmark	81.9		31	Macau[a]	57.9
7	Luxembourg	80.1		32	Latvia	52.8
8	Japan	79.8		33	Spain	51.0
9	Switzerland[a]	78.9		34	Lithuania	50.9
10	Singapore	76.0		35	Hungary	48.4
11	Canada[a]	75.1		36	Bahrain[a]	48.0
12	Germany	74.9		37	Poland	47.6
13	Finland	72.4		38	Italy	46.9
14	United Kingdom	71.1		39	Portugal	46.0
15	Hong Kong	70.9		40	Czech Republic	45.9
16	Austria	68.9		41	Croatia[a]	45.3
17	New Zealand[a]	67.5		42	Cyprus[a]	42.9
18	Australia	66.6		43	Saudi Arabia[a]	41.5
19	United Arab Emirates	66.4		44	Syria	31.2
20	Brunei[a]	65.2		45	Greece	31.0
21	Belgium	63.6		46	Romania	30.4
22	Israel	63.3		47	Russia	30.0
23	Ireland	63.0		48	Argentina[a]	29.9
	Qatar	63.0		49	Kuwait[a]	29.7
25	United States[a]	62.5		50	Macedonia	29.4

Internet users per 100 population, 2008

1	Iceland	90.6		23	Slovakia	66.0
2	Sweden	87.8		24	United Arab Emirates	65.2
3	Netherlands	86.5		25	Ireland	62.5
4	Denmark	83.9		26	Latvia	60.6
5	Finland	82.6		27	Hungary	58.7
	Norway	82.6		28	Czech Republic	58.4
7	Luxembourg	80.5		29	Jamaica	56.9
8	Switzerland	77.0		30	Spain	56.7
9	South Korea	76.5		31	South Africa	55.9
10	United Kingdom	76.2		32	Malaysia	55.8
11	Canada[a]	75.4		33	Brunei	55.3
	Japan	75.4		34	Lithuania	55.0
13	Germany	75.3		35	Bahrain	51.9
14	United States[a]	74.0		36	Croatia	50.6
15	Singapore[a]	73.0		37	Israel[a]	49.6
16	Australia	72.0		38	Macau[a]	49.2
	New Zealand[a]	72.0		39	Poland	49.0
18	Austria	71.2		40	Malta	48.8
19	Belgium	68.9		41	Montenegro[a]	47.2
20	France	68.2		42	Greece	43.5
21	Hong Kong	67.0		43	Italy	41.9
22	Estonia	66.2			Portugal	41.9

a Estimate.

Cinema and films

Cinema attendances

Total visits, m, 2008			Visits per head, 2008	
1	China	1,535.3	1 New Zealand	9.5
2	United States	1,459.3	2 Australia	7.2
3	India	1,221.4	3 United States	4.7
4	Indonesia	310.4	4 Iceland	4.6
5	France	195.4	5 Canada	4.3
6	Mexico	188.4	6 Ireland	4.2
7	United Kingdom	166.2	7 Singapore	3.4
8	Japan	163.6	8 France	3.2
9	Australia	152.2	9 United Kingdom	2.7
10	Canada	144.3	10 Spain	2.5
11	Germany	117.6	11 Belgium	2.3
12	Italy	116.4	Denmark	2.3
13	Russia	113.1	Luxembourg	2.3
14	Spain	109.3	14 Norway	2.2
15	Philippines	89.1	Malta	2.2
16	South Africa	76.5	Switzerland	2.2
17	Venezuela	59.0	17 Venezuela	2.1
18	Argentina	54.7	18 Austria	2.0
19	South Korea	46.2	Italy	2.0
20	New Zealand	39.9	20 Ecuador	1.7
21	Poland	39.7	Mexico	1.7
22	Brazil	38.8	22 South Africa	1.6
23	Turkey	31.5	Sweden	1.6
24	Belgium	24.3	24 Portugal	1.5
25	Netherlands	23.1	25 Argentina	1.4
26	Ecuador	22.9	Germany	1.4
27	Ireland	18.3	Netherlands	1.4
28	Taiwan	17.6		
29	Austria	16.8		
30	Malaysia	16.7		
31	Switzerland	16.3		
32	Portugal	16.2		

Top Oscar winners

	Film	Awards	Nominations
1	Ben-Hur (1959)	11	12
	Titanic (1997)	11	14
	The Lord of the Rings: The Return of the King (2003)	11	11
4	West Side Story (1961)	10	11
5	Gigi (1958)	9	9
	The Last Emperor (1987)	9	9
	The English Patient (1996)	9	12
8	Gone with the Wind (1939)	8	13
	From Here to Eternity (1953)	8	13
	On the Waterfront (1954)	8	12
	My Fair Lady (1964)	8	12
	Cabaret[a] (1972)	8	10
	Gandhi (1982)	8	11
	Amadeus (1984)	8	11
	Slumdog Millionaire (2009)	8	10

a Did not win best picture award.

The press

Daily newspapers

Copies per '000 population, 2008

1	Iceland	812	16	Malta	265
2	Denmark	777	17	Slovenia	253
3	Sweden	541	18	Germany	250
4	Japan	534	19	Ireland	248
5	Switzerland	490	20	Spain	245
6	Norway	462	21	Luxembourg	239
7	Finland	455	22	United Arab Emirates	237
8	Hong Kong	435	23	Croatia	224
	South Korea	435	24	Italy	215
10	Austria	406	25	Canada	202
11	Czech Republic	349	26	Taiwan	183
12	Singapore	348	27	United States	180
13	Estonia	316	28	Hungary	174
	United Kingdom	316	29	Latvia	173
15	Netherlands	284	30	Poland	172

Press freedom[a]

Scores, 2009

Most free

1	Denmark	0.00
	Finland	0.00
	Ireland	0.00
	Norway	0.00
	Sweden	0.00
6	Estonia	0.50
7	Netherlands	1.00
	Switzerland	1.00
9	Iceland	2.00
10	Lithuania	2.25
11	Belgium	2.50
	Malta	2.50
13	Austria	3.00
	Latvia	3.00
	New Zealand	3.00
16	Australia	3.13
17	Japan	3.25
18	Germany	3.50
19	Canada	3.70
20	Luxembourg	4.00
	United Kingdom	4.00
	United States	4.00
23	Jamaica	4.75
24	Czech Republic	5.00
25	Cyprus	5.50
	Hungary	5.50
27	Ghana	6.00
28	Trinidad & Tobago	7.00
29	Uruguay	7.63

Least free

1	Eritrea	115.50
2	North Korea	112.50
3	Turkmenistan	107.00
4	Iran	104.14
5	Burma	102.67
6	Cuba	94.00
7	Laos	92.00
8	China	84.50
9	Yemen	83.38
10	Vietnam	81.67
11	Syria	78.00
12	Somalia	77.50
13	Saudia Arabia	76.50
14	Sri Lanka	75.00
15	Uzbekistan	67.67
16	Pakistan	66.50
17	Equatorial Guinea	65.50
18	Rwanda	64.67
19	Libya	64.50
20	Brunei	63.50
21	Tunisia	61.50
22	Russia	60.88
23	Fiji	60.00
24	Belarus	59.50
25	Afghanistan	54.25
26	Azerbaijan	53.50
	Congo-Kinshasa	53.50
	Sudan	53.50
29	Iraq	53.30

a Based on 40 questions on topics such as threats, censorship, monopolies, pressure and new media, answered by journalists and media experts.

Nobel prize winners: 1901–2009

Peace (two or more)

1	United States	19
2	United Kingdom	11
3	France	9
4	Sweden	5
5	Belgium	4
	Germany	4
7	Austria	3
	Norway	3
	South Africa	3
	Switzerland	3
11	Argentina	2
	Egypt	2
	Israel	2
	Russia	2

Economics[a]

1	United States	33
2	United Kingdom	8
3	Norway	2
	Sweden	2
5	France	1
	Germany	1
	Israel	1
	Netherlands	1
	Russia	1

Literature (three or more)

1	France	15
2	United States	12
3	United Kingdom	11
4	Germany	8
5	Sweden	6
6	Italy	5
	Spain	5
8	Norway	3
	Poland	3
	Russia	3

Medicine (three or more)

1	United States	52
2	United Kingdom	22
3	Germany	15
4	France	7
	Sweden	7
6	Switzerland	6
7	Austria	5
	Denmark	5
9	Australia	3
	Belgium	3
	Italy	3

Physics

1	United States	50
2	Germany	19
	United Kingdom	19
4	France	9
5	Netherlands	6
	Russia	6
7	Japan	5
8	Sweden	4
	Switzerland	4
10	Austria	3
	Italy	3
12	Canada	2
	Denmark	2
14	Colombia	1
	India	1
	Ireland	1
	Pakistan	1
	Poland	1

Chemistry

1	United States	44
2	United Kingdom	23
3	Germany	15
4	France	7
5	Switzerland	6
6	Sweden	5
7	Canada	4
	Japan	4
9	Argentina	1
	Austria	1
	Belgium	1
	Czech Republic	1
	Denmark	1
	Finland	1
	Israel	1
	Italy	1
	Netherlands	1
	Norway	1
	Russia	1

a Since 1969.
Notes: Prizes by country of residence at time awarded. When prizes have been shared in the same field, one credit given to each country.

Olympics

Winter Olympics

1956 to 2010	Gold	Silver	Bronze
1 Germany	139	130	100
2 Norway	105	117	88
3 United States	87	96	72
4 Austria	54	70	76
5 Canada	52	45	49
6 Sweden	51	34	38
7 Switzerland	43	37	46
8 Finland	42	58	56
9 Russia	38	31	28
10 Italy	37	32	36
11 Netherlands	29	31	26
12 France	27	27	38
13 South Korea	23	14	8
14 China	9	18	17
15 Japan	9	13	15
16 United Kingdom	9	5	15
17 Czech Republic	5	3	7
18 Australia	5	1	2
19 Croatia	4	5	1
20 Estonia	4	2	1
21 Poland	2	6	6
22 Spain	2	0	0
23 Belarus	1	2	4
24 Bulgaria	1	2	2
25 Slovakia	1	2	1

Winter Olympics

2010	Gold	Silver	Bronze
1 Canada	14	7	5
2 Germany	10	13	7
3 United States	9	15	13
4 Norway	9	8	6
5 South Korea	6	6	2
6 Switzerland	6	0	3
7 China	5	2	4
Sweden	5	2	4
9 Austria	4	6	6
10 Netherlands	4	1	3
11 Russia	3	5	7
12 France	2	3	6
13 Australia	2	1	0
14 Czech Republic	2	0	4
15 Poland	1	3	2
16 Italy	1	1	3
17 Belarus	1	1	1
Slovakia	1	1	1
19 United Kingdom	1	0	0
20 Japan	0	3	2

Note: Table excludes Soviet Union medals (1956 to 1988) and as the Unified Team in 1992: Gold 87, Silver 63 and Bronze 67.

Drinking and smoking

Beer drinkers
Retail sales, litres per head of population, 2008

1	Czech Republic	82.2
2	Venezuela	74.4
3	Russia	73.0
4	Poland	71.5
5	Australia	68.7
6	Finland	68.2
7	Romania	67.8
8	Slovakia	67.2
9	Austria	66.1
10	Germany	64.2
11	United States	61.0
12	Ukraine	58.1
13	Denmark	56.6
14	Canada	55.3
15	Netherlands	54.6
	New Zealand	54.6
17	Hungary	51.9
18	Bulgaria	51.3
19	Mexico	48.9
20	South Africa	43.6
21	Italy	42.9
22	Belgium	42.7

Wine drinkers
Retail sales, litres per head of population, 2008

1	Portugal	28.8
2	Switzerland	28.4
3	France	27.7
4	Italy	27.1
5	Denmark	26.6
6	Argentina	25.0
7	Germany	21.3
8	Belgium	20.5
9	Netherlands	20.3
10	Hungary	20.0
11	New Zealand	18.5
12	Austria	18.4
13	Sweden	18.1
14	United Kingdom	18.0
15	Australia	17.1
16	Greece	14.9
17	Ireland	13.3
18	Chile	13.2
19	Norway	12.7
20	Spain	11.2
21	Finland	11.1

Alcoholic drink
Retail sales, litres per head of population, 2008

1	Finland	99.8
2	Australia	99.7
3	Czech Republic	98.3
4	Russia	97.2
5	Germany	96.3
6	Austria	89.0
7	Denmark	86.3
8	Poland	85.7
9	New Zealand	83.0
10	Slovakia	82.0
11	Romania	79.5
12	Venezuela	78.7
13	Netherlands	78.3
14	Hungary	75.5
15	United States	73.2
16	Ukraine	73.0
17	Canada	72.7
18	Argentina	68.2
19	Ireland	66.6
20	Belgium	66.3
	Sweden	66.3
22	United Kingdom	65.1
23	Bulgaria	61.4

Cigarettes
Av. ann. consumption of cigarettes per head per day, 2009

1	Greece	8.1
2	Russia	7.6
3	Bulgaria	7.1
4	Bosnia	6.7
5	Ukraine	6.6
6	Slovenia	6.5
7	Czech Republic	6.2
8	Belarus	5.8
	Cyprus	5.8
10	Kazakhstan	5.7
11	Serbia	5.6
12	Lebanon	5.5
	Spain	5.5
14	Azerbaijan	5.3
	Moldova	5.3
	South Korea	5.3
17	Armenia	5.2
	Macedonia	5.2
19	Japan	5.0
20	Croatia	4.9
21	China	4.6
22	Austria	4.5
	Switzerland	4.5

Crime and punishment

Police

Personnel per 100,000 pop., 2008 or latest

1	Honduras	60.9
2	Jamaica	59.5
3	Venezuela	52.0
4	El Salvador	51.8
5	Guatemala	45.2
6	Trinidad & Tobago	39.7
7	Colombia	38.8
8	Lesotho	36.7
9	South Africa	36.5
10	Belize	34.3
11	Brazil	22.0
12	Dominican Republic	21.5
13	Guyana	20.7
14	Puerto Rico	20.4
15	Ecuador	18.1
16	Namibia	17.9
17	Saint Lucia	16.0
18	Russia	14.2
19	Bahamas	13.7
	Suriname	13.7

Robberies

Per 100,000 population, 2008

1	Belgium	1,837
2	Spain	1,067
3	Maldives	196
4	Chile	180
5	Russia	173
6	France	172
7	United Kingdom[a]	147
8	United States	142
9	Lithuania	104
10	Mauritius	99
11	Canada	97
	Sweden	97
13	Australia	78
14	Morocco	74
15	Kazakhstan	72
16	Zimbabwe	71
17	Belarus	69
18	Estonia	68
	Luxembourg	68
20	Latvia	64

Prisoners

Total prison pop., latest available year

1	United States	2,304,115
2	China	1,565,771
3	Russia	862,300
4	Brazil	469,546
5	India	376,396
6	Mexico	224,749
7	Thailand	212,058
8	Iran	166,979
9	South Africa	164,526
10	Ukraine	144,380
11	Indonesia	140,740
12	Turkey	118,929
13	Philippines	102,267
14	Pakistan	95,016
15	United Kingdom	94,258
16	Vietnam	92,153
17	Poland	85,530
18	Bangladesh	83,000
19	Japan	80,523
20	Ethiopia	80,487
21	Spain	76,753
22	Colombia	76,500
23	Germany	72,043
24	Myanmar	64,930

Per 100,000 pop., latest available year

1	United States	753
2	Russia	660
3	Rwanda	593
4	Virgin Islands (US)	561
5	Cuba	531
6	British Virgin Islands	488
7	Georgia	483
8	Belize	449
9	Bermuda	394
10	Belarus	385
11	Kazakhstan	382
12	Bahamas	376
13	El Salvador	370
14	French Guiana	365
15	Suriname	356
16	Cayman Islands	346
17	Maldives	343
18	South Africa	331
19	Antigua & Barbuda	329
20	Barbados	326
21	Israel	325
22	Latvia	319
	Netherlands Antilles	319
24	Ukraine	314

a England and Wales.

Stars...

Space missions

Firsts and selected events

1957 Dog in space, Laika

1961 Human in space, Yuri Gagarin
Entire day in space, Gherman Titov

1963 Woman in space, Valentina Tereshkova

1964 Space crew, one pilot and two passengers

1965 Space walk, Alexei Leonov
Eight days in space achieved (needed to travel to moon and back)

1966 Docking between space craft and target vehicle
Autopilot re-entry and landing

1968 Live television broadcast from space
Moon orbit

1969 Astronaut transfer from one craft to another in space
Moon landing

1971 Space station, Salyut
Drive on the moon

1973 Space laboratory, Skylab

1978 Non-American, non-Soviet, Vladimir Remek (Czechoslovakia)

1982 Space shuttle, Columbia (first craft to carry four crew members)

1983 Five-crew mission

1984 Space walk, untethered
Capture, repair and redeployment of satellite in space
Seven-crew mission

1985 Classified US Defence Department mission

1986 Space shuttle explosion, Challenger
Mir space station activated

1990 Hubble telescope deployed

2001 Dennis Tito, first paying space tourist

2003 Space shuttle explosion, Columbia. Shuttle programme suspended
China's first manned space flight, Yang Liwei

2004 SpaceShipOne, first successful private manned space flight

2005 Space shuttle, resumption of flights

2008 *Phoenix* lander, mission on Mars

Space vehicle launches[a]

2006			2007		
1 United States	20		**1** Russia	22	
2 Russia	19		**2** United States	20	
3 Japan	7		**3** China	6	
4 France	5		**4** France	5	
5 China	4		**5** India	3	
6 Sweden	3		Japan	3	
2008			2009		
1 Russia	25		**1** Russia	30	
2 United States	13		**2** United States	27	
3 China	10		**3** China	5	
4 France	4		**4** France	7	
5 India	3		**5** India	2	
6 Iran	2		**6** Iran	1	

a By host country and including
   suborbital launches.

...and Wars

Defence spending
As % of GDP, 2008

1	Jordan	10.6		Chile	3.3
2	Oman	8.5		Namibia	3.3
3	Saudi Arabia	8.2	18	Azerbaijan	3.2
4	Georgia	8.1	19	Algeria	3.0
5	Israel	7.4		Pakistan	3.0
6	Yemen	6.4	21	Egypt	2.9
7	United Arab Emirates	5.1		Greece	2.9
8	United States	4.9	23	Bahrain	2.8
9	Kuwait	4.4		Iran	2.8
10	Cuba	4.0		Taiwan	2.8
11	Colombia	3.9	26	Lebanon	2.7
12	Syria	3.8	27	Bulgaria	2.6
13	Guinea-Bissau	3.7		India	2.6
14	Morocco	3.5		South Korea	2.6
15	Armenia	3.3			

Defence spending

$bn, 2008 — *Per head, $, 2008*

	$bn, 2008			Per head, $, 2008	
1	United States	696.3	1	United Arab Emirates	2,972
2	France	67.2	2	Kuwait	2,623
3	United Kingdom	60.8	3	United States	2,290
4	China[a]	60.2	4	Qatar	2,129
5	Germany	46.9	5	Israel	2,077
6	Russia	40.5	6	Oman	1,410
7	Saudi Arabia	38.2	7	Saudi Arabia	1,357
8	India	31.5	8	Norway	1,264
9	Italy	30.9	9	Australia	1,056
10	Brazil	26.3	10	France	1,049
11	South Korea	24.2	11	United Kingdom	998
12	Australia	22.2	12	Greece	946
13	Canada	19.8	13	Denmark	815
14	Spain	19.3	14	Bahrain	768
15	Israel	14.8	15	Netherlands	738

Armed forces
'000, 2008

		Regulars	Reserves			Regulars	Reserves
1	China	2,285	510	13	Brazil	328	1,340
2	United States	1,580	865	14	Syria	325	314
3	India	1,325	1,155	15	Indonesia	302	400
4	North Korea	1,106	4,700	16	Italy	293	42
5	Russia	1,027	20,000	17	Taiwan	290	1,657
6	South Korea	687	4,500	18	Colombia	285	62
7	Pakistan	617	0	19	Germany	251	162
8	Iraq	578	0	20	Saudi Arabia	234	0
9	Iran	523	350	21	Morocco	196	150
10	Turkey	511	379	22	Israel	177	565
11	Egypt	469	479	23	United Kingdom	175	199
12	France	353	70	24	Greece	157	238

a Official budget only at market exchange rates.

Environment

Environmental performance index[a], 2010

Highest			Lowest		
1	Iceland	93.5	1	Sierra Leone	32.1
2	Switzerland	89.1	2	Central African Republic	33.3
3	Costa Rica	86.4	3	Mauritania	33.7
4	Sweden	86.0	4	Angola	36.3
5	Norway	81.1	5	Togo	36.4
6	Mauritius	80.6	6	Niger	37.6
7	France	78.2	7	Turkmenistan	38.4
8	Austria	78.1	8	Mali	39.4
	Cuba	78.1	9	Haiti	39.5
10	Colombia	76.8	10	Benin	39.6
11	Malta	76.3	11	Nigeria	40.2
12	Finland	74.7	12	United Arab Emirates	40.7
13	Slovakia	74.5	13	Chad	40.8
14	United Kingdom	74.2	14	Iraq	41.0
15	New Zealand	73.4	15	Botswana	41.3
16	Chile	73.3	16	Cambodia	41.7
17	Germany	73.2	17	North Korea	41.8
18	Italy	73.1	18	Equatorial Guinea	41.9
19	Portugal	73.0	19	Bahrain	42.0
20	Japan	72.5	20	Senegal	42.3
	Latvia	72.5		Uzbekistan	42.3
22	Czech Republic	71.6	22	Mongolia	42.8
23	Albania	71.4	23	Ethiopia	43.1
	Panama	71.4	24	Burundi	43.9
25	Spain	70.6	25	Bangladesh	44.0
26	Belize	69.9	26	Bolivia	44.3
	Singapore	69.6		Papua New Guinea	44.3
28	Serbia	69.4	28	Guinea	44.4

Biggest emitters of carbon dioxide

Millions of tonnes, 2006

1	China	6,099.1	17	Brazil	352.3
2	United States	5,748.1	18	Spain	352.0
3	Russia	1,563.5	19	Indonesia	333.2
4	India	1,509.3	20	Ukraine	318.9
5	Japan	1,292.5	21	Poland	318.0
6	Germany	804.5	22	Thailand	272.3
7	United Kingdom	568.1	23	Turkmenistan	269.3
8	Canada	544.3	24	Kazakhstan	193.4
9	South Korea	474.9	25	Malawi	187.7
10	Italy	473.8	26	Argentina	173.4
11	Iran	466.6	27	Venezuela	171.5
12	Mexico	435.8	28	Netherlands	168.4
13	South Africa	414.3	29	Egypt	166.7
14	France	382.9	30	Pakistan	142.6
15	Saudi Arabia	381.3	31	United Arab Emirates	139.5
16	Australia	371.7	32	Algeria	132.6

a Based on a range of factors including environmental health, biodiversity, air
   pollution, water use, agricultural methods, tackling climate change.

Largest amount of carbon dioxide emitted per person
Tonnes, 2006

1	Qatar	46.1	25	Libya	9.2
2	Kuwait	33.3	26	Turkmenistan	9.0
3	United Arab Emirates	32.9	27	Austria	8.7
4	Trinidad & Tobago	25.4		South Africa	8.7
5	United States	19.3	29	Greece	8.6
6	Australia	18.0		Norway	8.6
7	Canada	16.7	31	Poland	8.3
8	Saudi Arabia	16.1	32	Italy	8.0
9	Oman	15.5		Spain	8.0
10	Estonia	13.0	34	Slovenia	7.6
11	Singapore	12.8	35	Bosnia	7.3
12	Finland	12.7		New Zealand	7.3
13	Kazakhstan	12.6	37	Malaysia	7.2
14	Czech Republic	11.2	38	Belarus	7.1
15	Russia	11.0	39	Slovakia	6.9
16	Ireland	10.3	40	Ukraine	6.8
	Netherlands	10.3	41	Iran	6.7
18	Belgium	10.2	42	Venezuela	6.3
19	Japan	10.1	43	Bulgaria	6.2
20	Israel	10.0		France	6.2
21	Denmark	9.9	45	Hong Kong	5.7
22	Germany	9.8		Hungary	5.7
	South Korea	9.8		Portugal	5.7
24	United Kingdom	9.4			

Average annual % change in carbon emissions

	Biggest increase, 1990–2006			*Biggest decrease, 1990–2006*	
1	Namibia	47.2	1	North Korea	-9.6
2	Somalia	31.0	2	Afghanistan	-8.6
3	West Bank and Gaza	24.1	3	Tajikistan	-8.2
4	Cambodia	16.7	4	Georgia	-7.4
5	Bosnia	14.7	5	Moldova	-7.3
6	Laos	14.5	6	Gabon	-7.0
7	Vietnam	11.8	7	Mauritania	-5.5
8	Swaziland	10.9	8	Latvia	-5.0
9	Chad	10.3	9	Kyrgyzstan	-4.8
10	Kuwait	9.6		Ukraine	-4.8
11	Eritrea	8.9	11	Congo-Kinshasa	-4.7
12	Nepal	8.5	12	Burundi	-4.6
	Oman	8.5	13	Congo-Brazzaville	-4.1
14	Benin	8.3	14	Lithuania	-3.7
15	Sri Lanka	7.9	15	Zimbabwe	-3.2
16	Uganda	7.8	16	Kazakhstan	-3.1
17	Madagascar	7.7		Romania	-3.1
18	Honduras	7.4	18	Belarus	-3.0
19	Malaysia	6.7	19	Estonia	-2.6
20	Bangladesh	6.6	20	Bulgaria	-2.5
	Haiti	6.6	21	Azerbaijan	-2.4
	United Arab Emirates	6.6		Russia	-2.4

Biggest emitters of carbon dioxide per $ of GDP

Kg of carbon dioxide emitted in 2006 per $ of GDP (PPP) in 2005

1	Zimbabwe	5.0		Liberia	0.7
2	Uzbekistan	2.1		Macedonia	0.7
3	Turkmenistan	1.7		Qatar	0.7
4	Kazakhstan	1.3	26	Algeria	0.6
	Mongolia	1.3		India	0.6
6	Bosnia	1.2		Jamaica	0.6
	Trinidad & Tobago	1.2		Kyrgyzstan	0.6
8	Ukraine	1.1		Libya	0.6
9	China	1.0		Malaysia	0.6
	South Africa	1.0		Poland	0.6
11	Moldova	0.9		Tajikistan	0.6
	Russia	0.9		Thailand	0.6
	Syria	0.9		United Arab Emirates	0.6
14	Jordan	0.8		Venezuela	0.6
	Oman	0.8		Vietnam	0.6
	Saudi Arabia	0.8	38	Australia	0.5
17	Azerbaijan	0.7		Canada	0.5
	Belarus	0.7		Czech Republic	0.5
	Bulgaria	0.7		Egypt	0.5
	Estonia	0.7		Romania	0.5
	Indonesia	0.7		United States	0.5
	Kuwait	0.7			

Non-carbon dioxide emitting energy[a]

As % of total energy use, 2006

1	Paraguay	109.9	24	Czech Republic	15.4
2	Sweden	46.2	25	Japan	15.3
3	France	45.6	26	Brazil	15.1
4	Norway	43.2		Mozambique	15.1
5	Kyrgyzstan	41.2	28	Hungary	14.8
6	Syria	40.9	29	Spain	13.3
7	Tajikistan	37.7	30	Colombia	13.2
8	Costa Rica	35.0	31	Germany	12.8
9	Armenia	29.0	32	Peru	12.0
10	Lithuania	28.7	33	Zambia	11.3
11	El Salvador	27.4	34	Panama	11.2
12	New Zealand	25.9		Venezuela	11.2
13	Slovakia	24.9	36	Albania	11.1
14	Slovenia	24.1	37	United States	10.8
15	Philippines	23.8	38	Austria	10.3
16	Belgium	22.2	39	Namibia	8.7
17	Uruguay	21.9		Romania	8.7
18	Canada	20.9	41	Russia	8.6
19	Bulgaria	20.4	42	United Kingdom	8.2
20	Finland	20.1	43	Nicaragua	6.8
21	Ukraine	18.2	44	Ecuador	6.6
22	Georgia	18.0	45	Chile	6.5
23	South Korea	16.9	46	Kenya	6.4

a Includes nuclear, hydropower, solar power and other alternative energy sources.

Biggest forest areas
000 sq km, 2007

1	Russia	8,086	25	Finland	225
2	Brazil	4,715	26	Congo-Brazzaville	220
3	Canada	3,101	27	Gabon	218
4	United States	3,034	28	Cameroon	208
5	China	2,054	29	Malaysia	206
6	Australia	1,633	30	Mozambique	192
7	Congo-Kinshasa	1,330	31	South Korea	185
8	Indonesia	848	32	Paraguay	181
9	Peru	686	33	Zimbabwe	169
10	India	678	34	Chile	162
11	Sudan	664	35	Laos	160
12	Mexico	637	36	France	156
13	Colombia	606	37	Thailand	144
14	Angola	589	38	Vietnam	134
15	Bolivia	582	39	Madagascar	128
16	Venezuela	471	40	Ethiopia	127
17	Zambia	416	41	Mali	124
18	Tanzania	344	42	Chad	118
19	Argentina	327	43	Botswana	117
20	Myanmar	313	44	Germany	111
21	Papua New Guinea	292		Iran	111
22	Sweden	275	46	Ecuador	105
23	Japan	249	47	Côte d'Ivoire	104
24	Central African Rep	227	48	Nigeria	103

Biggest forest area as % of land
2007

1	Gabon	84.4	24	North Korea	49.3
2	Finland	74.0	25	Myanmar	47.9
3	Guinea-Bissau	73.0	26	Latvia	47.6
4	Laos	69.3	27	Gambia	47.5
5	Japan	68.2	28	Angola	47.2
6	Sweden	67.1	29	Austria	47.0
7	Congo-Brazzaville	65.7	30	Costa Rica	46.9
8	South Korea	64.5	31	Indonesia	46.8
9	Papua New Guinea	64.4	32	Puerto Rico	46.0
10	Slovenia	63.3	33	Paraguay	45.6
11	Malaysia	62.7	34	Senegal	44.6
12	Congo-Kinshasa	58.7	35	Cameroon	44.0
13	Panama	57.7	36	Trinidad & Tobago	43.9
14	Cambodia	56.7	37	Zimbabwe	43.7
15	Zambia	55.9	38	Vietnam	43.3
16	Brazil	55.7	39	Bosnia	42.7
17	Colombia	54.6	40	Portugal	42.2
18	Estonia	54.3	41	Nicaragua	41.5
19	Bolivia	53.7	42	Kosovo	41.3
20	Philippines	53.6	43	Slovakia	40.2
21	Venezuela	53.4	44	Georgia	39.7
22	Timor-Leste	52.2	45	Croatia	39.6
23	Russia	49.4	46	Belarus	39.0

Fastest rate of deforestation

Average annual % rate, 2000-07

1	Burundi	5.5	15	Ecuador	1.8
2	Togo	4.7		Liberia	1.8
3	Mauritania	3.5	17	El Salvador	1.7
	Nigeria	3.5		Zimbabwe	1.7
5	Afghanistan	3.2	19	Armenia	1.5
	Honduras	3.2		Nicaragua	1.5
7	Benin	2.6		Sri Lanka	1.5
8	Uganda	2.3	22	Myanmar	1.4
9	Pakistan	2.2		Nepal	1.4
10	Philippines	2.1		Timor-Leste	1.4
11	Cambodia	2.0	25	Guatemala	1.3
	Ghana	2.0	26	Ethiopia	1.1
	Indonesia	2.0		Somalia	1.1
	North Korea	2.0		Tanzania	1.1

Fastest rate of forestation

Average annual % increase, 2000-07

1	Rwanda	6.5	17	Swaziland	0.9
2	Lesotho	2.6	18	Greece	0.8
3	Egypt	2.5		Israel	0.8
4	Kuwait	2.4		Lebanon	0.8
5	China	2.1		Libya	0.8
	Cuba	2.1	22	Hungary	0.7
7	Ireland	1.9	23	Albania	0.6
	Tunisia	1.9		Czech Republic	0.6
9	Spain	1.7	25	Uzbekistan	0.5
10	Vietnam	1.6	26	Chile	0.4
11	Bulgaria	1.4		Estonia	0.4
12	Syria	1.3		Gambia	0.4
	Uruguay	1.3		Latvia	0.4
14	Algeria	1.2		Slovenia	0.4
15	Italy	1.1		Switzerland	0.4
	Portugal	1.1		United Kingdom	0.4

Biggest nationally protected land area[a]

As % of surface area, 2008

1	Venezuela	71.3	13	Brazil	29.6
2	Germany	56.2	14	New Zealand	29.5
3	Estonia	46.8	15	Switzerland	28.6
4	Hong Kong	44.1	16	Dominican Republic	28.5
5	Zambia	41.1	17	Panama	28.1
6	Tanzania	38.8	18	Austria	28.0
7	Saudi Arabia	38.4	19	United States	27.1
8	Trinidad & Tobago	35.0	20	Colombia	26.2
9	Israel	34.5	21	Uganda	26.1
10	Guatemala	32.7	22	Ecuador	25.4
11	Costa Rica	31.0	23	Senegal	25.0
12	Botswana	30.1	24	Poland	24.3

a Scientific reserves with limited access, national parks, nature reserves and protected landscapes.

Country
profiles

ALGERIA

Area	2,381,741 sq km	Capital	Algiers
Arable as % of total land	3	Currency	Algerian dinar (AD)

People

Population	34.4m	Life expectancy: men	71.9 yrs
Pop. per sq km	14.4	women	75.0 yrs
Av. ann. growth		Adult literacy	72.6%
in pop. 2010–15	1.51%	Fertility rate (per woman)	2.4
Pop. under 15	27.0%	Urban population	66.5%
Pop. over 60	6.9%		per 1,000 pop.
No. of men per 100 women	101.9	Crude birth rate	20.8
Human Development Index	75.4	Crude death rate	4.9

The economy

GDP	AD10,756bn	GDP per head	$4,850
GDP	$167bn	GDP per head in purchasing	
Av. ann. growth in real		power parity (USA=100)	17.3
GDP 2003–08	3.5%	Economic freedom index	56.9

Origins of GDP		Components of GDP	
	% of total		% of total
Agriculture	7	Private consumption	29
Industry, of which:	62	Public consumption	13
manufacturing	5	Investment	34
Services	31	Exports	48
		Imports	-24

Structure of employment

	% of total		% of labour force
Agriculture	21	Unemployed 2007	13.8
Industry	27	Av. ann. rate 1995–2007	23.7
Services	52		

Energy

	m TOE		
Total output	164.3	Net energy imports as %	
Total consumption	36.9	of energy use	-346
Consumption per head,			
kg oil equivalent	1,089		

Inflation and finance

Consumer price			av. ann. increase 2003–08
inflation 2009	5.7%	Narrow money (M1)	24.9%
Av. ann. inflation 2004–09	3.5%	Broad money	16.1%
Treasury bill rate, 2009	0.94%		

Exchange rates

	end 2009		December 2009
AD per $	72.73	Effective rates	2005 = 100
AD per SDR	114.02	– nominal	91.1
AD per €	104.77	– real	96.9

Trade

Principal exports		Principal imports	
	$bn fob		*$bn cif*
Hydrocarbons	76.7	Capital goods	13.6
Semi-finished goods	1.4	Semi-finished goods	10.4
Raw materials	0.4	Food	8.1
Total incl. others	**78.6**	**Total incl. others**	**41.0**

Main export destinations		Main origins of imports	
	% of total		*% of total*
United States	24.1	France	15.8
Italy	15.7	Italy	10.5
Spain	11.5	China	9.9
France	8.1	Spain	7.1

Balance of payments, reserves and debt, $bn

Visible exports fob	78.6	Change in reserves	33.1
Visible imports fob	-38.1	Level of reserves	
Trade balance	40.5	end Dec.	148.1
Invisibles inflows	8.6	No. months of import cover	32.0
Invisibles outflows	-17.5	Official gold holdings, m oz	5.6
Net transfers	2.8	Foreign debt	5.5
Current account balance	34.5	– as % of GDP	3.2
– as % of GDP	20.7	– as % of total exports	6
Capital balance	2.5	Debt service ratio	9
Overall balance	37.0		

Health and education

Health spending, % of GDP	4.4	Education spending, % of GDP	...
Doctors per 1,000 pop.	1.2	Enrolment, %: primary	108
Hospital beds per 1,000 pop.	1.7	secondary	83
Improved-water source access,		tertiary	24
% of pop.	83		

Society

No. of households	5.9m	Colour TVs per 100 households	90.6
Av. no. per household	5.8	Telephone lines per 100 pop.	9.6
Marriages per 1,000 pop.	9.0	Mobile telephone subscribers	
Divorces per 1,000 pop.	...	per 100 pop.	92.7
Cost of living, Feb. 2010		Computers per 100 pop.	1.1
New York = 100	57	Internet hosts per 1,000 pop.	...

ARGENTINA

Area	2,766,889 sq km	Capital	Buenos Aires
Arable as % of total land	12	Currency	Peso (P)

People

Population	39.9m	Life expectancy: men		72.5 yrs
Pop. per sq km	14.4	women		80.0 yrs
Av. ann. growth		Adult literacy		97.7%
in pop. 2010–15	0.98%	Fertility rate (per woman)		2.3
Pop. under 15	24.9%	Urban population		92.4%
Pop. over 60	14.7%			per 1,000 pop.
No. of men per 100 women	96.3	Crude birth rate		17.4
Human Development Index	86.6	Crude death rate		7.7

The economy

GDP	P1,033bn	GDP per head	$8,240
GDP	$328bn	GDP per head in purchasing	
Av. ann. growth in real		power parity (USA=100)	30.9
GDP 2003–08	8.4%	Economic freedom index	51.2

Origins of GDP		**Components of GDP**	
	% of total		% of total
Agriculture	10	Private consumption	59
Industry, of which:	32	Public consumption	13
manufacturing	21	Investment	23
Services	58	Exports	24
		Imports	-21

Structure of employment

	% of total		% of labour force
Agricultural	1	Unemployed 2008	7.3
Industry	23	Av. ann. rate 1995–2008	13.9
Services	76		

Energy

	m TOE		
Total output	81.9	Net energy imports as %	
Total consumption	73.1	of energy use	-12
Consumption per head			
kg oil equivalent	1,850		

Inflation and finance

Consumer price		av. ann. increase 2003–08	
inflation 2009	6.3%	Narrow money (M1)	21.1%
Av. ann. inflation 2004–09	8.8%	Broad money	18.9%
Money market rate, 2009	10.23%		

Exchange rates

	end 2009		December 2009
P per $	3.78	Effective rates	2005 = 100
P per SDR	5.93	– nominal	...
P per €	5.45	– real	...

Trade

Principal exports		Principal imports	
	$bn fob		*$bn cif*
Agricultural products	23.9	Intermediate goods	20.2
Manufactures	22.1	Capital goods	12.6
Primary products	16.1	Consumer goods	6.3
Fuels	8.0	Fuels	4.3
Total incl. others	**70.0**	Total incl. others	**57.4**

Main export destinations		Main origins of imports	
	% of total		*% of total*
Brazil	18.9	Brazil	31.3
China	9.1	China	12.4
United States	7.9	United States	12.2
Chile	6.7	Germany	4.4

Balance of payments, reserves and debt, $bn

Visible exports fob	70.0	Change in reserves	0.2
Visible imports fob	-54.6	Level of reserves	
Trade balance	13.5	end Dec.	46.4
Invisibles inflows	17.7	No. months of import cover	6.9
Invisibles outflows	-26.2	Official gold holdings, m oz	1.8
Net transfers	0.1	Foreign debt	128.3
Current account balance	7.1	– as % of GDP	40
– as % of GDP	2.2	– as % of total exports	171
Capital balance	-11.0	Debt service ratio	11
Overall balance	-3.6		

Health and education

Health spending, % of GDP	10.0	Education spending, % of GDP	4.6
Doctors per 1,000 pop.	3.2	Enrolment, %: primary	115
Hospital beds per 1,000 pop.	4.0	secondary	85
Improved-water source access,		tertiary	68
% of pop.	97		

Society

No. of households	10.8m	Colour TVs per 100 households	95.9
Av. no. per household	3.7	Telephone lines per 100 pop.	24.4
Marriages per 1,000 pop.	3.0	Mobile telephone subscribers	
Divorces per 1,000 pop.	...	per 100 pop.	116.6
Cost of living, Feb. 2010		Computers per 100 pop.	9.0
New York = 100	60	Internet hosts per 1,000 pop.	150.7

AUSTRALIA

Area	7,682,300 sq km	Capital	Canberra
Arable as % of total land	6	Currency	Australian dollar (A$)

People

Population	21.0m	Life expectancy: men	80.0 yrs
Pop. per sq km	2.7	women	84.4 yrs
Av. ann. growth		Adult literacy	...
in pop. 2010–15	1.07%	Fertility rate (per woman)	1.8
Pop. under 15	18.9%	Urban population	89.1%
Pop. over 60	19.5%		per 1,000 pop.
No. of men per 100 women	98.9	Crude birth rate	12.7
Human Development Index	97.0	Crude death rate	7.1

The economy

GDP	A$1,232bn	GDP per head	$47,370
GDP	$1,015bn	GDP per head in purchasing	
Av. ann. growth in real		power parity (USA=100)	83.7
GDP 2003–08	3.3%	Economic freedom index	82.6

Origins of GDP		Components of GDP	
	% of total		% of total
Agriculture	3	Private consumption	55
Industry, of which:	29	Public consumption	18
manufacturing	10	Investment	29
Services	68	Exports	21
		Imports	-23

Structure of employment

	% of total		% of labour force
Agriculture	3	Unemployed 2008	4.2
Industry	19	Av. ann. rate 1995–2008	6.4
Services	78		

Energy

	m TOE		
Total output	289.2	Net energy imports as %	
Total consumption	124.1	of energy use	-133
Consumption per head,			
kg oil equivalent	5,888		

Inflation and finance

Consumer price		av. ann. increase 2003–08	
inflation 2009	1.8%	Narrow money (M1)	8.1%
Av. ann. inflation 2004–09	2.9%	Broad money	12.6%
Money market rate, 2009	3.28%	Household saving rate, 2009	2.5%

Exchange rates

	end 2009		December 2009
A$ per $	1.12	Effective rates	2005 = 100
A$ per SDR	1.75	– nominal	108.8
A$ per €	1.61	– real	113.3

Trade

Principal exports		Principal imports	
	$bn fob		*$bn cif*
Coal	38.5	Intermediate & other goods	100.0
Meat & meat products	7.8	Capital goods	40.8
Wheat	3.2	Consumption goods	30.2
Total incl. others	**186.5**	**Total incl. others**	**190.9**

Main export destinations		Main origins of imports	
	% of total		*% of total*
Japan	22.1	China	17.0
China	14.5	United States	13.3
South Korea	8.2	Japan	10.0
India	6.1	Singapore	7.7
United States	5.5	Germany	5.6

Balance of payments, reserves and aid, $bn

Visible exports fob	189.1	Overall balance	3.7
Visible imports fob	-194.0	Change in reserves	6.0
Trade balance	-4.9	Level of reserves	
Invisibles inflows	82.6	end Dec.	32.9
Invisibles outflows	-125.1	No. months of import cover	1.2
Net transfers	-0.4	Official gold holdings, m oz	2.6
Current account balance	-47.8	Aid given	2.95
– as % of GDP	-4.7	– as % of GDP	0.29
Capital balance	51.1		

Health and education

Health spending, % of GDP	8.9	Education spending, % of GDP	4.9
Doctors per 1,000 pop.	2.5	Enrolment, %: primary	105
Hospital beds per 1,000 pop.	4.0	secondary	148
Improved-water source access,		tertiary	75
% of pop.	100		

Society

No. of households	7.9m	Colour TVs per 100 households	99.1
Av. no. per household	2.7	Telephone lines per 100 pop.	44.7
Marriages per 1,000 pop.	5.3	Mobile telephone subscribers	
Divorces per 1,000 pop.	2.3	per 100 pop.	105.0
Cost of living, Feb. 2010		Computers per 100 pop.	68.1
New York = 100	120	Internet hosts per 1,000 pop.	625.1

AUSTRIA

Area	83,855 sq km	Capital	Vienna
Arable as % of total land	17	Currency	Euro (€)

People

Population	8.4m	Life expectancy: men	78.2 yrs
Pop. per sq km	100.2	women	83.2 yrs
Av. ann. growth		Adult literacy	...
in pop. 2010–15	0.37%	Fertility rate (per woman)	1.4
Pop. under 15	14.7%	Urban population	67.6%
Pop. over 60	23.1%		per 1,000 pop.
No. of men per 100 women	95.3	Crude birth rate	9.1
Human Development Index	95.5	Crude death rate	9.5

The economy

GDP	€282bn	GDP per head	$49,600
GDP	$414bn	GDP per head in purchasing	
Av. ann. growth in real		power parity (USA=100)	81.8
GDP 2003–08	2.8%	Economic freedom index	71.6

Origins of GDP		**Components of GDP**	
	% of total		% of total
Agriculture	2	Private consumption	53
Industry, of which:	31	Public consumption	18
manufacturing	20	Investment	23
Services	67	Exports	59
		Imports	-54

Structure of employment

	% of total		% of labour force
Agriculture	6	Unemployed 2007	3.8
Industry	26	Av. ann. rate 1995–2007	4.2
Services	68		

Energy

	m TOE		
Total output	10.9	Net energy imports as %	
Total consumption	33.2	of energy use	67
Consumption per head,			
kg oil equivalent	3,997		

Inflation and finance

Consumer price		*av. ann. increase 2003–08*	
inflation 2009	0.5%	Euro area:	
Av. ann. inflation 2004–09	1.9%	Narrow money (M1)	8.2%
Deposit rate, h'holds, 2009	2.43%	Broad money	8.8%
		Household saving rate, 2009	14.2%

Exchange rates

	end 2009		December 2009
€ per $	0.69	Effective rates	2005 = 100
€ per SDR	1.09	– nominal	102.9
		– real	102.4

Trade

Principal exports		**Principal imports**	
	$bn fob		*$bn cif*
Machinery & transport equip.	71.4	Machinery & transport equip.	63.6
Chemicals & related products	19.1	Chemicals & related products	20.9
Food, drink & tobacco	11.8	Mineral fuels & lubricants	19.9
Mineral fuels & lubricants	6.1	Food, drink & tobacco	11.6
Raw materials	5.7	Raw materials	8.2
Total incl. others	**173.3**	Total incl. others	**176.0**

Main export destinations		**Main origins of imports**	
	% of total		*% of total*
Germany	31.0	Germany	46.6
Italy	9.0	Italy	7.4
United States	4.5	Switzerland	5.4
Switzerland	4.4	Netherlands	4.3
EU27	72.2	EU27	78.0

Balance of payments, reserves and aid, $bn

Visible exports fob	179.2	Overall balance	-0.8
Visible imports fob	-179.8	Change in reserves	-1.5
Trade balance	-0.6	Level of reserves	
Invisibles inflows	107.3	end Dec.	16.7
Invisibles outflows	-90.9	No. months of import cover	0.7
Net transfers	-2.6	Official gold holdings, m oz	9.0
Current account balance	13.2	Aid given	1.71
– as % of GDP	3.2	– as % of GDP	0.41
Capital balance	-27.0		

Health and education

Health spending, % of GDP	10.1	Education spending, % of GDP	5.8
Doctors per 1,000 pop.	3.8	Enrolment, %: primary	101
Hospital beds per 1,000 pop.	7.8	secondary	100
Improved-water source access,		tertiary	50
% of pop.	100		

Society

No. of households	3.6m	Colour TVs per 100 households	98.9
Av. no. per household	2.4	Telephone lines per 100 pop.	39.4
Marriages per 1,000 pop.	4.9	Mobile telephone subscribers	
Divorces per 1,000 pop.	2.2	per 100 pop.	129.7
Cost of living, Feb. 2010		Computers per 100 pop.	60.7
New York = 100	121	Internet hosts per 1,000 pop.	383.5

BANGLADESH

Area	143,998 sq km	Capital	Dhaka
Arable as % of total land	61	Currency	Taka (Tk)

People

Population	161.3m	Life expectancy: men	66.5 yrs
Pop. per sq km	1,120.1	women	69.0 yrs
Av. ann. growth		Adult literacy	55.0%
in pop. 2010–15	1.42%	Fertility rate (per woman)	2.4
Pop. under 15	30.9%	Urban population	28.1%
Pop. over 60	6.2%		per 1,000 pop.
No. of men per 100 women	102.3	Crude birth rate	21.6
Human Development Index	54.3	Crude death rate	6.3

The economy

GDP	Tk5,458bn	GDP per head	$500
GDP	$79.6bn	GDP per head in purchasing	
Av. ann. growth in real		power parity (USA=100)	2.9
GDP 2003–08	6.3%	Economic freedom index	51.1

Origins of GDP		**Components of GDP**	
	% of total		% of total
Agriculture	19	Private consumption	79
Industry, of which:	29	Public consumption	5
manufacturing	18	Investment	24
Services	52	Exports	20
		Imports	-29

Structure of employment

	% of total		% of labour force
Agriculture	52	Unemployed 2003	4.3
Industry	14	Av. ann. rate 1995–2003	2.7
Services	35		

Energy

			m TOE
Total output	21.3	Net energy imports as %	
Total consumption	25.8	of energy use	17
Consumption per head,			
kg oil equivalent	163		

Inflation and finance

Consumer price		av. ann. increase 2003–08	
inflation 2009	5.4%	Narrow money (M1)	18.8%
Av. ann. inflation 2004–09	7.4%	Broad money	16.1%
Deposit rate, 2009	8.21%		

Exchange rates

	end 2009		December 2009
Tk per $	69.27	Effective rates	2005 = 100
Tk per SDR	108.59	– nominal	...
Tk per €	99.78	– real	...

Trade

Principal exports[a]		Principal imports[a]	
	$bn fob		*$bn cif*
Clothing	8.3	Capital goods	4.3
Fish & fish products	0.6	Textiles & yarns	3.9
Jute goods	0.4	Fuels	2.8
Leather	0.4	Iron & steel	1.2
Total incl. others	**12.6**	Total incl. others	**21.6**

Main export destinations		Main origins of imports	
	% of total		*% of total*
United States	20.7	China	14.7
Germany	13.2	India	14.7
United Kingdom	8.6	Kuwait	7.5
France	6.3	Singapore	7.1
Netherlands	4.7	Hong Kong	4.1

Balance of payments, reserves and debt, $bn

Visible exports fob	15.4	Change in reserves	0.5
Visible imports fob	-21.5	Level of reserves	
Trade balance	-6.1	end Dec.	5.8
Invisibles inflows	2.2	No. months of import cover	2.6
Invisibles outflows	-4.8	Official gold holdings, m oz	0.1
Net transfers	9.8	Foreign debt	23.6
Current account balance	1.0	– as % of GDP	28
– as % of GDP	1.3	– as % of total exports	67
Capital balance	-0.0	Debt service ratio	4
Overall balance	1.1		

Health and education

Health spending, % of GDP	3.4	Education spending, % of GDP	2.3
Doctors per 1,000 pop.	0.3	Enrolment, %: primary	94
Hospital beds per 1,000 pop.	0.4	secondary	44
Improved-water source access,		tertiary	7
% of pop.	80		

Society

No. of households	26.5m	Colour TVs per 100 households	...
Av. no. per household	6.1	Telephone lines per 100 pop.	0.8
Marriages per 1,000 pop.	...	Mobile telephone subscribers	
Divorces per 1,000 pop.	...	per 100 pop.	27.9
Cost of living, Feb. 2010		Computers per 100 pop.	2.3
New York = 100	59	Internet hosts per 1,000 pop.	0.3

a Fiscal year ending June 30 2008.

BELGIUM

Area	30,520 sq km	Capital	Brussels
Arable as % of total land	28	Currency	Euro (€)

People

Population	10.5m	Life expectancy: men	77.7 yrs
Pop. per sq km	344.0	women	83.9 yrs
Av. ann. growth		Adult literacy	...
in pop. 2010–15	0.54%	Fertility rate (per woman)	1.8
Pop. under 15	16.7%	Urban population	97.4%
Pop. over 60	23.4%		per 1,000 pop.
No. of men per 100 women	96	Crude birth rate	11.3
Human Development Index	95.3	Crude death rate	9.7

The economy

GDP	€344bn	GDP per head	$47,090
GDP	$504bn	GDP per head in purchasing	
Av. ann. growth in real		power parity (USA=100)	76.0
GDP 2003–08	2.3%	Economic freedom index	70.1

Origins of GDP		**Components of GDP**	
	% of total		% of total
Agriculture	1	Private consumption	54
Industry, of which:	23	Public consumption	23
manufacturing	16	Investment	24
Services	76	Exports	92
		Imports	-93

Structure of employment

	% of total		% of labour force
Agriculture	2	Unemployed 2008	7.0
Industry	25	Av. ann. rate 1995–2008	8.1
Services	73		

Energy

	m TOE		
Total output	14.4	Net energy imports as %	
Total consumption	57.0	of energy use	75
Consumption per head,			
kg oil equivalent	5,366		

Inflation and finance

Consumer price		*av. ann. increase 2003–08*	
inflation 2009	-0.1%	Euro area:	
Av. ann. inflation 2004–09	2.1%	Narrow money (M1)	8.2%
Treasury bill rate, 2009	0.58%	Broad money	8.8%
		Household saving rate, 2009	12.7%

Exchange rates

	end 2009		December 2009
€ per $	0.69	Effective rates	2005 = 100
€ per SDR	1.09	– nominal	105.6
		– real	105.3

Trade

Principal exports		Principal imports	
	$bn fob		*$bn cif*
Chemicals & related products	131.7	Machinery & transport equip.	114.9
Machinery & transport equip.	108.6	Chemicals & related products	104.4
Minerals, fuels & lubricants	43.7	Minerals, fuels & lubricants	71.1
Food, drink & tobacco	38.7	Food, drink & tobacco	33.7
Raw materials	13.3	Raw materials	20.8
Total incl. others	**473.3**	Total incl. others	**467.3**

Main export destinations		Main origins of imports	
	% of total		*% of total*
Germany	19.8	Netherlands	19.3
France	17.4	Germany	17.2
Netherlands	12.2	France	11.0
United Kingdom	7.2	United Kingdom	5.7
EU27	76.9	EU27	69.9

Balance of payments, reserves and aid, $bn

Visible exports fob	373.4	Overall balance	-1.3
Visible imports fob	-388.4	Change in reserves	-0.8
Trade balance	-15.0	Level of reserves	
Invisibles inflows	202.2	end Dec.	15.7
Invisibles outflows	-191.0	No. months of import cover	0.3
Net transfers	-8.3	Official gold holdings, m oz	7.3
Current account balance	-12.1	Aid given	2.39
– as % of GDP	-2.4	– as % of GDP	0.47
Capital balance	12.6		

Health and education

Health spending, % of GDP	9.4	Education spending, % of GDP	5.9
Doctors per 1,000 pop.	4.2	Enrolment, %: primary	102
Hospital beds per 1,000 pop.	5.3	secondary	110
Improved-water source access,		tertiary	62
% of pop.	100		

Society

No. of households	4.6m	Colour TVs per 100 households	99.0
Av. no. per household	2.3	Telephone lines per 100 pop.	42.1
Marriages per 1,000 pop.	4.2	Mobile telephone subscribers	
Divorces per 1,000 pop.	3.0	per 100 pop.	111.6
Cost of living, Feb. 2010		Computers per 100 pop.	41.7
New York = 100	119	Internet hosts per 1,000 pop.	416.6

BRAZIL

Area	8,511,965 sq km	Capital	Brasilia
Arable as % of total land	7	Currency	Real (R)

People

Population	194.2m	Life expectancy: men	69.9 yrs
Pop. per sq km	22.8	women	77.2 yrs
Av. ann. growth		Adult literacy	90.0%
in pop. 2010–15	0.98%	Fertility rate (per woman)	1.9
Pop. under 15	25.5%	Urban population	86.5%
Pop. over 60	10.2%		per 1,000 pop.
No. of men per 100 women	97	Crude birth rate	16.4
Human Development Index	81.3	Crude death rate	6.5

The economy

GDP	R2,890bn	GDP per head	$8,210
GDP	$1,575bn	GDP per head in purchasing	
Av. ann. growth in real		power parity (USA=100)	22.2
GDP 2003–08	4.8%	Economic freedom index	55.6

Origins of GDP		Components of GDP	
	% of total		% of total
Agriculture	7	Private consumption	61
Industry, of which:	28	Public consumption	20
manufacturing	16	Investment	19
Services	65	Exports	14
		Imports	-14

Structure of employment

	% of total		% of labour force
Agriculture	21	Unemployed 2006	8.4
Industry	19	Av. ann. rate 1995–2006	8.6
Services	60		

Energy

			m TOE
Total output	215.6	Net energy imports as %	
Total consumption	235.6	of energy use	8
Consumption per head,			
kg oil equivalent	1,239		

Inflation and finance

			av. ann. increase 2003–08
Consumer price			
inflation 2009	4.9%	Narrow money (M1)	15.3%
Av. ann. inflation 2004–09	5.1%	Broad money	17.9%
Money market rate, 2009	10.06%		

Exchange rates

	end 2009		December 2009
R per $	1.74	Effective rates	2005 = 100
R per sdr	2.73	– nominal	...
R per €	2.51	– real	...

Trade

Principal exports	$bn fob	Principal imports	$bn cif
Metal goods	27.5	Machines & electrical	
Transport equipment & parts	22.2	equipment	45.9
Soyabeans, meal & oils	18.6	Oil & derivatives	31.5
Chemical products	3.9	Chemical products	24.7
		Transport equipment & parts	21.8
Total incl. others	**197.9**	Total incl. others	**173.1**

Main export destinations	% of total	Main origins of imports	% of total
United States	13.9	United States	14.8
Argentina	8.9	China	11.6
China	8.3	Argentina	7.7
Netherlands	5.3	Germany	6.9

Balance of payments, reserves and debt, $bn

Visible exports fob	197.9	Change in reserves	13.5
Visible imports fob	-173.1	Level of reserves	
Trade balance	24.8	end Dec.	193.8
Invisibles inflows	43.0	No. months of import cover	8.5
Invisibles outflows	-100.2	Official gold holdings, m oz	1.1
Net transfers	4.2	Foreign debt	255.6
Current account balance	-28.2	– as % of GDP	16
– as % of GDP	-1.8	– as % of total exports	121
Capital balance	29.4	Debt service ratio	16
Overall balance	3.0		

Health and education

Health spending, % of GDP	8.4	Education spending, % of GDP	4.3
Doctors per 1,000 pop.	1.7	Enrolment, %: primary	130
Hospital beds per 1,000 pop.	2.4	secondary	100
Improved-water source access,		tertiary	39
% of pop.	97		

Society

No. of households	53.5m	Colour TVs per 100 households	95.6
Av. no. per household	3.6	Telephone lines per 100 pop.	21.4
Marriages per 1,000 pop.	3.9	Mobile telephone subscribers	
Divorces per 1,000 pop.	0.8	per 100 pop.	78.5
Cost of living, Feb. 2010		Computers per 100 pop.	14.1
New York = 100	94	Internet hosts per 1,000 pop.	97.1

BULGARIA

Area	110,994 sq km	Capital	Sofia
Arable as % of total land	28	Currency	Lev (BGL)

People

Population	7.6m	Life expectancy: men	70.9 yrs
Pop. per sq km	68.5	women	77.7 yrs
Av. ann. growth		Adult literacy	98.3%
in pop. 2010–15	0.64%	Fertility rate (per woman)	1.4
Pop. under 15	13.5%	Urban population	71.5%
Pop. over 60	24.5%		per 1,000 pop.
No. of men per 100 women	93.5	Crude birth rate	9.6
Human Development Index	84.0	Crude death rate	14.6

The economy

GDP	BGL66.7bn	GDP per head	$6,550
GDP	$49.9bn	GDP per head in purchasing	
Av. ann. growth in real		power parity (USA=100)	25.4
GDP 2003–08	6.3%	Economic freedom index	62.3

Origins of GDP		Components of GDP	
	% of total		% of total
Agriculture	7	Private consumption	68
Industry, of which:	31	Public consumption	16
manufacturing	15	Investment	38
Services	62	Exports	60
		Imports	-83

Structure of employment

	% of total		% of labour force
Agriculture	9	Unemployed 2008	7.9
Industry	34	Av. ann. rate 1995–2008	13.5
Services	57		

Energy

		m TOE	
Total output	10.0	Net energy imports as %	
Total consumption	20.2	of energy use	51
Consumption per head,			
kg oil equivalent	2,641		

Inflation and finance

Consumer price		av. ann change 2003–08	
inflation 2009	2.8%	Narrow money (M1)	19.9%
Av. ann. inflation 2004–09	7.1%	Broad money	22.5%
Money market rate, 2009	2.01%		

Exchange rates

	end 2009		December 2009
BGL per $	1.36	Effective rates	2005 = 100
BGL per SDR	2.14	– nominal	107.3
BGL per €	1.96	– real	125.1

Trade

Principal exports		Principal imports	
	$bn fob		*$bn cif*
Other metals	2.6	Crude oil & natural gas	6.3
Clothing	2.1	Machinery & equipment	3.6
Iron & steel	1.4	Chemicals, plastics & rubber	2.2
Chemicals, plastics & rubber	1.1	Textiles	1.8
Total incl. others	**22.7**	Total incl. others	**35.1**

Main export destinations		Main origins of imports	
	% of total		*% of total*
Greece	9.8	Russia	15.2
Germany	9.0	Germany	12.5
Turkey	8.8	Italy	8.4
Italy	8.3	Ukraine	7.8
EU27	60.0	EU27	56.7

Balance of payments, reserves and debt, $bn

Visible exports fob	22.6	Change in reserves	0.4
Visible imports fob	-35.5	Level of reserves	
Trade balance	-12.9	end Dec.	17.9
Invisibles inflows	10.6	No. months of import cover	4.6
Invisibles outflows	-11.2	Official gold holdings, m oz	1.3
Net transfers	0.8	Foreign debt	38.0
Current account balance	-12.6	– as % of GDP	79
– as % of GDP	-25.2	– as % of total exports	128
Capital balance	17.3	Debt service ratio	15
Overall balance	1.6		

Health and education

Health spending, % of GDP	7.3	Education spending, % of GDP	3.5
Doctors per 1,000 pop.	3.7	Enrolment, %: primary	101
Hospital beds per 1,000 pop.	6.4	secondary	105
Improved-water source access,		tertiary	50
% of pop.	100		

Society

No. of households	2.9m	Colour TVs per 100 households	90.0
Av. no. per household	2.6	Telephone lines per 100 pop.	28.8
Marriages per 1,000 pop.	4.0	Mobile telephone subscribers	
Divorces per 1,000 pop.	2.5	per 100 pop.	138.3
Cost of living, Feb. 2010		Computers per 100 pop.	11.0
New York = 100	72	Internet hosts per 1,000 pop.	102.3

CAMEROON

Area	475,442 sq km	Capital	Yaoundé
Arable as % of total land	13	Currency	CFA franc (CFAfr)

People

Population	18.9m	Life expectancy: men	52.0 yrs
Pop. per sq km	39.8	women	53.4 yrs
Av. ann. growth		Adult literacy	75.9%
in pop. 2010–15	2.20%	Fertility rate (per woman)	4.7
Pop. under 15	40.8%	Urban population	58.4%
Pop. over 60	5.4%		per 1,000 pop.
No. of men per 100 women	100	Crude birth rate	37.1
Human Development Index	52.3	Crude death rate	13.2

The economy

GDP	CFAfr10,477bn	GDP per head	$1,230
GDP	$23.4bn	GDP per head in purchasing	
Av. ann. growth in real		power parity (USA=100)	4.7
GDP 2003–08	3.1%	Economic freedom index	52.3

Origins of GDP		Components of GDP	
	% of total		% of total
Agriculture	19	Private consumption	72
Industry, of which:	31	Public consumption	9
manufacturing	17	Investment	18
Services	50	Exports	30
		Imports	-29

Structure of employment

	% of total		% of labour force
Agriculture	70	Unemployed 2008	...
Industry	13	Av. ann. rate 1995–2008	...
Services	17		

Energy

	m TOE		
Total output	10.2	Net energy imports as %	
Total consumption	7.3	of energy use	-39
Consumption per head,			
kg oil equivalent	391		

Inflation and finance

Consumer price		av. ann. change 2003–08	
inflation 2009	3.0%	Narrow money (M1)	12.0%
Av. ann. inflation 2004–09	3.2%	Broad money	10.0%
Deposit rate, 2009	3.25%		

Exchange rates

	end 2009		December 2009
			2005 = 100
CFAfr per $	455.34	Effective rates	
CFAfr per SDR	713.83	– nominal	103.8
CFAfr per €	655.92	– real	110.0

Trade

Principal exports[a]		Principal imports[a]	
	$bn fob		$bn cif
Crude oil	1.9	Minerals & raw materials	1.2
Timber	0.5	Intermediate goods	0.6
Cocoa	0.2	Food, drink & tobacco	0.5
Cotton	0.1	Capital goods	0.4
Total incl. others	**5.0**	Total incl. others	**3.8**

Main export destinations		Main origins of imports	
	% of total		% of total
Spain	20.1	France	23.4
Italy	15.9	Nigeria	12.8
France	11.9	Belgium	5.9
South Korea	9.6	Germany	3.9

Balance of payments, reserves and debt, $bn

Visible exports fob	5.9	Change in reserves	0.2
Visible imports fob	-5.4	Level of reserves	
Trade balance	0.5	end Dec.	3.1
Invisible inflows	1.6	No. months of import cover	4.3
Invisible outflows	-3.3	Official gold holdings, m oz	0
Net transfers	0.6	Foreign debt	2.8
Current account balance	-0.5	– as % of GDP	12
– as % of GDP	-2.2	– as % of total exports	15
Capital balance	0.2	Debt service ratio	10
Overall balance	0.1		

Health and education

Health spending, % of GDP	4.9	Education spending, % of GDP	3.2
Doctors per 1,000 pop.	0.2	Enrolment, %: primary	111
Hospital beds per 1,000 pop.	1.5	secondary	37
Improved-water source access,		tertiary	8
% of pop.	74		

Society

No. of households	3.8m	Colour TVs per 100 households	...
Av. no. per household	5.0	Telephone lines per 100 pop.	1.0
Marriages per 1,000 pop.	...	Mobile telephone subscribers	
Divorces per 1,000 pop.	...	per 100 pop.	32.3
Cost of living, Feb. 2010		Computers per 100 pop.	1.1
New York = 100	...	Internet hosts per 1,000 pop.	...

a 2007

CANADA

Area[a]	9,970,610 sq km	Capital	Ottawa
Arable as % of total land	5	Currency	Canadian dollar (C$)

People

Population	33.2m	Life expectancy:	men	79.2 yrs
Pop. per sq km	3.3		women	83.6 yrs
Av. ann. growth		Adult literacy		...
in pop. 2010–15	0.96%	Fertility rate (per woman)		1.6
Pop. under 15	16.3%	Urban population		80.6%
Pop. over 60	20.0%			per 1,000 pop.
No. of men per 100 women	98.2	Crude birth rate		10.6
Human Development Index	96.6	Crude death rate		7.6

The economy

GDP	C$1,602bn	GDP per head	$45,070
GDP	$1,501bn	GDP per head in purchasing	
Av. ann. growth in real		power parity (USA=100)	84.3
GDP 2003–08	2.4%	Economic freedom index	80.4

Origins of GDP[b]		**Components of GDP**	
	% of total		% of total
Agriculture	3	Private consumption	55
Industry, of which:	32	Public consumption	19
manufacturing & mining	...	Investment	23
Services	69	Exports	35
		Imports	-33

Structure of employment

	% of total		% of labour force
Agriculture	3	Unemployed 2008	6.1
Industry	21	Av. ann. rate 1995–2008	7.6
Services	76		

Energy

	m TOE		
Total output	413.2	Net energy imports as %	
Total consumption	269.4	of energy use	-53
Consumption per head,			
kg oil equivalent	8,169		

Inflation and finance

Consumer price		av. ann. increase 2003–08	
inflation 2009	0.3%	Narrow money (M1)	9.1%
Av. ann. inflation 2004–09	1.8%	Broad money	2.2%
Money market rate, 2009	0.39%	Household saving rate, 2009	4.3%

Exchange rates

	end 2009		December 2009
C$ per $	1.05	Effective rates	2005 = 100
C$ per SDR	1.64	– nominal	112.8
C$ per €	1.51	– real	109.8

Trade

Principal exports		Principal imports	
	$bn fob		*$bn fob*
Energy products	118.1	Machinery & equipment	114.8
Other industrial goods	104.2	Other industrial goods	85.8
Machinery & equipment	87.0	Motor vehicles & parts	67.4
Motor vehicles and parts	57.2	Consumer goods	53.9
Total incl. others	**448.9**	Total incl. others	**405.1**

Main export destinations		Main origins of imports	
	% of total		*% of total*
United States	77.7	United States	52.4
United Kingdom	2.7	China	9.8
China	2.3	Mexico	4.1
Japan	2.1	Japan	3.5
EU 27	7.5	EU 27	12.5

Balance of payments, reserves and aid, $bn

Visible exports fob	462.7	Overall balance	1.8
Visible imports fob	-399.0	Change in reserves	2.8
Trade balance	63.7	Level of reserves	
Invisibles inflows	134.4	end Dec.	43.9
Invisibles outflows	-169.8	No. months of import cover	0.9
Net transfers	-1.1	Official gold holdings, m oz	0.1
Current account balance	27.3	Aid given	4.78
– as % of GDP	1.8	– as % of GDP	0.32
Capital balance	-7.0		

Health and education

Health spending, % of GDP	10.1	Education spending, % of GDP	5.3
Doctors per 1,000 pop.	1.9	Enrolment, %: primary	99
Hospital beds per 1,000 pop.	3.4	secondary	101
Improved-water source access,		tertiary	62
% of pop.	100		

Society

No. of households	12.8m	Colour TVs per 100 households	98.9
Av. no. per household	2.6	Telephone lines per 100 pop.	54.9
Marriages per 1,000 pop.	4.4	Mobile telephone subscribers	
Divorces per 1,000 pop.	2.1	per 100 pop.	66.4
Cost of living, Feb. 2010		Computers per 100 pop.	94.3
New York = 100	99	Internet hosts per 1,000 pop.	234.9

a Including freshwater.
b 2005

CHILE

Area	756,945 sq km	Capital	Santiago
Arable as % of total land	2	Currency	Chilean peso (Ps)

People

Population	16.8m	Life expectancy: men	76.2 yrs
Pop. per sq km	22.2	women	82.3 yrs
Av. ann. growth		Adult literacy	98.6%
in pop. 2010–15	1.00%	Fertility rate (per woman)	1.9
Pop. under 15	22.3%	Urban population	89.0%
Pop. over 60	13.2%		per 1,000 pop.
No. of men per 100 women	97.8	Crude birth rate	15.0
Human Development Index	87.8	Crude death rate	5.8

The economy

GDP	88.5trn pesos	GDP per head	$10,080
GDP	$169bn	GDP per head in purchasing	
Av. ann. growth in real		power parity (USA=100)	31.1
GDP 2003–08	4.9%	Economic freedom index	77.2

Origins of GDP		**Components of GDP**	
	% of total		% of total
Agriculture	4	Private consumption	59
Industry, of which:	44	Public consumption	12
manufacturing	13	Investment	25
Services	52	Exports	45
		Imports	-41

Structure of employment

	% of total		% of labour force
Agriculture	13	Unemployed 2008	7.8
Industry	23	Av. ann. rate 1995–2008	7.0
Services	64		

Energy

	m TOE		
Total output	8.5	Net energy imports as %	
Total consumption	30.8	of energy use	73
Consumption per head,			
kg oil equivalent	1,851		

Inflation and finance

Consumer price		av. ann. increase 2003–08	
inflation 2009	1.5%	Narrow money (M1)	13.9%
Av. ann. inflation 2004–09	4.2%	Broad money	13.8%
Money market rate, 2009	1.95%		

Exchange rates

	end 2009		December 2009
Ps per $	506.40	Effective rates	2005 = 100
Ps per SDR	793.93	– nominal	103.6
Ps per €	729.47	– real	109.0

Trade

Principal exports		Principal imports	
	$bn fob		*$bn cif*
Copper	32.8	Intermediate goods	35.7
Fruit	3.3	Consumer goods	11.6
Paper products	3.3	Capital goods	9.2
Total incl. others	**66.5**	Total incl. others	**61.9**

Main export destinations		Main origins of imports	
	% of total		*% of total*
China	14.8	United States	17.3
United States	11.8	China	10.8
Japan	10.7	Brazil	8.4
Brazil	6.2	Argentina	7.9
South Korea	5.9	South Korea	5.0

Balance of payments, reserves and debt, $bn

Visible exports fob	66.5	Change in reserves	6.2
Visible imports fob	-57.6	Level of reserves	
Trade balance	8.8	end Dec.	23.1
Invisibles inflows	16.9	No. months of import cover	3.1
Invisibles outflows	-32.2	Official gold holdings, m oz	0.0
Net transfers	2.9	Foreign debt	64.3
Current account balance	-3.4	– as % of GDP	41
– as % of GDP	-2.0	– as % of total exports	74
Capital balance	12.0	Debt service ratio	18
Overall balance	6.5		

Health and education

Health spending, % of GDP	6.2	Education spending, % of GDP	4.4
Doctors per 1,000 pop.	1.3	Enrolment, %: primary	106
Hospital beds per 1,000 pop.	2.3	secondary	91
Improved-water source access,		tertiary	52
% of pop.	96		

Society

No. of households	4.6m	Colour TVs per 100 households	94.6
Av. no. per household	3.7	Telephone lines per 100 pop.	21.0
Marriages per 1,000 pop.	3.3	Mobile telephone subscribers	
Divorces per 1,000 pop.	0.5	per 100 pop.	88.1
Cost of living, Feb. 2010		Computers per 100 pop.	14.1
New York = 100	71	Internet hosts per 1,000 pop.	62.1

CHINA

Area	9,560,900 sq km	Capital	Beijing
Arable as % of total land	15	Currency	Yuan

People

Population	1,336.3m	Life expectancy: men		72.3 yrs
Pop. per sq km	139.7		women	75.9 yrs
Av. ann. growth		Adult literacy		93.7%
in pop. 2010–15	0.63%	Fertility rate (per woman)		1.0
Pop. under 15	19.9%	Urban population		47.0%
Pop. over 60	12.3%			per 1,000 pop.
No. of men per 100 women	107.9	Crude birth rate		13.5
Human Development Index	77.2	Crude death rate		7.3

The economy

GDP	Yuan30.1trn	GDP per head	$3,270
GDP	$4,327bn	GDP per head in purchasing	
Av. ann. growth in real		power parity (USA=100)	12.9
GDP 2003–08	10.9%	Economic freedom index	51.0

Origins of GDP		**Components of GDP**	
	% of total		% of total
Agriculture	11	Private consumption	34
Industry, of which:	49	Public consumption	14
manufacturing	34	Investment	44
Services	40	Exports	37
		Imports	-28

Structure of employment

	% of total		% of labour force
Agriculture	41	Unemployed 2008	4.2
Industry	25	Av. ann. rate 1995–2008	3.6
Services	34		

Energy

	m TOE		
Total output	1,814.0	Net energy imports as %	
Total consumption	1,955.8	of energy use	7
Consumption per head,			
kg oil equivalent	1,484		

Inflation and finance

		av. ann. increase 2003–08	
Consumer price			
inflation 2009	-0.7%	Narrow money (M1)	14.6%
Av. ann. inflation 2004–09	2.6%	Broad money	17.6%
Deposit rate, 2009	2.25%		

Exchange rates

	end 2009		December 2009
Yuan per $	6.83	Effective rates	2005 = 100
Yuan per SDR	10.71	– nominal	111.2
Yuan per €	9.84	– real	115.7

Trade

Principal exports		Principal imports	
	$bn fob		*$bn cif*
Telecoms equipment	179.0	Electrical machinery	216.7
Office machinery	159.7	Petroleum & products	161.8
Electrical goods	152.8	Multiferous ores & scrap	99.4
Clothing & apparel	120.0	Professional instruments	66.1
Total incl. others	**1,429.5**	Total incl. others	**1,132.3**

Main export destinations		Main origins of imports	
	% of total		*% of total*
United States	19.1	Japan	13.1
Hong Kong	13.1	South Korea	10.7
Japan	8.4	Taiwan	9.1
South Korea	5.3	United States	7.1
EU27	20.5	EU27	11.7

Balance of payments, reserves and debt, $bn

Visible exports fob	1,434.61	Change in reserves	419.7
Visible imports fob	-1,073.9	Level of reserves	
Trade balance	360.7	end Dec.	1,966.0
Invisibles inflows	238.7	No. months of import cover	18.2
Invisibles outflows	-219.1	Official gold holdings, m oz	19.3
Net transfers	45.8	Foreign debt	378.2
Current account balance	426.1	– as % of GDP	9
– as % of GDP	9.8	– as % of total exports	25
Capital balance	19.0	Debt service ratio	2
Overall balance	419.0		

Health and education

Health spending, % of GDP	4.3	Education spending, % of GDP	2.1
Doctors per 1,000 pop.	1.5	Enrolment, %: primary	112
Hospital beds per 1,000 pop.	2.2	secondary	74
Improved-water source access,		tertiary	22
% of pop.	89		

Society

No. of households	384.8m	Colour TVs per 100 households	96.1
Av. no. per household	3.5	Telephone lines per 100 pop.	25.5
Marriages per 1,000 pop.	5.7	Mobile telephone subscribers	
Divorces per 1,000 pop.	1.5	per 100 pop.	48.0
Cost of living, Feb. 2010		Computers per 100 pop.	5.7
New York = 100	89	Internet hosts per 1,000 pop.	11.5

Note: Data excludes Special Administrative Regions ie, Hong Kong and Macau.

COLOMBIA

Area	1,141,748 sq km	Capital	Bogota
Arable as % of total land	2	Currency	Colombian peso (peso)

People

Population	46.7m	Life expectancy: men	70.4 yrs
Pop. per sq km	40.9	women	77.7 yrs
Av. ann. growth		Adult literacy	93.4%
in pop. 2010–15	1.46%	Fertility rate (per woman)	2.5
Pop. under 15	28.6%	Urban population	75.1%
Pop. over 60	8.6%		per 1,000 pop.
No. of men per 100 women	96.9	Crude birth rate	20.6
Human Development Index	80.7	Crude death rate	5.6

The economy

GDP	480trn pesos	GDP per head	$5,420
GDP	$244bn	GDP per head in purchasing	
Av. ann. growth in real		power parity (USA=100)	19.0
GDP 2003–08	5.4%	Economic freedom index	65.5

Origins of GDP		**Components of GDP**	
	% of total		% of total
Agriculture	9	Private consumption	63
Industry, of which:	36	Public consumption	16
manufacturing	16	Investment	25
Services	53	Exports	18
		Imports	-22

Structure of employment

	% of total		% of labour force
Agriculture	21	Unemployed 2008	11.7
Industry	20	Av. ann. rate 1995–2008	13.8
Services	59		

Energy

	m TOE		
Total output	87.6	Net energy imports as %	
Total consumption	29.0	of energy use	-202
Consumption per head,			
kg oil equivalent	655		

Inflation and finance

		av. ann. increase 2003–08	
Consumer price			
inflation 2009	4.2%	Narrow money (M1)	14.4%
Av. ann. inflation 2004–09	5.2%	Broad money	18.1%
Money market rate, 2009	5.65%		

Exchange rates

	end 2009		December 2009
Peso per $	2,044	Effective rates	2005 = 100
Peso per SDR	3,205	– nominal	109.1
Peso per €	2,945	– real	110.2

Trade

Principal exports		Principal imports	
	$bn fob		$bn cif
Petroleum & products	12.2	Intermediate goods &	
Coal	5.0	raw materials	17.7
Coffee	1.8	Capital goods	14.4
Nickel	0.9	Consumer goods	7.6
Total incl. others	37.6	Total	39.7

Main export destinations		Main origins of imports	
	% of total		% of total
United States	38.0	United States	29.2
Venezuela	16.2	China	11.5
Ecuador	4.0	Mexico	7.9
Switzerland	2.5	Brazil	5.9

Balance of payments, reserves and debt, $bn

Visible exports fob	38.5	Change in reserves	2.7
Visible imports fob	-37.6	Level of reserves	
Trade balance	1.0	end Dec.	23.7
Invisibles inflows	5.7	No. months of import cover	5.0
Invisibles outflows	-18.9	Official gold holdings, m oz	0.2
Net transfers	5.5	Foreign debt	46.9
Current account balance	-6.7	– as % of GDP	20
– as % of GDP	-2.8	– as % of total exports	108
Capital balance	9.4	Debt service ratio	16
Overall balance	2.6		

Health and education

Health spending, % of GDP	6.1	Education spending, % of GDP	4.4
Doctors per 1,000 pop.	1.4	Enrolment, %: primary	120
Hospital beds per 1,000 pop.	1.0	secondary	91
Improved-water source access,		tertiary	35
% of pop.	92		

Society

No. of households	11.6m	Colour TVs per 100 households	80.7
Av. no. per household	4.0	Telephone lines per 100 pop.	17.9
Marriages per 1,000 pop.	1.7	Mobile telephone subscribers	
Divorces per 1,000 pop.	...	per 100 pop.	91.9
Cost of living, Feb. 2010		Computers per 100 pop.	11.2
New York = 100	89	Internet hosts per 1,000 pop.	54.3

CÔTE D'IVOIRE

Area	322,463 sq km	Capital	Abidjan/Yamoussoukro
Arable as % of total land	9	Currency	CFA franc (CFAfr)

People

Population	19.6m	Life expectancy:	men	58.4 yrs
Pop. per sq km	60.8		women	61.0 yrs
Av. ann. growth		Adult literacy		54.6%
in pop. 2010–15	2.28%	Fertility rate (per woman)		4.6
Pop. under 15	40.4%	Urban population		50.6%
Pop. over 60	6.1%			per 1,000 pop.
No. of men per 100 women	103.6	Crude birth rate		35.1
Human Development Index	48.4	Crude death rate		9.8

The economy

GDP	CFAfr10,485bn	GDP per head	$1,140
GDP	$23.4bn	GDP per head in purchasing	
Av. ann. growth in real		power parity (USA=100)	3.6
GDP 2003–08	1.6%	Economic freedom index	54.1

Origins of GDP		Components of GDP	
	% of total		% of total
Agriculture	25	Private consumption	74
Industry, of which:	26	Public consumption	9
manufacturing	18	Investment	10
Services	49	Exports	47
		Imports	-39

Structure of employment

	% of total		% of labour force
Agriculture	...	Unemployed 2008	...
Industry	...	Av. ann. rate 1995–2008	...
Services	...		

Energy

	m TOE		
Total output	11.2	Net energy imports as %	
Total consumption	10.0	of energy use	-13
Consumption per head,			
kg oil equivalent	496		

Inflation and finance

Consumer price		av. ann. change 2003–08	
inflation 2009	1.0%	Narrow money (M1)	11.8%
Av. ann. inflation 2004–09	3.1%	Broad money	11.2%
Money market rate, 2009	3.47%		

Exchange rates

	end 2009		December 2009
CFAfr per $	455.34	Effective rates	2005 = 100
CFAfr per SDR	713.83	– nominal	103.9
CFAfr per €	655.92	– real	105.3

Trade

Principal exports[a]		Principal imports[a]	
	$bn fob		$bn cif
Petroleum products	3.2	Capital equipment	
Cocoa beans & products	2.2	& raw materials	2.6
Timber	0.4	Fuel & lubricants	1.9
Coffee & products	0.2	Foodstuffs	1.2
Total incl. others	**8.7**	**Total incl. others**	**6.8**

Main export destinations		Main origins of imports	
	% of total		% of total
Germany	11.8	Nigeria	27.8
United States	10.9	France	15.9
Netherlands	10.5	China	7.6
Nigeria	8.4	Thailand	4.1
France	6.9	Venezuela	3.7

Balance of payments, reserves and debt, $bn

Visible exports fob	10.1	Change in reserves	-0.3
Visible imports fob	-6.8	Level of reserves	
Trade balance	3.3	end Dec.	2.3
Invisibles inflows	1.3	No. months of import cover	2.6
Invisibles outflows	-3.7	Official gold holdings, m oz	0.0
Net transfers	-0.4	Foreign debt	12.6
Current account balance	0.5	– as % of GDP	56
– as % of GDP	2.1	– as % of total exports	144
Capital balance	-0.2	Debt service ratio	9
Overall balance	0.2		

Health and education

Health spending, % of GDP	4.2	Education spending, % of GDP	4.6
Doctors per 1,000 pop.	0.1	Enrolment, %: primary	74
Hospital beds per 1,000 pop.	0.4	secondary	25
Improved-water source access,		tertiary	8
% of pop.	80		

Society

No. of households	3.8m	Colour TVs per 100 households	...
Av. no. per household	5.2	Telephone lines per 100 pop.	1.7
Marriages per 1,000 pop.	...	Mobile telephone subscribers	
Divorces per 1,000 pop.	...	per 100 pop.	50.7
Cost of living, Feb. 2010		Computers per 100 pop.	1.7
New York = 100	85	Internet hosts per 1,000 pop.	0.5

a 2007

CZECH REPUBLIC

Area	78,864 sq km	Capital	Prague
Arable as % of total land	39	Currency	Koruna (Kc)

People

Population	10.2m	Life expectancy: men	74.3 yrs
Pop. per sq km	129.3	women	80.3 yrs
Av. ann. growth		Adult literacy	...
in pop. 2010–15	0.42%	Fertility rate (per woman)	1.4
Pop. under 15	14.1%	Urban population	73.5%
Pop. over 60	22.2%		per 1,000 pop.
No. of men per 100 women	96.6	Crude birth rate	10.6
Human Development Index	90.3	Crude death rate	10.9

The economy

GDP	Kc3,689bn	GDP per head	$20,670
GDP	$215bn	GDP per head in purchasing	
Av. ann. growth in real		power parity (USA=100)	53.2
GDP 2003–08	5.2%	Economic freedom index	69.8

Origins of GDP		**Components of GDP**	
	% of total		% of total
Agriculture	3	Private consumption	50
Industry, of which:	38	Public consumption	20
manufacturing	25	Investment	25
Services	60	Exports	77
		Imports	-73

Structure of employment

	% of total		% of labour force
Agriculture	3	Unemployed 2008	4.4
Industry	41	Av. ann. rate 1995–2008	6.6
Services	56		

Energy

	m TOE		
Total output	33.7	Net energy imports as %	
Total consumption	45.8	of energy use	26
Consumption per head,			
kg oil equivalent	4,428		

Inflation and finance

		av. ann. increase 2003–08	
Consumer price			
inflation 2009	1.0%	Narrow money (M1)	11.7%
Av. ann. inflation 2004–09	2.9%	Broad money	12.2%
Money market rate, 2009	1.54%	Household saving rate, 2009	4.1%

Exchange rates

	end 2009		December 2009
Kc per $	18.37	Effective rates	2005 = 100
Kc per SDR	28.80	– nominal	117.9
Kc per €	26.46	– real	121.6

Trade

Principal exports		Principal imports	
	$bn fob		*$bn cif*
Machinery & transport		Machinery & transport	
equipment	78.8	equipment	58.8
Semi-manufactures	28.6	Semi-manufactures	28.0
Raw materials & fuels	8.8	Raw materials & fuels	18.6
Chemicals	8.7	Chemicals	14.6
Total incl. others	**146.4**	Total incl. others	**142.2**

Main export destinations		Main origins of imports	
	% of total		*% of total*
Germany	30.7	Germany	30.3
Slovakia	9.2	Slovakia	6.5
Poland	6.5	Poland	6.4
United Kingdom	4.8	Russia	6.2
EU27	84.9	EU27	76.9

Balance of payments, reserves and debt, $bn

Visible exports fob	145.7	Change in reserves	2.1
Visible imports fob	-139.3	Level of reserves	
Trade balance	6.4	end Dec.	37.0
Invisibles inflows	30.2	No. months of import cover	2.4
Invisibles outflows	-42.6	Official gold holdings, m oz	0.4
Net transfers	-0.6	Foreign debt	80.8
Current account balance	-6.6	– as % of GDP	37
– as % of GDP	-3.1	– as % of total exports	46
Capital balance	10.8	Debt service ratio	10
Overall balance	2.4	Aid given	0.25
		– as % of GDP	0.12

Health and education

Health spending, % of GDP	6.8	Education spending, % of GDP	4.4
Doctors per 1,000 pop.	3.6	Enrolment, %: primary	102
Hospital beds per 1,000 pop.	8.1	secondary	95
Improved-water source access,		tertiary	54
% of pop.	100		

Society

No. of households	4.5m	Colour TVs per 100 households	98.2
Av. no. per household	2.3	Telephone lines per 100 pop.	21.9
Marriages per 1,000 pop.	5.1	Mobile telephone subscribers	
Divorces per 1,000 pop.	3.4	per 100 pop.	133.5
Cost of living, Feb. 2010		Computers per 100 pop.	27.4
New York = 100	100	Internet hosts per 1,000 pop.	337.3

DENMARK

Area	43,075 sq km	Capital	Copenhagen
Arable as % of total land	54	Currency	Danish krone (DKr)

People

Population	5.5m	Life expectancy: men	76.7 yrs
Pop. per sq km	127.7	women	81.4 yrs
Av. ann. growth		Adult literacy	...
in pop. 2010–15	0.24%	Fertility rate (per woman)	1.8
Pop. under 15	18.0%	Urban population	86.9%
Pop. over 60	23.4%		per 1,000 pop.
No. of men per 100 women	98.4	Crude birth rate	11.5
Human Development Index	95.5	Crude death rate	10.4

The economy

GDP	DKr1,740bn	GDP per head	$62,120
GDP	$341bn	GDP per head in purchasing	
Av. ann. growth in real		power parity (USA=100)	79.5
GDP 2003–08	1.8%	Economic freedom index	77.9

Origins of GDP		Components of GDP	
	% of total		% of total
Agriculture	1	Private consumption	49
Industry, of which:	26	Public consumption	27
manufacturing	15	Investment	22
Services	73	Exports	55
		Imports	-52

Structure of employment

	% of total		% of labour force
Agriculture	3	Unemployed 2008	3.3
Industry	23	Av. ann. rate 1995–2008	5.2
Services	74		

Energy

	m TOE		
Total output	27.0	Net energy imports as %	
Total consumption	19.6	of energy use	-38
Consumption per head,			
kg oil equivalent	3,598		

Inflation and finance

Consumer price		av. ann. increase 2003–08	
inflation 2009	1.3%	Narrow money (M1)	10.0%
Av. ann. inflation 2004–09	2.0%	Broad money	10.5%
Money market rate, 2009	1.81%	Household saving rate, 2009	8.1%

Exchange rates

	end 2009		December 2009
DKr per $	5.19	Effective rates	2005 = 100
DKr per SDR	8.14	– nominal	106.2
DKr per €	7.48	– real	106.9

Trade

Principal exports		**Principal imports**	
	$bn fob		*$bn cif*
Machinery & transport equip.	30.5	Machinery & transport equip.	36.7
Food, drinks & tobacco	19.9	Food, drinks & tobacco	12.7
Chemicals & related products	15.0	Chemicals & related products	12.1
Minerals, fuels & lubricants	13.5	Minerals, fuels & lubricants	8.1
Total incl. others	**115.7**	Total incl. others	**109.8**

Main export destinations		**Main origins of imports**	
	% of total		*% of total*
Germany	18.0	Germany	21.3
Sweden	14.7	Sweden	14.0
United Kingdom	8.2	Netherlands	6.8
Norway	5.8	Norway	6.3
United States	5.4	China	5.7
EU27	69.7	EU27	71.8

Balance of payments, reserves and aid, $bn

Visible exports fob	114.7	Overall balance	7.4
Visible imports fob	-115.4	Change in reserves	8.0
Trade balance	-0.6	Level of reserves	
Invisibles inflows	109.9	end Dec.	42.3
Invisibles outflows	-96.0	No. months of import cover	2.4
Net transfers	-5.7	Official gold holdings, m oz	2.1
Current account balance	7.5	Aid given	2.80
– as % of GDP	2.2	– as % of GDP	0.82
Capital balance	9.8		

Health and education

Health spending, % of GDP	9.8	Education spending, % of GDP	8.4
Doctors per 1,000 pop.	3.2	Enrolment, %: primary	99
Hospital beds per 1,000 pop.	3.5	secondary	119
Improved-water source access,		tertiary	80
% of pop.	100		

Society

No. of households	2.5m	Colour TVs per 100 households	98.1
Av. no. per household	2.2	Telephone lines per 100 pop.	45.6
Marriages per 1,000 pop.	7.2	Mobile telephone subscribers	
Divorces per 1,000 pop.	3.1	per 100 pop.	125.7
Cost of living, Feb. 2010		Computers per 100 pop.	54.9
New York = 100	138	Internet hosts per 1,000 pop.	749.1

EGYPT

Area	1,000,250 sq km	Capital	Cairo
Arable as % of total land	3	Currency	Egyptian pound (£E)

People

Population	76.8m	Life expectancy: men		69.3 yrs
Pop. per sq km	76.8		women	73.0 yrs
Av. ann. growth		Adult literacy		66.4%
in pop. 2010–15	1.81%	Fertility rate (per woman)		2.9
Pop. under 15	32.1%	Urban population		43.4%
Pop. over 60	7.5%			per 1,000 pop.
No. of men per 100 women	101.1	Crude birth rate		24.8
Human Development Index	70.3	Crude death rate		5.7

The economy

GDP	£E893bn	GDP per head	$1,990
GDP	$162bn	GDP per head in purchasing	
Av. ann. growth in real		power parity (USA=100)	11.7
GDP 2003–08	5.9%	Economic freedom index	59.0

Origins of GDP		Components of GDP[a]	
	% of total		% of total
Agriculture	13	Private consumption	72
Industry, of which:	38	Public consumption	11
manufacturing	16	Investment	22
Services	49	Exports	33
		Imports	-39

Structure of employment

	% of total		% of labour force
Agriculture	30	Unemployed 2008	8.7
Industry	21	Av. ann. rate 1995–2008	9.8
Services	49		

Energy

	m TOE		
Total output	82.3	Net energy imports as %	
Total consumption	67.2	of energy use	-22
Consumption per head,			
kg oil equivalent	840		

Inflation and finance

		av. ann. increase 2003–08	
Consumer price			
inflation 2009	11.8%	Narrow money (M1)	18.9%
Av. ann. inflation 2004–09	10.3%	Broad money	14.0%
Treasury bill rate, 2009	9.84%		

Exchange rates

	end 2009		December 2009
£E per $	5.20	Effective rates	2005 = 100
£E per SDR	8.20	– nominal	...
£E per €	7.49	– real	...

Trade

Principal exports[a]		Principal imports[a]	
	$bn fob		*$bn fob*
Petroleum & products	14.8	Intermediate goods	18.0
Finished goods incl. textiles	11.4	Capital goods	13.0
Semi-finished products	2.0	Consumer goods	9.3
Iron & steel	0.7	Fuels	5.6
Total incl. others	**29.8**	**Total incl. others**	**56.6**

Main export destinations		Main origins of imports	
	% of total		*% of total*
Italy	9.4	United States	10.3
United States	7.1	China	9.9
Spain	6.5	Italy	7.3
India	5.9	Germany	6.8

Balance of payments, reserves and debt, $bn

Visible exports fob	29.8	Change in reserves	2.1
Visible imports fob	-49.6	Level of reserves	
Trade balance	-19.8	end Dec.	34.3
Invisibles inflows	28.0	No. months of import cover	6.0
Invisibles outflows	-19.4	Official gold holdings, m oz	2.4
Net transfers	9.8	Foreign debt	32.6
Current account balance	-1.4	– as % of GDP	20
– as % of GDP	-0.9	– as % of total exports	49
Capital balance	5.3	Debt service ratio	5
Overall balance	0.9		

Health and education

Health spending, % of GDP	6.3	Education spending, % of GDP	3.8
Doctors per 1,000 pop.	2.4	Enrolment, %: primary	100
Hospital beds per 1,000 pop.	2.1	secondary	88
Improved-water source access,		tertiary	31
% of pop.	99		

Society

No. of households	18.4m	Colour TVs per 100 households	85.3
Av. no. per household	4.2	Telephone lines per 100 pop.	14.6
Marriages per 1,000 pop.	6.2	Mobile telephone subscribers	
Divorces per 1,000 pop.	0.7	per 100 pop.	50.6
Cost of living, Feb. 2010		Computers per 100 pop.	3.9
New York = 100	70	Internet hosts per 1,000 pop.	2.4

a Year ending June 30, 2008.

ESTONIA

Area	45,200 sq km	Capital	Tallinn
Arable as % of total land	14	Currency	Kroon (EEK)

People

Population	1.3m	Life expectancy:	men	68.9 yrs
Pop. per sq km	28.8		women	79.3 yrs
Av. ann. growth		Adult literacy		99.8%
in pop. 2010–15	-0.11%	Fertility rate (per woman)		1.6
Pop. under 15	15.4%	Urban population		69.5%
Pop. over 60	22.6%			per 1,000 pop.
No. of men per 100 women	85.6	Crude birth rate		11.8
Human Development Index	88.3	Crude death rate		13.0

The economy

GDP	EEK251bn	GDP per head	$17,450
GDP	$23.4bn	GDP per head in purchasing	
Av. ann. growth in real		power parity (USA=100)	44.6
GDP 2003–08	5.9%	Economic freedom index	74.7

Origins of GDP		**Components of GDP**	
	% of total		% of total
Agriculture	3	Private consumption	55
Industry, of which:	29	Public consumption	19
manufacturing	17	Investment	30
Services	68	Exports	76
		Imports	-80

Structure of employment

	% of total		% of labour force
Agriculture	4	Unemployed 2008	5.5
Industry	36	Av. ann. rate 1995–2008	9.3
Services	60		

Energy

	m TOE		
Total output	4.4	Net energy imports as %	
Total consumption	5.6	of energy use	22
Consumption per head,			
kg oil equivalent	4,198		

Inflation and finance

Consumer price		av. ann. increase 2003–08	
inflation 2009	-0.1%	Narrow money (M1)	13.2%
Av. ann. inflation 2004–09	5.0%	Broad money	20.0%
Money market rate, 2009	5.93%		

Exchange rates

	end 2009		December 2009
EEK per $	10.87	Effective rates	2005 = 100
EEK per SDR	17.03	– nominal	...
EEK per €	15.66	– real	...

Trade

Principal exports	
	$bn fob
Machinery & equipment	2.7
Mineral products	1.5
Non-precious metals & products	1.5
Wood & paper	1.4
Foodstuffs	1.1
Total incl. others	**12.4**

Principal imports	
	$bn cif
Machinery & equipment	3.4
Mineral products	2.5
Chemicals	2.0
Transport equipment	1.8
Non-precious metals & products	1.7
Total incl. others	**15.9**

Main export destinations	
	% of total
Finland	18.3
Sweden	13.8
Russia	10.4
Latvia	10.0
Lithuania	5.7
EU27	70.0

Main origins of imports	
	% of total
Finland	14.1
Germany	13.4
Sweden	10.0
Latvia	9.0
Lithuania	9.0
EU27	79.7

Balance of payments, reserves and debt, $bn

Visible exports fob	12.6	Change in reserves	0.7
Visible imports fob	-15.3	Level of reserves	
Trade balance	-2.8	end Dec.	4.0
Invisibles inflows	6.8	No. months of import cover	2.2
Invisibles outflows	-6.6	Official gold holdings, m oz	0.0
Net transfers	0.3	Foreign debt	26.0
Current account balance	-2.2	– as % of GDP	111.2
– as % of GDP	-9.6	– as % of total exports	134.4
Capital balance	3.1	Debt service ratio	20
Overall balance	0.7		

Health and education

Health spending, % of GDP	5.4	Education spending, % of GDP	5.9
Doctors per 1,000 pop.	3.3	Enrolment, %: primary	99
Hospital beds per 1,000 pop.	5.6	secondary	100
Improved-water source access,		tertiary	65
% of pop.	98		

Society

No. of households	0.6m	Colour TVs per 100 households	96.9
Av. no. per household	2.2	Telephone lines per 100 pop.	37.1
Marriages per 1,000 pop.	4.7	Mobile telephone subscribers	
Divorces per 1,000 pop.	3.2	per 100 pop.	182.2
Cost of living, Feb. 2010		Computers per 100 pop.	25.5
New York = 100	...	Internet hosts per 1,000 pop.	558.5

FINLAND

Area	338,145 sq km	Capital	Helsinki
Arable as % of total land	7	Currency	Euro (€)

People

Population	5.3m	Life expectancy: men	77.2 yrs
Pop. per sq km	15.7	women	83.6 yrs
Av. ann. growth		Adult literacy	...
in pop. 2010–15	0.38%	Fertility rate (per woman)	1.8
Pop. under 15	16.6%	Urban population	85.1%
Pop. over 60	24.7%		per 1,000 pop.
No. of men per 100 women	96.2	Crude birth rate	11.1
Human Development Index	95.9	Crude death rate	9.7

The economy

GDP	€186bn	GDP per head	$51,320
GDP	$273bn	GDP per head in purchasing	
Av. ann. growth in real		power parity (USA=100)	78.1
GDP 2003–08	3.5%	Economic freedom index	73.8

Origins of GDP		Components of GDP	
	% of total		% of total
Agriculture	3	Private consumption	53
Industry, of which:	32	Public consumption	22
manuf., mining & utilities	24	Investment	21
Services	65	Exports	44
		Imports	-40

Structure of employment

	% of total		% of labour force
Agriculture	5	Unemployed 2008	6.4
Industry	25	Av. ann. rate 1995–2008	9.9
Services	70		

Energy

	m TOE		
Total output	15.9	Net energy imports as %	
Total consumption	36.5	of energy use	56
Consumption per head,			
kg oil equivalent	6,895		

Inflation and finance

Consumer price		av. ann. increase 2003–08	
inflation 2009	0.0%	Euro area:	
Av. ann. inflation 2004–09	1.8%	Narrow money (M1)	8.2%
Money market rate, 2009	1.23%	Broad money	8.8%
		Household saving rate, 2009	4.9%

Exchange rates

	end 2009		December 2009
€ per $	0.69	Effective rates	2005 = 100
€ per SDR	1.09	– nominal	106.7
		– real	104.7

Trade

Principal exports		Principal imports	
	$bn fob		*$bn cif*
Machinery & transport equipment	42.3	Machinery & transport equipment	33.5
Mineral fuels & lubricants	6.7	Minerals & fuels	16.1
Chemicals & related products	5.8	Chemical & related products	8.9
Raw materials	4.7	Raw materials	7.8
Total incl. others	**96.9**	Total incl. others	**92.1**

Main export destinations		Main origins of imports	
	% of total		*% of total*
Russia	11.6	Russia	16.3
Germany	10.0	Germany	15.7
Sweden	10.0	Sweden	13.6
United States	6.4	Netherlands	6.3
United Kingdom	5.5	China	5.1
Netherlands	5.1	United Kingdom	4.2
EU27	55.9	EU27	62.0

Balance of payments, reserves and aid, $bn

Visible exports fob	97.0	Overall balance	0.2
Visible imports fob	-88.3	Change in reserves	-0.0
Trade balance	8.7	Level of reserves	
Invisibles inflows	55.4	end Dec.	8.4
Invisibles outflows	-53.8	No. months of import cover	0.7
Net transfers	-2.3	Official gold holdings, m oz	1.6
Current account balance	8.0	Aid given	1.17
– as % of GDP	2.9	– as % of GDP	0.43
Capital balance	8.2		

Health and education

Health spending, % of GDP	8.2	Education spending, % of GDP	6.3
Doctors per 1,000 pop.	3.3	Enrolment, %: primary	98
Hospital beds per 1,000 pop.	6.8	secondary	111
Improved-water source access, % of pop.	100	tertiary	94

Society

No. of households	2.5m	Colour TVs per 100 households	95.1
Av. no. per household	2.1	Telephone lines per 100 pop.	31.1
Marriages per 1,000 pop.	5.8	Mobile telephone subscribers	
Divorces per 1,000 pop.	2.4	per 100 pop.	128.8
Cost of living, Feb. 2010		Computers per 100 pop.	50.0
New York = 100	132	Internet hosts per 1,000 pop.	826.7

FRANCE

Area	543,965 sq km	Capital	Paris
Arable as % of total land	34	Currency	Euro (€)

People

Population	61.9m	Life expectancy: men	78.6 yrs
Pop. per sq km	113.8	women	85.1 yrs
Av. ann. growth		Adult literacy	...
in pop. 2010–15	0.53%	Fertility rate (per woman)	1.9
Pop. under 15	18.4%	Urban population	85.3%
Pop. over 60	23.2%		per 1,000 pop.
No. of men per 100 women	94.7	Crude birth rate	12.2
Human Development Index	96.1	Crude death rate	9.0

The economy

GDP	€1,907bn	GDP per head	$44,510
GDP	$2,857bn	GDP per head in purchasing	
Av. ann. growth in real		power parity (USA=100)	71.3
GDP 2003–08	1.8%	Economic freedom index	64.2

Origins of GDP		Components of GDP	
	% of total		% of total
Agriculture	2	Private consumption	57
Industry, of which:	20	Public consumption	23
manufacturing	12	Investment	22
Services	78	Exports	26
		Imports	-29

Structure of employment

	% of total		% of labour force
Agriculture	3	Unemployed 2008	7.4
Industry	23	Av. ann. rate 1995–2008	10.0
Services	73		

Energy

	m TOE		
Total output	135.5	Net energy imports as %	
Total consumption	263.7	of energy use	49
Consumption per head,			
kg oil equivalent	4,258		

Inflation and finance

Consumer price		av. ann. increase 2003–08	
inflation 2009	0.1%	Euro area:	
Av. ann. inflation 2004–09	1.6%	Narrow money (M1)	8.2%
Treasury bill rate, 2009	0.65%	Broad money	8.8%
		Household saving rate, 2009	13.5%

Exchange rates

	end 2009		December 2009
€ per $	0.69	Effective rates	2005 = 100
€ per SDR	1.09	– nominal	105.5
		– real	103.3

Trade

Principal exports	
	$bn fob
Machinery & transport equip.	225.5
Chemicals & related products	107.1
Food, drink & tobacco	66.3
Mineral fuels & lubricants	29.9
Raw materials	16.0
Total incl. others	**598.6**

Principal imports	
	$bn cif
Machinery & transport equip.	228.6
Mineral fuels & lubricants	116.0
Chemicals & related products	90.0
Food, drink & tobacco	51.4
Raw materials	20.4
Total incl. others	**702.6**

Main export destinations	
	% of total
Germany	14.6
Italy	8.8
Spain	8.4
United Kingdom	7.8
Belgium	7.7
United States	5.9
EU27	63.5

Main origins of imports	
	% of total
Germany	17.9
Belgium	11.8
Italy	8.3
Spain	6.9
Netherlands	6.8
United Kingdom	5.1
EU27	67.6

Balance of payments, reserves and aid, $bn

Visible exports fob	605.2	Overall balance	-12.0
Visible imports fob	-692.1	Change in reserves	-12.2
Trade balance	-86.9	Level of reserves	
Invisibles inflows	425.9	end Dec.	103.3
Invisibles outflows	-368.2	No. months of import cover	1.2
Net transfers	-35.1	Official gold holdings, m oz	80.1
Current account balance	-64.2	Aid given	10.91
– as % of GDP	-2.2	– as % of GDP	0.38
Capital balance	96.1		

Health and education

Health spending, % of GDP	11.0	Education spending, % of GDP	5.7
Doctors per 1,000 pop.	3.7	Enrolment, %: primary	110
Hospital beds per 1,000 pop.	7.2	secondary	113
Improved-water source access,		tertiary	55
% of pop.	100		

Society

No. of households	26.6m	Colour TVs per 100 households	97.3
Av. no. per household	2.3	Telephone lines per 100 pop.	56.4
Marriages per 1,000 pop.	3.9	Mobile telephone subscribers	
Divorces per 1,000 pop.	2.2	per 100 pop.	93.5
Cost of living, Feb. 2010		Computers per 100 pop.	65.2
New York = 100	150	Internet hosts per 1,000 pop.	242.4

GERMANY

Area	357,868 sq km	Capital	Berlin
Arable as % of total land	34	Currency	Euro (€)

People

Population	82.5m	Life expectancy: men	77.8 yrs
Pop. per sq km	230.5	women	83.1 yrs
Av. ann. growth		Adult literacy	...
in pop. 2010–15	-0.09%	Fertility rate (per woman)	1.3
Pop. under 15	13.4%	Urban population	73.8%
Pop. over 60	26.0%		per 1,000 pop.
No. of men per 100 women	96.3	Crude birth rate	8.1
Human Development Index	94.7	Crude death rate	11.0

The economy

GDP	€2,491bn	GDP per head	$44,450
GDP	$3,649bn	GDP per head in purchasing	
Av. ann. growth in real		power parity (USA=100)	76.3
GDP 2003–08	1.8%	Economic freedom index	71.1

Origins of GDP		**Components of GDP**	
	% of total		% of total
Agriculture	1	Private consumption	56
Industry, of which:	30	Public consumption	18
manufacturing	24	Investment	19
Services	69	Exports	47
		Imports	-41

Structure of employment

	% of total		% of labour force
Agriculture	2	Unemployed 2008	7.5
Industry	30	Av. ann. rate 1995–2008	9.1
Services	68		

Energy

	m TOE		
Total output	137.0	Net energy imports as %	
Total consumption	331.3	of energy use	59
Consumption per head,			
kg oil equivalent	4,027		

Inflation and finance

Consumer price		av. ann. increase 2003–08	
inflation 2009	0.3%	Euro area:	
Av. ann. inflation 2004–09	1.7%	Narrow money (M1)	8.2%
Money market rate, 2009	0.63%	Broad money	8.8%
		Household saving rate, 2009	11.7%

Exchange rates

	end 2009		December 2009
€ per $	0.69	Effective rates	2005 = 100
€ per SDR	1.09	– nominal	105.8
		– real	103.8

Trade

Principal exports		Principal imports	
	$bn fob		*$bn cif*
Machinery & transport equip.	697.9	Machinery & transport equip.	406.9
Chemicals & related products	205.6	Mineral fuels & lubricants	166.6
Food, drink & tobacco	70.1	Chemicals & related products	149.8
Mineral fuels & lubricants	38.6	Food, drink & tobacco	78.3
Raw materials	30.4	Raw materials	49.8
Total incl. others	**1,443.8**	Total incl. others	**1,184.1**

Main export destinations		Main origins of imports	
	% of total		*% of total*
France	9.6	Netherlands	12.4
United States	7.2	France	8.1
Netherlands	6.7	Belgium	7.2
United Kingdom	6.6	China	6.3
Italy	6.3	Italy	5.9
Austria	5.6	United Kingdom	5.2
Belgium	5.1	Russia	4.4
EU27	63.3	EU27	63.6

Balance of payments, reserves and aid, $bn

Visible exports fob	1,498.3	Overall balance	2.7
Visible imports fob	-1,232.8	Change in reserves	2.6
Trade balance	266.3	Level of reserves	
Invisibles inflows	607.7	end Dec.	138.6
Invisibles outflows	-581.3	No. months of import cover	0.9
Net transfers	-48.7	Official gold holdings, m oz	109.7
Current account balance	243.9	Aid given	13.98
– as % of GDP	6.7	– as % of GDP	0.38
Capital balance	-300.8		

Health and education

Health spending, % of GDP	10.4	Education spending, % of GDP	4.6
Doctors per 1,000 pop.	3.5	Enrolment, %: primary	106
Hospital beds per 1,000 pop.	8.3	secondary	101
Improved-water source access,		tertiary	46
% of pop.	100		

Society

No. of households	39.9m	Colour TVs per 100 households	98.0
Av. no. per household	2.1	Telephone lines per 100 pop.	62.4
Marriages per 1,000 pop.	4.9	Mobile telephone subscribers	
Divorces per 1,000 pop.	2.9	per 100 pop.	128.3
Cost of living, Feb. 2010		Computers per 100 pop.	65.6
New York = 100	116	Internet hosts per 1,000 pop.	260.1

GREECE

Area	131,957 sq km	Capital	Athens
Arable as % of total land	20	Currency	Euro (€)

People

Population	11.2m	Life expectancy: men	77.7 yrs
Pop. per sq km	84.9	women	82.5 yrs
Av. ann. growth		Adult literacy	97.0%
in pop. 2010–15	0.22%	Fertility rate (per woman)	1.4
Pop. under 15	14.2%	Urban population	61.4%
Pop. over 60	24.3%		per 1,000 pop.
No. of men per 100 women	98.4	Crude birth rate	9.7
Human Development Index	94.2	Crude death rate	10.4

The economy

GDP	€243bn	GDP per head	$31,670
GDP	$356bn	GDP per head in purchasing	
Av. ann. growth in real		power parity (USA=100)	63.3
GDP 2003–08	3.6%	Economic freedom index	62.7

Origins of GDP		**Components of GDP**	
	% of total		% of total
Agriculture	3	Private consumption	71
Industry, of which:	20	Public consumption	17
mining & manufacturing	10	Investment	21
Services	77	Exports	23
		Imports	-32

Structure of employment

	% of total		% of labour force
Agriculture	12	Unemployed 2008	7.7
Industry	22	Av. ann. rate 1995–2008	9.9
Services	66		

Energy

	m TOE		
Total output	12.1	Net energy imports as %	
Total consumption	32.2	of energy use	62
Consumption per head,			
kg oil equivalent	2,875		

Inflation and finance

Consumer price		*av. ann. increase 2003–08*	
inflation 2009	1.2%	Euro area:	
Av. ann. inflation 2004–09	3.0%	Narrow money (M1)	8.2%
Treasury bill rate, 2009	1.62%	Broad money	8.8%

Exchange rates

	end 2009		December 2009
€ per $	0.69	Effective rates	2005 = 100
€ per SDR	1.09	– nominal	105.7
		– real	107.8

Trade

Principal exports		Principal imports	
	$bn fob		*$bn cif*
Food, drink & tobacco	4.7	Machinery & transport equip.	23.7
Machinery & transport equip.	3.5	Mineral fuels & lubricants	17.7
Chemical & related products	3.3	Chemicals & related products	12.1
Mineral fuels & lubricants	2.7	Food, drink & tobacco	8.7
Total incl. others	**25.7**	Total incl. others	**88.3**

Main export destinations		Main origins of imports	
	% of total		*% of total*
Germany	11.5	Germany	11.9
Italy	10.5	Italy	11.5
United Kingdom	7.0	Russia	7.3
Bulgaria	6.2	China	5.6
Cyprus	5.0	France	5.1
EU27	64.3	EU27	55.2

Balance of payments, reserves and debt, $bn

Visible exports fob	29.2	Overall balance	0.0
Visible imports fob	-94.2	Change in reserves	-0.2
Trade balance	-65.0	Level of reserves	
Invisibles inflows	58.9	end Dec.	3.5
Invisibles outflows	-49.3	No. months of import cover	0.3
Net transfers	4.2	Official gold holdings, m oz	3.6
Current account balance	-51.3	Aid given	0.70
– as % of GDP	-14.4	– as % of GDP	0.20
Capital balance	50.2		

Health and education

Health spending, % of GDP	9.6	Education spending, % of GDP	3.9
Doctors per 1,000 pop.	5.4	Enrolment, %: primary	101
Hospital beds per 1,000 pop.	4.8	secondary	102
Improved-water source access,		tertiary	91
% of pop.	100		

Society

No. of households	4.0m	Colour TVs per 100 households	99.7
Av. no. per household	2.8	Telephone lines per 100 pop.	53.7
Marriages per 1,000 pop.	5.3	Mobile telephone subscribers	
Divorces per 1,000 pop.	1.2	per 100 pop.	123.9
Cost of living, Feb. 2010		Computers per 100 pop.	9.4
New York = 100	92	Internet hosts per 1,000 pop.	223.3

HONG KONG

Area	1,075 sq km	Capital	Victoria
Arable as % of total land	5	Currency	Hong Kong dollar (HK$)

People

Population	7.3m	Life expectancy: men	79.9 yrs
Pop. per sq km	6,790.7	women	85.7 yrs
Av. ann. growth		Adult literacy	...
in pop. 2010–15	0.54%	Fertility rate (per woman)	1.0
Pop. under 15	11.5%	Urban population	100.0%
Pop. over 60	18.4%		per 1,000 pop.
No. of men per 100 women	90	Crude birth rate	8.2
Human Development Index	94.4	Crude death rate	6.7

The economy

GDP	HK$1,677bn	GDP per head	$30,860
GDP	$215bn	GDP per head in purchasing	
Av. ann. growth in real		power parity (USA=100)	94.8
GDP 2003–08	6.2%	Economic freedom index	89.7

Origins of GDP		**Components of GDP**	
	% of total		% of total
Agriculture	0	Private consumption	60
Industry, of which:	8	Public consumption	8
manufacturing	3	Investment	20
Services	92	Exports	212
		Imports	-202

Structure of employment

	% of total		% of labour force
Agriculture	0	Unemployed 2008	3.5
Industry	15	Av. ann. rate 1995–2008	4.9
Services	85		

Energy

	m TOE		
Total output	0.0	Net energy imports as %	
Total consumption	13.7	of energy use	100
Consumption per head,			
kg oil equivalent	1,985		

Inflation and finance

Consumer price		av. ann. increase 2003–08	
inflation 2009	0.6%	Narrow money (M1)	6.1%
Av. ann. inflation 2004–09	2.0%	Broad money	9.9%
Money market rate, 2009	0.13%		

Exchange rates

	end 2009		December 2009
HK$ per $	7.76	Effective rates	2005 = 100
HK$ per SDR	12.16	– nominal	...
HK$ per €	11.18	– real	...

Trade

Principal exports[a]		**Principal imports**[a]	
	$bn fob		*$bn cif*
Clothing & apparel	2.9	Raw materials &	
Misc. manufactured goods	1.9	semi-manufactures	33.8
Telecoms equipment	1.1	Capital goods	21.6
Electrical goods	0.9	Consumer goods	20.5
Plastics	0.8	Fuel	13.6
		Food	9.2
Total incl. others	**11.6**	Total incl. others	**98.8**

Main export destinations		**Main origins of imports**	
	% of total		*% of total*
China	48.5	China	46.6
United States	12.7	Japan	9.8
Japan	4.3	Taiwan	6.4
United Kingdom	3.3	Singapore	5.0

Balance of payments, reserves and debt, $bn

Visible exports fob	365.2	Change in reserves	29.8
Visible imports fob	-388.4	Level of reserves	
Trade balance	-23.1	end Dec.	182.5
Invisibles inflows	213.1	No. months of import cover	4.0
Invisibles outflows	-156.2	Official gold holdings, m oz	0.1
Net transfers	-3.3	Foreign debt[b]	77.3
Current account balance	30.5	– as % of GDP[b]	36
– as % of GDP	14.2	– as % of total exports[b]	13
Capital balance	6.2	Debt service ratio[b]	2
Overall balance	33.9		

Health and education

Health spending, % of GDP	...	Education spending, % of GDP	4.1
Doctors per 1,000 pop.	...	Enrolment, %: primary	101
Hospital beds per 1,000 pop.	...	secondary	83
Improved-water source access,		tertiary	34
% of pop.	...		

Society

No. of households	2.3m	Colour TVs per 100 households	99.5
Av. no. per household	3.2	Telephone lines per 100 pop.	58.7
Marriages per 1,000 pop.	6.3	Mobile telephone subscribers	
Divorces per 1,000 pop.	2.7	per 100 pop.	165.9
Cost of living, Feb. 2010		Computers per 100 pop.	69.3
New York = 100	110	Internet hosts per 1,000 pop.	111.9

a Domestic, excluding re-exports.
b 2005
Note: Hong Kong became a Special Administrative Region of China on July 1 1997.

HUNGARY

Area	93,030 sq km	Capital	Budapest
Arable as % of total land	51	Currency	Forint (Ft)

People

Population	10.0m	Life expectancy: men	70.4 yrs
Pop. per sq km	107.5	women	78.3 yrs
Av. ann. growth		Adult literacy	99.0
in pop. 2010–15	-0.20%	Fertility rate (per woman)	1.4
Pop. under 15	14.7%	Urban population	68.1%
Pop. over 60	22.4%		per 1,000 pop.
No. of men per 100 women	90.4	Crude birth rate	9.9
Human Development Index	87.9	Crude death rate	13.4

The economy

GDP	Ft26,621bn	GDP per head	$15,410
GDP	$155bn	GDP per head in purchasing	
Av. ann. growth in real		power parity (USA=100)	42.7
GDP 2003–08	2.8%	Economic freedom index	66.1

Origins of GDP		**Components of GDP**	
	% of total		% of total
Agriculture	4	Private consumption	67
Industry, of which:	29	Public consumption	9
manufacturing	22	Investment	22
Services	66	Exports	81
		Imports	-80

Structure of employment

	% of total		% of labour force
Agriculture	5	Unemployed 2008	7.8
Industry	32	Av. ann. rate 1995–2008	7.3
Services	63		

Energy

	m TOE		
Total output	10.2	Net energy imports as %	
Total consumption	26.7	of energy use	62
Consumption per head,			
kg oil equivalent	2,658		

Inflation and finance

Consumer price		av. ann. increase 2003–08	
inflation 2009	4.2%	Narrow money (M1)	8.9%
Av. ann. inflation 2004–09	5.1%	Broad money	11.9%
Treasury bill rate, 2009	8.48%	Household saving rate, 2009	2.9%

Exchange rates

	end 2009		December 2009
Ft per $	188.07	Effective rates	2005 = 100
Ft per SDR	294.84	– nominal	94.1
Ft per €	270.91	– real	109.4

Trade

Principal exports		Principal imports	
	$bn fob		*$bn cif*
Machinery & equipment	65.1	Machinery & equipment	52.8
Other manufactures	28.6	Other manufactures	34.1
Food, drink & tobacco	7.2	Fuels	13.9
Raw materials	2.5	Food, drink & tobacco	5.0
Total incl. others	**107.1**	Total incl. others	**107.5**

Main export destinations		Main origins of imports	
	% of total		*% of total*
Germany	26.7	Germany	25.9
Italy	5.5	Russia	9.1
Romania	5.3	China	7.6
Austria	4.9	Austria	6.3
EU27	78.2	EU27	68.2

Balance of payments, reserves and debt, $bn

Visible exports fob	107.2	Change in reserves	9.8
Visible imports fob	-107.3	Level of reserves	
Trade balance	-0.1	end Dec.	33.9
Invisibles inflows	35.2	No. months of import cover	2.7
Invisibles outflows	-45.1	Official gold holdings, m oz	0.1
Net transfers	-1.0	Foreign debt	165.0
Current account balance	-10.9	– as % of GDP	106.7
– as % of GDP	-7.1	– as % of total exports	115.2
Capital balance	18.4	Debt service ratio	31
Overall balance	4.2	Aid given	0.11
		% of GDP	0.07

Health and education

Health spending, % of GDP	7.4	Education spending, % of GDP	5.1
Doctors per 1,000 pop.	2.8	Enrolment, %: primary	98
Hospital beds per 1,000 pop.	7.1	secondary	97
Improved-water source access,		tertiary	67
% of pop.	100		

Society

No. of households	4.1m	Colour TVs per 100 households	97.3
Av. no. per household	2.4	Telephone lines per 100 pop.	30.9
Marriages per 1,000 pop.	4.1	Mobile telephone subscribers	
Divorces per 1,000 pop.	2.3	per 100 pop.	122.1
Cost of living, Feb. 2010		Computers per 100 pop.	25.6
New York = 100	81	Internet hosts per 1,000 pop.	262.5

INDIA

Area	3,287,263 sq km	Capital	New Delhi
Arable as % of total land	53	Currency	Indian rupee (Rs)

People

Population	1,186.2m	Life expectancy: men	63.7 yrs
Pop. per sq km	360.8	women	66.9 yrs
Av. ann. growth		Adult literacy	62.8%
in pop. 2010–15	1.43%	Fertility rate (per woman)	2.8
Pop. under 15	30.8%	Urban population	30.0%
Pop. over 60	7.5%		per 1,000 pop.
No. of men per 100 women	106.8	Crude birth rate	23.0
Human Development Index	61.2	Crude death rate	8.1

The economy

GDP	Rs53.2trn	GDP per head	$1,020
GDP	$1,159bn	GDP per head in purchasing	
Av. ann. growth in real		power parity (USA=100)	6.4
GDP 2003–08	8.7%	Economic freedom index	53.8

Origins of GDP		**Components of GDP**	
	% of total		% of total
Agriculture	17	Private consumption	54
Industry, of which:	29	Public consumption	12
manufacturing	16	Investment	40
Services	54	Exports	23
		Imports	-28

Structure of employment

	% of total		% of labour force
Agriculture	...	Unemployed 2004	5.0
Industry	...	Av. ann. rate 1995–2004	3.3
Services	...		

Energy

	m TOE		
Total output	450.9	Net energy imports as %	
Total consumption	594.9	of energy use	24
Consumption per head,			
kg oil equivalent	529		

Inflation and finance

Consumer price		av. ann. increase 2003–08	
inflation 2009	10.9%	Narrow money (M1)	17.0%
Av. ann. inflation 2004–09	7.1%	Broad money	19.3%
Lending rate, 2009	12.19%		

Exchange rates

	end 2009		December 2009
		Effective rates	2005 = 100
Rs per $	46.68	– nominal	...
Rs per SDR	73.18	– real	...
Rs per €	67.24		...

Trade

Principal exports[a]		Principal imports[a]	
	$bn fob		*$bn cif*
Engineering goods	47.0	Petroleum & products	91.3
Gems & jewellery	27.7	Electronic goods	23.1
Petroleum & products	26.9	Machinery	20.9
Textiles	20.0	Gold & silver	18.7
Agricultural goods	17.5	Gems	14.2
Total incl. others	**182.9**	**Total incl. others**	**290.7**

Main export destinations		Main origins of imports	
	% of total		*% of total*
United Arab Emirates	11.9	China	10.4
United States	11.4	Saudi Arabia	6.7
China	5.3	United Arab Emirates	6.5
United Kingdom	4.4	United States	6.5

Balance of payments, reserves and debt, $bn

Visible exports fob	187.9	Change in reserves	-19.2
Visible imports fob	-315.1	Level of reserves	
Trade balance	-127.2	end Dec.	257.4
Invisibles inflows	118.5	No. months of import cover	7.9
Invisibles outflows	-75.7	Official gold holdings, m oz	11.5
Net transfers	48.2	Foreign debt	230.6
Current account balance	-36.1	– as % of GDP	19
– as % of GDP	-3.1	– as % of total exports	102
Capital balance	40.5	Debt service ratio	9
Overall balance	5.0		

Health and education

Health spending, % of GDP	4.1	Education spending, % of GDP	4.1
Doctors per 1,000 pop.	0.6	Enrolment, %: primary	113
Hospital beds per 1,000 pop.	0.9	secondary	57
Improved-water source access,		tertiary	13
% of pop.	88		

Society

No. of households	218.5m	Colour TVs per 100 households	31.7
Av. no. per household	5.4	Telephone lines per 100 pop.	3.2
Marriages per 1,000 pop.	...	Mobile telephone subscribers	
Divorces per 1,000 pop.	...	per 100 pop.	29.4
Cost of living, Feb. 2010		Computers per 100 pop.	3.3
New York = 100	48	Internet hosts per 1,000 pop.	3.8

a Year ending March 31, 2009.

INDONESIA

Area	1,904,443 sq km	Capital	Jakarta
Arable as % of total land	12	Currency	Rupiah (Rp)

People

Population	234.3m	Life expectancy: men	70.2 yrs
Pop. per sq km	122.9	women	74.3 yrs
Av. ann. growth		Adult literacy	92.0%
In pop. 2010–15	1.18%	Fertility rate (per woman)	2.2
Pop. under 15	26.7%	Urban population	44.3%
Pop. over 60	8.9%		per 1,000 pop.
No. of men per 100 women	99.7	Crude birth rate	18.8
Human Development Index	73.4	Crude death rate	6.3

The economy

GDP	Rp4,954trn	GDP per head	$2,250
GDP	$511bn	GDP per head in purchasing	
Av. ann. growth in real		power parity (USA=100)	8.6
GDP 2003–08	5.7%	Economic freedom index	55.5

Origins of GDP		**Components of GDP**	
	% of total		% of total
Agriculture	14	Private consumption	63
Industry, of which:	48	Public consumption	8
manufacturing	28	Investment	28
Services	37	Exports	30
		Imports	-29

Structure of employment

	% of total		% of labour force
Agriculture	45	Unemployed 2008	8.4
Industry	18	Av. ann. rate 1995–2008	7.5
Services	37		

Energy

	m TOE		
Total output	331.1	Net energy imports as %	
Total consumption	190.6	of energy use	-74
Consumption per head,			
kg oil equivalent	849		

Inflation and finance

Consumer price		av. ann. increase 2003–08	
inflation 2009	4.6%	Narrow money (M1)	15.3%
Av. ann. inflation 2004–09	8.9%	Broad money	14.7%
Money market rate, 2009	7.16%		

Exchange rates

	end 2009		December 2009
Rp per $	9,400	Effective rates	2005 = 100
Rp per SDR	14,736	– nominal	...
Rp per €	13,541	– real	...

Trade

Principal exports		Principal imports	
	$bn fob		*$bn cif*
Fats, oils & waxes	15.1	Intermediate goods	99.5
Mineral products	14.0	Capital goods	21.4
Petroleum & products	12.4	Consumer goods	8.3
Total incl. others	**137.0**	Total incl. others	**129.2**

Main export destinations		Main origins of imports	
	% of total		*% of total*
Japan	20.2	Singapore	16.9
United States	9.5	China	11.8
Singapore	9.4	Japan	11.7
China	8.5	Malaysia	6.9

Balance of payments, reserves and debt, $bn

Visible exports fob	139.6	Change in reserves	-5.3
Visible imports fob	-116.7	Level of reserves	
Trade balance	22.9	end Dec.	51.6
Invisibles inflows	18.8	No. months of import cover	3.8
Invisibles outflows	-47.0	Official gold holdings, m oz	2.4
Net transfers	5.4	Foreign debt	150.9
Current account balance	0.1	– as % of GDP	30
– as % of GDP	0.0	– as % of total exports	102
Capital balance	-1.9	Debt service ratio	13
Overall balance	-1.9		

Health and education

Health spending, % of GDP	2.2	Education spending, % of GDP	3.5
Doctors per 1,000 pop.	0.1	Enrolment, %: primary	121
Hospital beds per 1,000 pop.	0.6	secondary	76
Improved-water source access,		tertiary	18
% of pop.	80		

Society

No. of households	65.6m	Colour TVs per 100 households	84.6
Av. no. per household	3.6	Telephone lines per 100 pop.	13.4
Marriages per 1,000 pop.	7.2	Mobile telephone subscribers	
Divorces per 1,000 pop.	0.9	per 100 pop.	61.8
Cost of living, Feb. 2010		Computers per 100 pop.	2.0
New York = 100	73	Internet hosts per 1,000 pop.	5.4

IRAN

Area	1,648,000 sq km	Capital	Tehran
Arable as % of total land	10	Currency	Rial (IR)

People

Population	72.2m	Life expectancy: men	71.1 yrs
Pop. per sq km	43.8	women	74.1 yrs
Av. ann. growth		Adult literacy	82.3%
in pop. 2010–15	1.18%	Fertility rate (per woman)	1.8
Pop. under 15	23.8%	Urban population	70.8%
Pop. over 60	7.1%		per 1,000 pop.
No. of men per 100 women	103.3	Crude birth rate	18.9
Human Development Index	78.2	Crude death rate	5.5

The economy

GDP	IR3,268trn	GDP per head	$4,820
GDP	$347bn	GDP per head in purchasing	
Av. ann. growth in real		power parity (USA=100)	23.7[a]
GDP 2003–08	5.1%	Economic freedom index	43.4

Origins of GDP		**Components of GDP**	
	% of total		% of total
Agriculture	10	Private consumption	45
Industry, of which:	44	Public consumption	11
manufacturing	11	Investment	33
Services	45	Exports	32
		Imports	-22

Structure of employment

	% of total		% of labour force
Agriculture	25	Unemployed 2007	10.5
Industry	30	Av. ann. rate 2000–2007	12.5
Services	45		

Energy

	m TOE		
Total output	323.1	Net energy imports as %	
Total consumption	184.9	of energy use	-75
Consumption per head,			
kg oil equivalent	2,604		

Inflation and finance

Consumer price		av. ann. increase 2003–08	
inflation 2009	13.5%	Narrow money (M1)	19.0%
Av. ann. inflation 2004–09	16.2%	Broad money	22.4%
Deposit rate, 2007	11.60%		

Exchange rates

	end 2009		December 2009
IR per $	9,984	Effective rates	2005 = 100
IR per SDR	15,652	– nominal	83.4
IR per €	14,382	– real	139.7

Trade

Principal exports[a]		Principal imports[a]	
	$bn fob		*$bn cif*
Oil & gas	81.6	Raw materials &	
Industrial goods	11.6	intermediate goods	33.0
Agricultural & traditional goods	3.5	Capital goods	8.8
Metallic mineral ores	0.2	Consumer goods	6.7
Total incl. others	**97.7**	**Total incl. others**	**48.4**

Main export destinations		Main origins of imports	
	% of total		*% of total*
China	15.2	United Arab Emirates	18.8
Japan	14.2	China	12.6
India	9.2	Germany	9.0
South Korea	6.4	South Korea	6.8
Turkey	6.4	Russia	5.2

Balance of payments[b], reserves and debt, $bn

Visible exports fob	100.6	Change in reserves	-3.3
Visible imports fob	-68.5	Level of reserves	
Trade balance	32.0	end Dec.	79.6
Net invisibles	-8.8	No. months of import cover	10.9
Net transfers	0.8	Official gold holdings, m oz	...
Current account balance	24.0	Foreign debt	14.0
– as % of GDP	6.9	– as % of GDP	4
Capital balance	-9.6	– as % of total exports	12
Overall balance	3.3	Debt service ratio	3

Health and education

Health spending, % of GDP	6.4	Education spending, % of GDP	5.0
Doctors per 1,000 pop.	0.9	Enrolment, %: primary	128
Hospital beds per 1,000 pop.	1.4	secondary	80
Improved-water source access,		tertiary	36
% of pop.	94		

Society

No. of households	19.0m	Colour TVs per 100 households	...
Av. no. per household	3.6	Telephone lines per 100 pop.	33.8
Marriages per 1,000 pop.	11.8	Mobile telephone subscribers	
Divorces per 1,000 pop.	1.5	per 100 pop.	58.7
Cost of living, Feb. 2010		Computers per 100 pop.	10.6
New York = 100	48	Internet hosts per 1,000 pop.	1.7

a   2007
b   Iranian year ending March 20, 2008.

IRELAND

Area	70,282 sq km	Capital	Dublin
Arable as % of total land	15	Currency	Euro (€)

People

Population	4.4m	Life expectancy: men	78.1 yrs
Pop. per sq km	62.6	women	82.9 yrs
Av. ann. growth		Adult literacy	...
in pop. 2010–15	1.83%	Fertility rate (per woman)	2.0
Pop. under 15	20.8%	Urban population	61.9%
Pop. over 60	16.1%		per 1,000 pop.
No. of men per 100 women	100.4	Crude birth rate	15.6
Human Development Index	96.5	Crude death rate	6.5

The economy

GDP	€183bn	GDP per head	$60,460
GDP	$268bn	GDP per head in purchasing	
Av. ann. growth in real		power parity (USA=100)	90.3
GDP 2003–08	3.8%	Economic freedom index	81.3

Origins of GDP		Components of GDP	
	% of total		% of total
Agriculture	2	Private consumption	47
Industry, of which:	34	Public consumption	16
manufacturing	22	Investment	26
Services	64	Exports	79
		Imports	-69

Structure of employment

	% of total		% of labour force
Agriculture	6	Unemployed 2008	6.0
Industry	26	Av. ann. rate 1995–2008	6.3
Services	68		

Energy

	m TOE		
Total output	1.4	Net energy imports as %	
Total consumption	15.1	of energy use	91
Consumption per head,			
kg oil equivalent	3,457		

Inflation and finance

Consumer price		av. ann. increase 2003–08	
inflation 2009	-4.5%	Euro area:	
Av. ann. inflation 2004–09	2.1%	Narrow money (M1)	8.2%
Money market rate, 2009	0.48%	Broad money	8.8%
		Household saving rate, 2009	12.3%

Exchange rates

	end 2009		December 2009
€ per $	0.69	Effective rates	2005 = 100
€ per SDR	1.09	– nominal	110.5
		– real	107.9

Trade

Principal exports		Principal imports	
	$bn fob		*$bn cif*
Chemicals & related products	64.4	Machinery & transport	
Machinery & transport		equipment	28.6
equipment	26.1	Chemicals	12.1
Food, drink & tobacco	11.7	Minerals, fuels & lubricants	9.6
Raw materials	2.0	Food, drink & tobacco	8.0
Total incl. others	**126.9**	Total incl. others	**84.9**

Main export destinations		Main origins of imports	
	% of total		*% of total*
United States	18.8	United Kingdom	37.3
United Kingdom	18.2	United States	11.5
Belgium	14.5	Germany	8.6
Germany	6.9	Netherlands	5.6
France	5.8	France	3.9
Spain	4.1	China	3.2
EU27	62.8	EU27	69.9

Balance of payments, reserves and aid, $bn

Visible exports fob	119.7	Overall balance	0.2
Visible imports fob	-85.0	Change in reserves	0.1
Trade balance	34.7	Level of reserves	
Invisibles inflows	225.1	end Dec.	1.0
Invisibles outflows	-272.2	No. months of import cover	0.0
Net transfers	-1.8	Official gold holdings, m oz	0.2
Current account balance	-14.2	Aid given	1.33
– as % of GDP	-5.3	– as % of GDP	0.50
Capital balance	25.0		

Health and education

Health spending, % of GDP	7.6	Education spending, % of GDP	4.3
Doctors per 1,000 pop.	3.1	Enrolment, %: primary	105
Hospital beds per 1,000 pop.	5.3	secondary	113
Improved-water source access,		tertiary	61
% of pop.	100		

Society

No. of households	1.6m	Colour TVs per 100 households	99.7
Av. no. per household	2.8	Telephone lines per 100 pop.	49.7
Marriages per 1,000 pop.	4.8	Mobile telephone subscribers	
Divorces per 1,000 pop.	0.8	per 100 pop.	120.7
Cost of living, Feb. 2010		Computers per 100 pop.	58.2
New York = 100	116	Internet hosts per 1,000 pop.	299.1

ISRAEL

Area	20,770 sq km	Capital	Jerusalem[a]
Arable as % of total land	14	Currency	New Shekel (NIS)

People

Population	7.0m	Life expectancy:	men	79.4 yrs
Pop. per sq km	337.0		women	83.4 yrs
Av. ann. growth		Adult literacy		...
in pop. 2010–15	1.70%	Fertility rate (per woman)		2.8
Pop. under 15	27.6%	Urban population		91.9%
Pop. over 60	14.6%			per 1,000 pop.
No. of men per 100 women	98.5	Crude birth rate		20.0
Human Development Index	93.5	Crude death rate		5.6

The economy

GDP	NIS725bn	GDP per head	$27,650
GDP	$202bn	GDP per head in purchasing	
Av. ann. growth in real		power parity (USA=100)	60.2
GDP 2003–08	4.9%	Economic freedom index	67.7

Origins of GDP[b]		**Components of GDP**	
	% of total		% of total
Agriculture	3	Private consumption	58
Industry, of which:	32	Public consumption	25
manufacturing	22	Investment	18
Services	64	Exports	40
		Imports	-42

Structure of employment

	% of total		% of labour force
Agriculture	2	Unemployed 2008	6.2
Industry	21	Av. ann. rate 1995–2008	8.5
Services	77		

Energy

	m TOE		
Total output	2.7	Net energy imports as %	
Total consumption	22.0	of energy use	88
Consumption per head,			
kg oil equivalent	3,059		

Inflation and finance

		av. ann. increase 2003–07	
Consumer price			
inflation 2009	3.3%	Narrow money (M1)	15.8%
Av. ann. inflation 2004–09	2.3%	Broad money	6.9%
Treasury bill rate, 2009	1.39%		

Exchange rates

	end 2009		December 2009
NIS per $	3.78	Effective rates	2005 = 100
NIS per SDR	5.92	– nominal	110.7
NIS per €	5.45	– real	113.2

Trade

Principal exports		Principal imports	
	$bn fob		*$bn fob*
Diamonds	15.5	Fuel	12.8
Chemicals	13.6	Diamonds	8.8
Communications, medical &		Machinery & equipment	7.1
scientific equipment	8.0	Chemicals	4.4
Electronics	2.5		
Total incl. others	**51.3**	Total incl. others	**64.5**

Main export destinations		Main origins of imports	
	% of total		*% of total*
United States	39.0	United States	12.4
Belgium	9.0	Belgium	6.6
Hong Kong	8.1	China	6.6
India	4.6	Switzerland	6.2
Netherlands	4.0	Germany	6.1

Balance of payments, reserves and debt, $bn

Visible exports fob	57.2	Change in reserves	14.0
Visible imports fob	-64.4	Level of reserves	
Trade balance	-7.2	end Dec.	42.5
Invisibles inflows	32.3	No. months of import cover	5.3
Invisibles outflows	-31.4	Official gold holdings, m oz	0.0
Net transfers	8.5	Foreign debt	86.1
Current account balance	2.1	– as % of GDP	43
– as % of GDP	1.0	– as % of total exports	94
Capital balance	10.4	Debt service ratio	13
Overall balance	15.3	Aid given	0.14
		% of GDP	0.07

Health and education

Health spending, % of GDP	8.0	Education spending, % of GDP	7.3
Doctors per 1,000 pop.	3.6	Enrolment, %: primary	111
Hospital beds per 1,000 pop.	5.8	secondary	91
Improved-water source access,		tertiary	60
% of pop.	100		

Society

No. of households	2.1m	Colour TVs per 100 households	95.0
Av. no. per household	3.3	Telephone lines per 100 pop.	45.7
Marriages per 1,000 pop.	5.0	Mobile telephone subscribers	
Divorces per 1,000 pop.	1.6	per 100 pop.	127.4
Cost of living, Feb. 2010		Computers per 100 pop.	...
New York = 100	107	Internet hosts per 1,000 pop.	239.9

a Sovereignty over the city is disputed.
b 2006

ITALY

Area	301,245 sq km	Capital	Rome
Arable as % of total land	24	Currency	Euro (€)

People

Population	58.9m	Life expectancy: men	78.6 yrs
Pop. per sq km	195.5	women	84.6 yrs
Av. ann. growth		Adult literacy	98.8%
in pop. 2010–15	0.49%	Fertility rate (per woman)	1.4
Pop. under 15	14.2%	Urban population	68.4%
Pop. over 60	26.7%		per 1,000 pop.
No. of men per 100 women	94.8	Crude birth rate	9.3
Human Development Index	95.1	Crude death rate	10.5

The economy

GDP	€1,572bn	GDP per head	$38,490
GDP	$2,303bn	GDP per head in purchasing	
Av. ann. growth in real		power parity (USA=100)	67.5
GDP 2003–08	0.9%	Economic freedom index	62.7

Origins of GDP		**Components of GDP**	
	% of total		% of total
Agriculture	2	Private consumption	59
Industry, of which:	27	Public consumption	20
manufacturing	18	Investment	21
Services	71	Exports	29
		Imports	-29

Structure of employment

	% of total		% of labour force
Agriculture	4	Unemployed 2008	6.7
Industry	30	Av. ann. rate 1995–2008	9.3
Services	66		

Energy

	m TOE		
Total output	26.4	Net energy imports as %	
Total consumption	178.2	of energy use	85
Consumption per head,			
kg oil equivalent	3,001		

Inflation and finance

Consumer price		av. ann. increase 2003–08	
inflation 2009	0.8%	Euro area:	
Av. ann. inflation 2004–09	2.0%	Narrow money (M1)	8.2%
Money market rate, 2009	1.28%	Broad money	8.8%
		Household saving rate, 2009	10.7%

Exchange rates

	end 2009		December 2009
€ per $	0.69	Effective rates	2005 = 100
€ per SDR	1.09	– nominal	105.1
		– real	104.6

Trade

Principal exports		Principal imports	
	$bn fob		*$bn cif*
Machinery & transport equip.	202.9	Machinery & transport equip.	148.3
Chemicals & related products	53.7	Mineral fuels & lubricants	111.5
Food, drink & tobacco	34.3	Chemicals & related products	68.5
Mineral fuels & lubricants	26.6	Food, drink & tobacco	41.8
Total incl. others	**545.0**	Total incl. others	**563.4**

Main export destinations		Main origins of imports	
	% of total		*% of total*
Germany	12.8	Germany	16.0
France	11.2	France	8.6
United States	6.3	Netherlands	5.4
United Kingdom	5.3	United Kingdom	3.0
EU27	58.9	EU27	54.6

Balance of payments, reserves and aid, $bn

Visible exports fob	546.3	Overall balance	8.2
Visible imports fob	-547.3	Change in reserves	11.5
Trade balance	-1.0	Level of reserves	
Invisibles inflows	220.5	end Dec.	105.7
Invisibles outflows	-274.4	No. months of import cover	1.5
Net transfers	-23.2	Official gold holdings, m oz	78.8
Current account balance	-78.1	Aid given	4.86
– as % of GDP	-3.4	– as % of GDP	0.21
Capital balance	82.5		

Health and education

Health spending, % of GDP	8.7	Education spending, % of GDP	5.0
Doctors per 1,000 pop.	3.7	Enrolment, %: primary	104
Hospital beds per 1,000 pop.	3.9	secondary	100
Improved-water source access,		tertiary	67
% of pop.	100		

Society

No. of households	24.1m	Colour TVs per 100 households	96.6
Av. no. per household	2.4	Telephone lines per 100 pop.	35.7
Marriages per 1,000 pop.	4.4	Mobile telephone subscribers	
Divorces per 1,000 pop.	0.8	per 100 pop.	151.6
Cost of living, Feb. 2010		Computers per 100 pop.	36.7
New York = 100	109	Internet hosts per 1,000 pop.	387.2

JAPAN

Area	377,727 sq km	Capital	Tokyo
Arable as % of total land	12	Currency	Yen (¥)

People

Population	127.9m	Life expectancy:	men	80.1 yrs
Pop. per sq km	339.2		women	87.2 yrs
Av. ann. growth		Adult literacy		...
in pop. 2010–15	-0.07%	Fertility rate (per woman)		1.3
Pop. under 15	13.2%	Urban population		66.8%
Pop. over 60	30.5%		per 1,000 pop.	
No. of men per 100 women	94.9	Crude birth rate		8.2
Human Development Index	96.0	Crude death rate		9.8

The economy

GDP	¥508trn	GDP per head	$38,460
GDP	$4,911bn	GDP per head in purchasing	
Av. ann. growth in real		power parity (USA=100)	73.6
GDP 2003–08	1.6%	Economic freedom index	72.9

Origins of GDP		**Components of GDP**	
	% of total		% of total
Agriculture	1	Private consumption	56
Industry, of which:	29	Public consumption	18
manufacturing	21	Investment	24
Services	69	Exports	18
		Imports	-16

Structure of employment

	% of total		% of labour force
Agriculture	4	Unemployed 2008	4.0
Industry	27	Av. ann. rate 1995–2008	4.3
Services	69		

Energy

	m TOE		
Total output	90.5	Net energy imports as %	
Total consumption	513.5	of energy use	82
Consumption per head,			
kg oil equivalent	4,019		

Inflation and finance

		av. ann. increase 2003–08	
Consumer price			
inflation 2009	-1.4%	Narrow money (M1)	1.8%
Av. ann. inflation 2004–09	0.0%	Broad money	0.4%
Money market rate, 2009	0.11%	Household saving rate, 2009	2.8%

Exchange rates

	end 2009		December 2009
¥ per $	92.06	Effective rates	2005 = 100
¥ per SDR	144.32	– nominal	115.3
¥ per €	132.61	– real	102.7

Trade

Principal exports		Principal imports	
	$bn fob		*$bn cif*
Capital equipment	398.2	Industrial supplies	434.0
Industrial supplies	187.7	Capital equipment	162.0
Consumer durable goods	146.4	Food & direct consumer goods	61.3
Consumer nondurable goods	4.9	Consumer durable goods	46.4
Total incl. others	**781.9**	**Total incl. others**	**762.5**

Main export destinations		Main origins of imports	
	% of total		*% of total*
United States	17.8	China	18.8
China	16.0	United States	10.4
South Korea	7.6	Saudi Arabia	6.7
Hong Kong	5.2	Australia	6.3
Thailand	3.8	United Arab Emirates	6.1
EU27	14.1	EU27	9.2

Balance of payments, reserves and aid, $bn

Visible exports fob	746.5	Overall balance	30.9
Visible imports fob	-708.3	Change in reserves	57.5
Trade balance	38.1	Level of reserves	
Invisibles inflows	360.9	end Dec.	1,030.8
Invisibles outflows	-77.3	No. months of import cover	13.2
Net transfers	-13.0	Official gold holdings, m oz	24.6
Current account balance	156.6	Aid given	9.58
– as % of GDP	3.2	– as % of GDP	0.20
Capital balance	-178.1		

Health and education

Health spending, % of GDP	8.0	Education spending, % of GDP	3.5
Doctors per 1,000 pop.	2.1	Enrolment, %: primary	102
Hospital beds per 1,000 pop.	14.0	secondary	101
Improved-water source access,		tertiary	58
% of pop.	100		

Society

No. of households	50.1m	Colour TVs per 100 households	99.0
Av. no. per household	2.4	Telephone lines per 100 pop.	38.0
Marriages per 1,000 pop.	5.5	Mobile telephone subscribers	
Divorces per 1,000 pop.	2.0	per 100 pop.	86.7
Cost of living, Feb. 2010		Computers per 100 pop.	...
New York = 100	146	Internet hosts per 1,000 pop.	422.7

KENYA

Area	582,646 sq km	Capital	Nairobi
Arable as % of total land	9	Currency	Kenyan shilling (KSh)

People

Population	38.6m	Life expectancy: men	56.3 yrs
Pop. per sq km	66.2	women	57.5 yrs
Av. ann. growth		Adult literacy	86.5%
in pop. 2010–15	2.64%	Fertility rate (per woman)	5.0
Pop. under 15	42.8%	Urban population	22.2%
Pop. over 60	4.1%		per 1,000 pop.
No. of men per 100 women	100	Crude birth rate	39.0
Human Development Index	54.1	Crude death rate	10.3

The economy

GDP	KSh2,100bn	GDP per head	$780
GDP	$30.4bn	GDP per head in purchasing	
Av. ann. growth in real		power parity (USA=100)	3.3
GDP 2003–08	5.0%	Economic freedom index	57.5

Origins of GDP		**Components of GDP**	
	% of total		% of total
Agriculture	27	Private consumption	78
Industry, of which:	19	Public consumption	17
manufacturing	12	Investment	19
Other	54	Exports	27
		Imports	-41

Structure of employment

	% of total		% of labour force
Agriculture	...	Unemployed 2008	...
Industry	...	Av. ann. rate 1995–2008	...
Services	...		

Energy

	m TOE		
Total output	14.7	Net energy imports as %	
Total consumption	18.3	of energy use	20
Consumption per head,			
kg oil equivalent	485		

Inflation and finance

		av. ann. increase 2003–08	
Consumer price			
inflation 2009	9.2%	Narrow money (M1)	15.2%
Av. ann. inflation 2004–09	13.8%	Broad money	14.7%
Treasury bill rate, 2009	7.38%		

Exchange rates

	end 2009		December 2009
KSh per $	75.82	Effective rates	2005 = 100
KSh per SDR	118.86	– nominal	...
KSh per €	109.22	– real	...

Trade

Principal exports		Principal imports	
	$bn fob		*$bn cif*
Horticultural products	1.0	Industrial supplies	3.6
Tea	0.9	Machinery & other equip.	1.8
Coffee	0.1	Transport equipment	1.3
Fish products	0.1	Consumer goods	0.8
		Food & drink	0.8
Total incl. others	**5.0**	Total incl. others	**10.7**

Main export destinations		Main origins of imports	
	% of total		*% of total*
United Kingdom	10.0	United Arab Emirates	11.8
Netherlands	9.2	India	11.7
Uganda	9.0	China	10.2
Tanzania	8.7	Saudi Arabia	8.3

Balance of payments, reserves and debt, $bn

Visible exports fob	5.0	Change in reserves	-0.5
Visible imports fob	-10.7	Level of reserves	
Trade balance	-5.6	end Dec.	2.9
Invisibles inflows	3.4	No. months of import cover	2.7
Invisibles outflows	-2.1	Official gold holdings, m oz	0.0
Net transfers	2.3	Foreign debt	7.4
Current account balance	-2.0	– as % of GDP	22
– as % of GDP	-6.5	– as % of total exports	68
Capital balance	1.2	Debt service ratio	5
Overall balance	-0.5		

Health and education

Health spending, % of GDP	4.7	Education spending, % of GDP	6.2
Doctors per 1,000 pop.	0.1	Enrolment, %: primary	112
Hospital beds per 1,000 pop.	1.4	secondary	58
Improved-water source access,		tertiary	4
% of pop.	59		

Society

No. of households	8.8m	Colour TVs per 100 households	...
Av. no. per household	4.4	Telephone lines per 100 pop.	0.6
Marriages per 1,000 pop.	...	Mobile telephone subscribers	
Divorces per 1,000 pop.	...	per 100 pop.	42.1
Cost of living, Feb. 2010		Computers per 100 pop.	1.4
New York = 100	72	Internet hosts per 1,000 pop.	1.2

LATVIA

Area	63,700 sq km	Capital	Riga
Arable as % of total land	19	Currency	Lats (LVL)

People

Population	2.3m	Life expectancy: men	68.7 yrs
Pop. per sq km	36.1	women	78.1 yrs
Av. ann. growth		Adult literacy	99.8%
in pop. 2010–15	-0.46%	Fertility rate (per woman)	1.4
Pop. under 15	13.8%	Urban population	67.7%
Pop. over 60	22.5%		per 1,000 pop.
No. of men per 100 women	85.6	Crude birth rate	10.1
Human Development Index	86.6	Crude death rate	13.9

The economy

GDP	LVL16.2bn	GDP per head	$14,910
GDP	$33.8bn	GDP per head in purchasing	
Av. ann. growth in real		power parity (USA=100)	35.3
GDP 2003–08	7.2%	Economic freedom index	66.2

Origins of GDP		Components of GDP	
	% of total		% of total
Agriculture	3	Private consumption	58
Industry, of which:	23	Public consumption	20
manufacturing	11	Investment	35
Services	74	Exports	42
		Imports	-55

Structure of employment

	% of total		% of labour force
Agriculture	8	Unemployed 2008	7.5
Industry	29	Av. ann. rate 1996–2008	11.8
Services	64		

Energy

			m TOE
Total output	1.8	Net energy imports as %	
Total consumption	4.7	of energy use	61
Consumption per head,			
kg oil equivalent	2,052		

Inflation and finance

Consumer price		av. ann. increase 2003–08	
inflation 2009	3.5%	Narrow money (M1)	16.0%
Av. ann. inflation 2004–09	8.4%	Broad money	22.1%
Money market rate, 2009	3.92%		

Exchange rates

	end 2009		December 2009
LVL per $	0.49	Effective rates	2005 = 100
LVL per SDR	0.77	– nominal	...
LVL per €	0.71	– real	...

Trade

Principal exports		Principal imports	
	$bn fob		$bn cif
Metals	1.6	Machinery & equipment	2.8
Wood & wood products	1.5	Mineral products	2.5
Machinery & equipment	1.1	Transport equipment	1.7
Chemicals	0.8	Base metals	1.6
Total incl. others	**9.3**	Total incl. others	**15.7**

Main export destinations		Main origins of imports	
	% of total		% of total
Lithuania	16.7	Lithuania	16.5
Estonia	14.0	Germany	13.0
Russia	10.0	Russia	10.6
Germany	8.1	Estonia	7.1
Sweden	6.6	Sweden	4.4
EU27	68.6	EU27	75.5

Balance of payments, reserves and debt, $bn

Visible exports fob	9.6	Change in reserves	-0.5
Visible imports fob	-15.6	Level of reserves	
Trade balance	-6.0	end Dec.	5.2
Invisibles inflows	5.3	No. months of import cover	3.0
Invisibles outflows	-5.6	Official gold holdings, m oz	0.2
Net transfers	0.8	Foreign debt	42.1
Current account balance	-4.5	– as % of GDP	127
– as % of GDP	-13.3	– as % of total exports	301
Capital balance	3.8	Debt service ratio	38
Overall balance	-1.3		

Health and education

Health spending, % of GDP	6.2	Education spending, % of GDP	5.9
Doctors per 1,000 pop.	3.0	Enrolment, %: primary	97
Hospital beds per 1,000 pop.	7.6	secondary	115
Improved-water source access,		tertiary	69
% of pop.	99		

Society

No. of households	0.8m	Colour TVs per 100 households	95.8
Av. no. per household	2.8	Telephone lines per 100 pop.	28.5
Marriages per 1,000 pop.	4.9	Mobile telephone subscribers	
Divorces per 1,000 pop.	2.4	per 100 pop.	98.9
Cost of living, Feb. 2010		Computers per 100 pop.	32.7
New York = 100	...	Internet hosts per 1,000 pop.	125.8

LITHUANIA

Area	65,200 sq km	Capital	Vilnius
Arable as % of total land	29	Currency	Litas (LTL)

People

Population	3.4m	Life expectancy: men	67.0 yrs
Pop. per sq km	52.1	women	78.3 yrs
Av. ann. growth		Adult literacy	99.7%
in pop. 2010–15	-0.97%	Fertility rate (per woman)	1.3
Pop. under 15	14.6%	Urban population	67.0%
Pop. over 60	21.5%		per 1,000 pop.
No. of men per 100 women	88.1	Crude birth rate	9.5
Human Development Index	87.0	Crude death rate	13.8

The economy

GDP	LTL111bn	GDP per head	$14,100
GDP	$47.3bn	GDP per head in purchasing	
Av. ann. growth in real		power parity (USA=100)	38.3
GDP 2003–08	7.1%	Economic freedom index	70.3

Origins of GDP		Components of GDP	
	% of total		% of total
Agriculture	4	Private consumption	66
Industry, of which:	33	Public consumption	18
manufacturing	19	Investment	27
Services	63	Exports	59
		Imports	-71

Structure of employment

	% of total		% of labour force
Agriculture	8	Unemployed 2008	5.8
Industry	30	Av. ann. rate 1995–2008	12.3
Services	62		

Energy

		m TOE	
Total output	3.8	Net energy imports as %	
Total consumption	9.3	of energy use	59
Consumption per head,			
kg oil equivalent	2,740		

Inflation and finance

Consumer price		av. ann. increase 2004–08	
inflation 2009	4.5%	Narrow money (M1)	11.4%
Av. ann. inflation 2004–09	5.5%	Broad money	18.2%
Money market rate, 2009	0.88%		

Exchange rates

	end 2009		December 2009
LTL per $	2.41	Effective rates	2005 = 100
LTL per SDR	3.77	– nominal	...
LTL per €	3.47	– real	...

Trade

Principal exports		Principal imports	
	$bn fob		*$bn cif*
Mineral products	5.9	Mineral products	9.1
Machinery & equipment	2.5	Machinery & equipment	4.4
Chemicals	2.3	Transport equipment	3.8
Transport equipment	2.0	Chemicals	2.8
Total incl. others	**23.5**	Total incl. others	**30.8**

Main export destinations		Main origins of imports	
	% of total		*% of total*
Russia	16.1	Russia	30.1
Latvia	11.6	Germany	11.9
Germany	7.2	Poland	10.0
Poland	5.8	Latvia	5.2
Estonia	5.7	Italy	3.6
EU27	60.3	EU25	57.6

Balance of payments, reserves and debt, $bn

Visible exports fob	23.8	Change in reserves	-1.3
Visible imports fob	-29.5	Level of reserves	
Trade balance	-5.7	end Dec.	6.4
Invisibles inflows	5.9	No. months of import cover	2.1
Invisibles outflows	-6.8	Official gold holdings, m oz	0.2
Net transfers	1.1	Foreign debt	31.7
Current account balance	-5.6	– as % of GDP	69
– as % of GDP	-11.9	– as % of total exports	120
Capital balance	4.6	Debt service ratio	31
Overall balance	-1.2		

Health and education

Health spending, % of GDP	6.2	Education spending, % of GDP	6.0
Doctors per 1,000 pop.	4.0	Enrolment, %: primary	96
Hospital beds per 1,000 pop.	8.1	secondary	99
Improved-water source access,		tertiary	76
% of pop.	...		

Society

No. of households	1.4m	Colour TVs per 100 households	97.5
Av. no. per household	2.4	Telephone lines per 100 pop.	23.6
Marriages per 1,000 pop.	6.4	Mobile telephone subscribers	
Divorces per 1,000 pop.	3.5	per 100 pop.	151.2
Cost of living, Feb. 2010		Computers per 100 pop.	24.2
New York = 100	...	Internet hosts per 1,000 pop.	331.7

MALAYSIA

Area	332,665 sq km	Capital	Kuala Lumpur
Arable as % of total land	5	Currency	Malaysian dollar/ringgit (M$)

People

Population	27.0m	Life expectancy: men	72.9 yrs
Pop. per sq km	81.1	women	77.6 yrs
Av. ann. growth		Adult literacy	92.1%
in pop. 2010–15	1.71%	Fertility rate (per woman)	2.6
Pop. under 15	29.1%	Urban population	72.2%
Pop. over 60	7.8%		per 1,000 pop.
No. of men per 100 women	103.1	Crude birth rate	20.5
Human Development Index	82.9	Crude death rate	4.6

The economy

GDP	M$741bn	GDP per head	$8,210
GDP	$222bn	GDP per head in purchasing	
Av. ann. growth in real		power parity (USA=100)	30.7
GDP 2003–08	5.8%	Economic freedom index	64.8

Origins of GDP		Components of GDP	
	% of total		% of total
Agriculture	10	Private consumption	46
Industry, of which:	48	Public consumption	12
manufacturing	28	Investment	22
Services	42	Exports	110
		Imports	-90

Structure of employment

	% of total		% of labour force
Agriculture	15	Unemployed 2008	3.2
Industry	30	Av. ann. rate 1995–2008	3.2
Services	55		

Energy

	m TOE		
Total output	94.4	Net energy imports as %	
Total consumption	72.6	of energy use	-30
Consumption per head,			
kg oil equivalent	2,733		

Inflation and finance

Consumer price		av. ann. increase 2003–08	
inflation 2009	0.6%	Narrow money (M1)	12.4%
Av. ann. inflation 2004–09	2.9%	Broad money	11.1%
Money market rate, 2009	2.12%		

Exchange rates

	end 2009		December 2009
M$ per $	3.42	Effective rates	2005 = 100
M$ per SDR	5.37	– nominal	101.6
M$ per €	4.93	– real	104.9

Trade

Principal exports[a]		Principal imports[a]	
	$bn fob		*$bn cif*
Electronics	62.0	Machinery	15.1
Electrical machinery	21.7	Transport equipment	6.4
Chemicals & products	10.9	Metal products	5.9
Palm oil	9.3	Foodstuffs	3.6
Total incl. others	**176.2**	Total incl. others	**147.0**

Main export destinations		Main origins of imports	
	% of total		*% of total*
Singapore	14.7	China	12.8
United States	12.5	Japan	12.5
Japan	10.8	Singapore	11.0
China	9.5	United States	10.8
Thailand	4.8	Thailand	5.6

Balance of payments, reserves and debt, $bn

Visible exports fob	199.7	Change in reserves	-9.8
Visible imports fob	-148.5	Level of reserves	
Trade balance	51.3	end Dec.	92.2
Invisibles inflows	42.4	No. months of import cover	5.6
Invisibles outflows	-49.5	Official gold holdings, m oz	1.2
Net transfers	-5.3	Foreign debt	66.2
Current account balance	38.9	– as % of GDP	35
– as % of GDP	17.5	– as % of total exports	30
Capital balance	-33.8	Debt service ratio	7
Overall balance	-3.5		

Health and education

Health spending, % of GDP	9.8	Education spending, % of GDP	7.9
Doctors per 1,000 pop.	...	Enrolment, %: primary	98
Hospital beds per 1,000 pop.	1.8	secondary	69
Improved-water source access,		tertiary	30
% of pop.	100		

Society

No. of households	6.2m	Colour TVs per 100 households	96.0
Av. no. per household	4.4	Telephone lines per 100 pop.	15.9
Marriages per 1,000 pop.	5.8	Mobile telephone subscribers	
Divorces per 1,000 pop.	...	per 100 pop.	102.6
Cost of living, Feb. 2010		Computers per 100 pop.	23.1
New York = 100	70	Internet hosts per 1,000 pop.	13.0

a 2007

MEXICO

Area	1,972,545 sq km	Capital	Mexico city
Arable as % of total land	13	Currency	Mexican peso (PS)

People

Population	107.8m	Life expectancy: men	74.9 yrs
Pop. per sq km	54.7	women	79.7 yrs
Av. ann. growth		Adult literacy	92.9%
in pop. 2010–15	0.99%	Fertility rate (per woman)	2.2
Pop. under 15	27.9%	Urban population	77.8%
Pop. over 60	9.4%		per 1,000 pop.
No. of men per 100 women	97.0	Crude birth rate	19.1
Human Development Index	85.4	Crude death rate	4.9

The economy

GDP	PS12,111bn	GDP per head	$10,230
GDP	$1,088bn	GDP per head in purchasing	
Av. ann. growth in real		power parity (USA=100)	31.4
GDP 2003–08	3.4%	Economic freedom index	68.3

Origins of GDP		Components of GDP	
	% of total		% of total
Agriculture	4	Private consumption	66
Industry, of which:	37	Public consumption	10
manufacturing & mining	19	Investment	26
Services	59	Exports	28
		Imports	-30

Structure of employment

	% of total		% of labour force
Agriculture	14	Unemployed 2008	4.0
Industry	27	Av. ann. rate 1995–2008	3.0
Services	59		

Energy

	m TOE		
Total output	251.1	Net energy imports as %	
Total consumption	184.3	of energy use	-36
Consumption per head,			
kg oil equivalent	1,750		

Inflation and finance

		av. ann. increase 2003–08	
Consumer price			
inflation 2009	5.3%	Narrow money (M1)	11.6%
Av. ann. inflation 2004–09	4.4%	Broad money	11.0%
Money market rate, 2009	5.93%		

Exchange rates

	end 2009		December 2009
PS per $	13.06	Effective rates	2005 = 100
PS per SDR	20.47	– nominal	...
PS per €	18.81	– real	...

Trade

Principal exports	$bn fob	Principal imports	$bn fob
Manufactured products	230.9	Intermediate goods	221.6
Crude oil & products	50.6	Consumer goods	47.9
Agricultural products	7.9	Capital goods	39.1
Total incl. others	**291.3**	Total	**308.6**

Main export destinations	% of total	Main origins of imports	% of total
United States	80.1	United States	49.0
Canada	2.4	China	11.2
Germany	1.7	South Korea	5.3
Spain	1.5	Japan	4.4

Balance of payments, reserves and debt, $bn

Visible exports fob	291.3	Change in reserves	8.1
Visible imports fob	-308.6	Level of reserves	
Trade balance	-17.3	end Dec.	95.3
Invisibles inflows	25.8	No. months of import cover	3.2
Invisibles outflows	-49.8	Official gold holdings, m oz	0.2
Net transfers	25.4	Foreign debt	204.0
Current account balance	-15.8	– as % of GDP	19
– as % of GDP	-1.5	– as % of total exports	62
Capital balance	24.3	Debt service ratio	12
Overall balance	7.7		

Health and education

Health spending, % of GDP	5.9	Education spending, % of GDP	5.1
Doctors per 1,000 pop.	2.9	Enrolment, %: primary	113
Hospital beds per 1,000 pop.	1.7	secondary	87
Improved-water source access,		tertiary	26
% of pop.	94		

Society

No. of households	26.9m	Colour TVs per 100 households	94.6
Av. no. per household	4.0	Telephone lines per 100 pop.	19.0
Marriages per 1,000 pop.	5.6	Mobile telephone subscribers	
Divorces per 1,000 pop.	0.7	per 100 pop.	69.4
Cost of living, Feb. 2010		Computers per 100 pop.	14.4
New York = 100	75	Internet hosts per 1,000 pop.	117.6

MOROCCO

Area	446,550 sq km	Capital	Rabat
Arable as % of total land	18	Currency	Dirham (Dh)

People

Population	31.6m	Life expectancy: men	70.2 yrs
Pop. per sq km	70.8	women	74.8 yrs
Av. ann. growth		Adult literacy	56.4%
in pop. 2010–15	1.20%	Fertility rate (per woman)	2.4
Pop. under 15	28.0%	Urban population	58.2%
Pop. over 60	8.1%		per 1,000 pop.
No. of men per 100 women	96.4	Crude birth rate	20.5
Human Development Index	65.4	Crude death rate	5.8

The economy

GDP	Dh689bn	GDP per head	$2,770
GDP	$88.9bn	GDP per head in purchasing	
Av. ann. growth in real		power parity (USA=100)	9.2
GDP 2003–08	4.7%	Economic freedom index	59.2

Origins of GDP		Components of GDP	
	% of total		% of total
Agriculture	15	Private consumption	60
Industry, of which:	30	Public consumption	17
manufacturing	14	Investment	36
Services	55	Exports	37
		Imports	-50

Structure of employment

	% of total		% of labour force
Agriculture	44	Unemployed 2008	9.6
Industry	20	Av. ann. rate 1995–2008	13.6
Services	36		

Energy

	m TOE		
Total output	0.7	Net energy imports as %	
Total consumption	14.4	of energy use	95
Consumption per head,			
kg oil equivalent	460		

Inflation and finance

		av. ann. increase 2003–08	
Consumer price			
inflation 2009	1.0%	Narrow money (M1)	13.4%
Av. ann. inflation 2004–09	2.2%	Broad money	13.1%
Money market rate, 2009	3.26%		

Exchange rates

	end 2009		December 2009
			2005 = 100
Dh per $	7.86	Effective rates	
Dh per SDR	12.32	– nominal	102.2
Dh per €	11.32	– real	92.9

Trade

Principal exports		Principal imports	
	$bn fob		*$bn cif*
Phosphoric acid	2.9	Fuel & lubricants	9.2
Textiles	2.5	Semi-finished goods	8.8
Phosphate rock	2.2	Capital goods	8.7
Electrical components	0.6	Consumer goods	6.9
Citrus fruits	0.4	Food, drink & tobacco	4.1
Total incl. others	**18.3**	Total incl. others	**40.3**

Main export destinations		Main origins of imports	
	% of total		*% of total*
Spain	19.2	France	16.3
France	17.4	Spain	13.7
Brazil	7.0	Italy	6.5
United States	4.5	China	6.1

Balance of payments, reserves and debt, $bn

Visible exports fob	20.3	Change in reserves	-2.0
Visible imports fob	-39.8	Level of reserves	
Trade balance	-19.5	end Dec.	22.7
Invisibles inflows	14.5	No. months of import cover	5.7
Invisibles outflows	-7.3	Official gold holdings, m oz	0.7
Net transfers	7.8	Foreign debt	20.8
Current account balance	-5.7	– as % of GDP	24
– as % of GDP	-6.4	– as % of total exports	51
Capital balance	0.4	Debt service ratio	10
Overall balance	-5.7		

Health and education

Health spending, % of GDP	5.0	Education spending, % of GDP	5.1
Doctors per 1,000 pop.	0.6	Enrolment, %: primary	107
Hospital beds per 1,000 pop.	1.1	secondary	56
Improved-water source access,		tertiary	12
% of pop.	81		

Society

No. of households	6.2m	Colour TVs per 100 households	80.7
Av. no. per household	5.1	Telephone lines per 100 pop.	9.5
Marriages per 1,000 pop.	...	Mobile telephone subscribers	
Divorces per 1,000 pop.	...	per 100 pop.	72.2
Cost of living, Feb. 2010		Computers per 100 pop.	5.7
New York = 100	80	Internet hosts per 1,000 pop.	8.8

NETHERLANDS

Areaª	41,526 sq km	Capital	Amsterdam
Arable as % of total land	31	Currency	Euro (€)

People

Population	16.5m	Life expectancy: men	78.5 yrs
Pop. per sq km	397.3	women	82.6 yrs
Av. ann. growth		Adult literacy	...
in pop. 2010–15	0.41%	Fertility rate (per woman)	1.7
Pop. under 15	17.6%	Urban population	82.9%
Pop. over 60	21.9%		per 1,000 pop.
No. of men per 100 women	98.4	Crude birth rate	11.3
Human Development Index	96.4	Crude death rate	8.8

The economy

GDP	€595bn	GDP per head	$52,960
GDP	$871bn	GDP per head in purchasing	
Av. ann. growth in real		power parity (USA=100)	88.4
GDP 2003–08	2.7%	Economic freedom index	75.0

Origins of GDP		Components of GDP	
	% of total		% of total
Agriculture	2	Private consumption	46
Industry, of which:	25	Public consumption	28
manufacturing	14	Investment	21
Services	73	Exports	77
		Imports	-69

Structure of employment

	% of total		% of labour force
Agriculture	3	Unemployed 2008	2.8
Industry	18	Av. ann. rate 1995–2008	4.4
Services	79		

Energy

	m TOE		
Total output	61.5	Net energy imports as %	
Total consumption	80.4	of energy use	24
Consumption per head,			
kg oil equivalent	4,909		

Inflation and finance

Consumer price			av. ann. increase 2003–08
inflation 2009	1.2%	Euro area:	
Av. ann. inflation 2004–09	1.6%	Narrow money (M1)	8.2%
Deposit rate, households, 2009	4.63%	Broad money	8.8%
		Household saving rate, 2009	10.1%

Exchange rates

	end 2009		December 2009
€ per $	0.69	Effective rates	2005 = 100
€ per SDR	1.09	– nominal	106.0
		– real	104.2

Trade

Principal exports		**Principal imports**	
	$bn fob		*$bn cif*
Machinery & transport equipment	190.6	Machinery & transport equipment	178.5
Mineral fuels & lubricants	106.0	Mineral fuels & lubricants	112.3
Chemicals & related products	88.2	Chemicals & related products	65.2
Food, drink & tobacco	73.9	Food, drink & tobacco	47.6
Total incl. others	**545.5**	Total incl. others	**494.7**

Main export destinations		**Main origins of imports**	
	% of total		*% of total*
Germany	29.8	Germany	19.5
Belgium	16.1	China	11.9
France	10.4	Belgium	10.2
United Kingdom	10.4	United States	8.8
EU27	78.9	EU27	48.1

Balance of payments, reserves and aid, $bn

Visible exports fob	532.8	Overall balance	0.8
Visible imports fob	-475.7	Change in reserves	1.7
Trade balance	-57.1	Level of reserves	
Invisibles inflows	239.3	end Dec.	28.6
Invisibles outflows	-241.0	No. months of import cover	0.5
Net transfers	-12.8	Official gold holdings, m oz	19.7
Current account balance	42.6	Aid given	6.99
– as % of GDP	4.9	– as % of GDP	0.80
Capital balance	0.7		

Health and education

Health spending, % of GDP	8.9	Education spending, % of GDP	5.0
Doctors per 1,000 pop.	3.9	Enrolment, %: primary	107
Hospital beds per 1,000 pop.	4.8	secondary	120
Improved-water source access,		tertiary	60
% of pop.	100		

Society

No. of households	7.2m	Colour TVs per 100 households	99.0
Av. no. per household	2.3	Telephone lines per 100 pop.	44.3
Marriages per 1,000 pop.	4.2	Mobile telephone subscribers	
Divorces per 1,000 pop.	1.7	per 100 pop.	124.8
Cost of living, Feb. 2010		Computers per 100 pop.	91.2
New York = 100	109	Internet hosts per 1,000 pop.	768.2

a Includes water.

NEW ZEALAND

Area	270,534 sq km	Capital	Wellington
Arable as % of total land	3	Currency	New Zealand dollar (NZ$)

People

Population	4.2m	Life expectancy:	men	79.1 yrs
Pop. per sq km	15.5		women	82.8 yrs
Av. ann. growth		Adult literacy		...
in pop. 2010–15	0.92%	Fertility rate (per woman)		2.0
Pop. under 15	20.2%	Urban population		86.2%
Pop. over 60	18.2%			*per 1,000 pop.*
No. of men per 100 women	97.7	Crude birth rate		13.8
Human Development Index	95.0	Crude death rate		7.2

The economy

GDP	NZ$182bn	GDP per head	$30,440
GDP	$130bn	GDP per head in purchasing	
Av. ann. growth in real		power parity (USA=100)	58.8
GDP 2003–08	2.2%	Economic freedom index	82.1

Origins of GDP		**Components of GDP**	
	% of total		*% of total*
Agriculture & mining	4	Private consumption	58
Industry	26	Public consumption	19
Services	70	Investment	24
		Exports	29
		Imports	-30

Structure of employment

	% of total		*% of labour force*
Agriculture	7	Unemployed 2008	4.1
Industry	22	Av. ann. rate 1995–2008	5.3
Services	71		

Energy

	m TOE		
Total output	14.0	Net energy imports as %	
Total consumption	16.8	of energy use	16
Consumption per head,			
kg oil equivalent	3,966		

Inflation and finance

Consumer price		*av. ann. increase 2003–08*	
inflation 2009	1.4%	Narrow money (M1)	-1.2%
Av. ann. inflation 2004–09	2.9%	Broad money	9.1%
Money market rate, 2009	2.82%		

Exchange rates

	end 2009		*December 2009*
NZ$ per $	1.39	Effective rates	*2005 = 100*
NZ$ per SDR	2.17	– nominal	91.1
NZ$ per €	2.00	– real	94.5

Trade

Principal exports		Principal imports	
	$bn fob		*$bn cif*
Dairy produce	6.6	Machinery & electrical	
Meat	3.7	equipment	7.2
Forestry products	1.6	Mineral fuels & lubricants	6.0
Wool	0.4	Transport equipment	3.6
Total incl. others	**30.6**	Total incl. others	**34.4**

Main export destinations		Main origins of imports	
	% of total		*% of total*
Australia	23.3	Australia	18.0
United States	10.2	China	13.3
Japan	8.4	United States	9.5
China	3.4	Japan	8.1

Balance of payments, reserves and aid, $bn

Visible exports fob	31.2	Overall balance	-4.9
Visible imports fob	-32.8	Change in reserves	-6.2
Trade balance	-1.6	Level of reserves	
Invisibles inflows	11.2	end Dec.	11.1
Invisibles outflows	-20.6	No. months of import cover	2.4
Net transfers	0.8	Official gold holdings, m oz	0.0
Current account balance	-11.2	Aid given	0.35
– as % of GDP	-8.6	– as % of GDP	0.27
Capital balance	0.2		

Health and education

Health spending, % of GDP	9.0	Education spending, % of GDP	6.9
Doctors per 1,000 pop.	2.1	Enrolment, %: primary	101
Hospital beds per 1,000 pop.	6.0	secondary	120
Improved-water source access,		tertiary	79
% of pop.	100		

Society

No. of households	1.5m	Colour TVs per 100 households	98.6
Av. no. per household	2.8	Telephone lines per 100 pop.	41.4
Marriages per 1,000 pop.	4.8	Mobile telephone subscribers	
Divorces per 1,000 pop.	2.7	per 100 pop.	109.2
Cost of living, Feb. 2010		Computers per 100 pop.	52.6
New York = 100	96	Internet hosts per 1,000 pop.	588.2

NIGERIA

Area	923,768 sq km	Capital	Abuja
Arable as % of total land	40	Currency	Naira (N)

People

Population	151.5m	Life expectancy: men	48.6 yrs
Pop. per sq km	164.1	women	49.7 yrs
Av. ann. growth		Adult literacy	60.1%
in pop. 2010–15	2.33%	Fertility rate (per woman)	5.3
Pop. under 15	42.4%	Urban population	49.8%
Pop. over 60	4.9%		per 1,000 pop.
No. of men per 100 women	100.5	Crude birth rate	40.1
Human Development Index	51.1	Crude death rate	15.3

The economy

GDP	N24,533bn	GDP per head	$1,370
GDP	$207bn	GDP per head in purchasing	
Av. ann. growth in real		power parity (USA=100)	4.5
GDP 2003–08	7.0%	Economic freedom index	56.8

Origins of GDP		**Components of GDP**[a]	
	% of total		% of total
Agriculture	33	Private and public consumption	56
Industry, of which:	41	Investment	22
manufacturing	3	Exports	56
Services	27	Imports	-35

Structure of employment

	% of total		% of labour force
Agriculture	...	Unemployed 2001	3.9
Industry	...	Av. ann. rate 1995–2001	3.7
Services	...		

Energy

	m TOE		
Total output	231.7	Net energy imports as %	
Total consumption	106.7	of energy use	-117
Consumption per head,			
kg oil equivalent	722		

Inflation and finance

Consumer price		av. ann. increase 2003–08	
inflation 2009	12.4%	Narrow money (M1)	30.7%
Av. ann. inflation 2004–09	11.0%	Broad money	35.1%
Treasury bill rate Oct. 2009	5.08%		

Exchange rates

	end 2009		December 2009
N per $	152.35	Effective rates	2005 = 100
N per SDR	237.84	– nominal	81.8
N per €	219.46	– real	110.2

Trade

Principal exports		Principal imports	
	$bn fob		*$bn cif*
Crude oil	74.3	Manufactured goods	14.0
Gas	5.5	Chemicals	10.6
		Machinery & transport equip.	9.3
		Food & live animals	3.4
Total incl. others	**80.6**	Total incl. others	**42.4**

Main export destinations		Main origins of imports	
	% of total		*% of total*
United States	44.2	China	13.9
Brazil	10.0	Netherlands	9.7
India	9.5	United States	8.4
Spain	7.8	United Kingdom	5.3

Balance of payments, reserves and debt, $bn

Visible exports fob	78.3	Change in reserves	1.7
Visible imports fob	-34.4	Level of reserves	
Trade balance	44.0	end Dec.	53.6
Invisibles inflows	4.1	No. months of import cover	10.5
Invisibles outflows	-26.7	Official gold holdings, m oz	0.7
Net transfers	18.0	Foreign debt	11.2
Current account balance	39.4	– as % of GDP	6
– as % of GDP	19.0	– as % of total exports	12
Capital balance	-8.5	Debt service ratio	1
Overall balance	1.6		

Health and education

Health spending, % of GDP	6.6	Education spending, % of GDP	...
Doctors per 1,000 pop.	0.4	Enrolment, %: primary	93
Hospital beds per 1,000 pop.	0.5	secondary	30
Improved-water source access,		tertiary	10
% of pop.	58		

Society

No. of households	30.5m	Colour TVs per 100 households	32.0
Av. no. per household	5.0	Telephone lines per 100 pop.	0.9
Marriages per 1,000 pop.	...	Mobile telephone subscribers	
Divorces per 1,000 pop.	...	per 100 pop.	41.7
Cost of living, Feb. 2010		Computers per 100 pop.	0.8
New York = 100	72	Internet hosts per 1,000 pop.	...

NORWAY

Area	323,878 sq km	Capital	Oslo
Arable as % of total land	3	Currency	Norwegian krone (Nkr)

People

Population	4.7m	Life expectancy:	men	79.2 yrs
Pop. per sq km	14.5		women	83.4 yrs
Av. ann. growth		Adult literacy		...
in pop. 2010–15	0.93%	Fertility rate (per woman)		1.9
Pop. under 15	18.8%	Urban population		79.4%
Pop. over 60	21.1%			per 1,000 pop.
No. of men per 100 women	99.0	Crude birth rate		12.3
Human Development Index	97.1	Crude death rate		8.5

The economy

GDP	Nkr2,548bn	GDP per head	$94,760
GDP	$452bn	GDP per head in purchasing	
Av. ann. growth in real		power parity (USA=100)	126.7
GDP 2003–08	2.7%	Economic freedom index	69.4

Origins of GDP		**Components of GDP**	
	% of total		% of total
Agriculture	1	Private consumption	39
Industry, of which:	46	Public consumption	19
manufacturing	9	Investment	23
Services	53	Exports	48
		Imports	-29

Structure of employment

	% of total		% of labour force
Agriculture	3	Unemployed 2008	2.6
Industry	21	Av. ann. rate 1995–2008	3.8
Services	76		

Energy

	m TOE		
Total output	213.9	Net energy imports as %	
Total consumption	26.9	of energy use	-696
Consumption per head,			
kg oil equivalent	5,704		

Inflation and finance

Consumer price		av. ann. increase 2003–08	
inflation 2009	2.2%	Narrow money (M1)	...
Av. ann. inflation 2004–09	2.1%	Broad money	...
Interbank rate, Sept. 2009	1.93%	Household saving rate, 2009	3.3%

Exchange rates

	end 2009		December 2009
Nkr per $	5.78	Effective rates	2005 = 100
Nkr per SDR	9.06	– nominal	102.3
Nkr per €	8.33	– real	103.6

Trade

Principal exports		Principal imports	
	$bn fob		*$bn cif*
Mineral, fuels & lubricants	117.4	Machinery & transport equip.	35.7
Manufactured goods	19.6	Manufactured goods	27.1
Machinery & transport equip.	15.5	Chemicals & mineral products	8.0
Chemicals	7.9	Food & beverages	5.5
Total incl. others	**172.4**	Total incl. others	**89.2**

Main export destinations		Main origins of imports	
	% of total		*% of total*
United Kingdom	26.4	Sweden	14.4
Germany	12.5	Germany	13.4
Netherlands	10.1	Denmark	6.9
France	9.2	China	6.4
Sweden	6.3	United Kingdom	5.9
United States	4.3	United States	5.4
EU27	83.4	EU27	68.2

Balance of payments, reserves and aid, $bn

Visible exports fob	173.6	Overall balance	4.6
Visible imports fob	-85.9	Change in reserves	-9.9
Trade balance	87.6	Level of reserves	
Invisibles inflows	93.9	end Dec.	51.0
Invisibles outflows	-89.8	No. months of import cover	3.5
Net transfers	-3.3	Official gold holdings, m oz	0.0
Current account balance	88.3	Aid given	3.96
– as % of GDP	19.6	– as % of GDP	0.88
Capital balance	-91.9		

Health and education

Health spending, % of GDP	8.9	Education spending, % of GDP	7.2
Doctors per 1,000 pop.	3.9	Enrolment, %: primary	98
Hospital beds per 1,000 pop.	3.9	secondary	113
Improved-water source access,		tertiary	76
% of pop.	100		

Society

No. of households	2.1m	Colour TVs per 100 households	98.3
Av. no. per household	2.2	Telephone lines per 100 pop.	39.8
Marriages per 1,000 pop.	5.0	Mobile telephone subscribers	
Divorces per 1,000 pop.	2.5	per 100 pop.	110.2
Cost of living, Feb. 2010		Computers per 100 pop.	62.9
New York = 100	144	Internet hosts per 1,000 pop.	707.7

PAKISTAN

Area	803,940 sq km	Capital	Islamabad
Arable as % of total land	28	Currency	Pakistan rupee (PRs)

People

Population	167.0m	Life expectancy: men	67.6 yrs
Pop. per sq km	208.0	women	68.3 yrs
Av. ann. growth		Adult literacy	53.7%
in pop. 2010–15	2.16%	Fertility rate (per woman)	4.0
Pop. under 15	36.6%	Urban population	35.9%
Pop. over 60	6.2%		per 1,000 pop.
No. of men per 100 women	106.1	Crude birth rate	30.2
Human Development Index	57.2	Crude death rate	6.4

The economy

GDP	PRs10,284bn	GDP per head	$990
GDP	$165bn	GDP per head in purchasing	
Av. ann. growth in real		power parity (USA=100)	5.5
GDP 2003–08	5.8%	Economic freedom index	55.2

Origins of GDP		**Components of GDP**	
	% of total		% of total
Agriculture	20	Private consumption	77
Industry, of which:	27	Public consumption	12
manufacturing	20	Investment	22
Services	53	Exports	13
		Imports	-24

Structure of employment

	% of total		% of labour force
Agriculture	44	Unemployed 2007	5.1
Industry	20	Av. ann. rate 1995–2007	6.2
Services	36		

Energy

	m TOE		
Total output	63.6	Net energy imports as %	
Total consumption	83.3	of energy use	24
Consumption per head,			
kg oil equivalent	512		

Inflation and finance

Consumer price		av. ann. increase 2003–08	
inflation 2009	13.6%	Narrow money (M1)	21.2%
Av. ann. inflation 2004–09	11.6%	Broad money (M2)	15.4%
Money market rate, 2009	11.96%		

Exchange rates

	end 2009		December 2009
PRs per $	84.26	Effective rates	2005 = 100
PRs per SDR	132.10	– nominal	65.6
PRs per €	121.38	– real	99.8

Trade[a]

Principal exports	$bn fob	Principal imports	$bn fob
Rice	2.4	Mineral fuels	13.9
Cotton fabrics	1.6	Machinery & transport equip.	9.2
Cotton yarn & thread	1.2	Chemicals	5.9
Raw cotton	0.1	Palm oil	1.9
Total incl. others	**20.3**	Total incl. others	**42.3**

Main export destinations	% of total	Main origins of imports	% of total
United States	17.1	China	15.6
United Arab Emirates	12.5	Saudi Arabia	13.3
Afghanistan	9.2	United Arab Emirates	12.3
United Kingdom	4.8	Kuwait	6.0
China	4.5	United States	5.2

Balance of payments, reserves and debt, $bn

Visible exports fob	21.3	Change in reserves	-6.8
Visible imports fob	-38.1	Level of reserves	
Trade balance	-16.8	end Dec.	9.0
Invisibles inflows	5.4	No. months of import cover	2.0
Invisibles outflows	-15.1	Official gold holdings, m oz	2.1
Net transfers	11.1	Foreign debt	49.3
Current account balance	-15.4	– as % of GDP	29
– as % of GDP	-9.4	– as % of total exports	120
Capital balance	6.3	Debt service ratio	9
Overall balance	-9.4		

Health and education

Health spending, % of GDP	2.7	Education spending, % of GDP	1.8
Doctors per 1,000 pop.	0.8	Enrolment, %: primary	85
Hospital beds per 1,000 pop.	0.6	secondary	33
Improved-water source access,		tertiary	5
% of pop.	90		

Society

No. of households	24.5m	Colour TVs per 100 households	35.4
Av. no. per household	6.8	Telephone lines per 100 pop.	2.5
Marriages per 1,000 pop.	...	Mobile telephone subscribers	
Divorces per 1,000 pop.	...	per 100 pop.	49.7
Cost of living, Feb. 2010		Computers per 100 pop.	...
New York = 100	40	Internet hosts per 1,000 pop.	2.0

a Fiscal year ending June 30, 2008.

PERU

Area	1,285,216 sq km	Capital	Lima
Arable as % of total land	3	Currency	Nuevo Sol (New Sol)

People

Population	28.2m	Life expectancy: men	71.6 yrs
Pop. per sq km	21.9	women	76.9 yrs
Av. ann. growth		Adult literacy	89.6%
in pop. 2010–15	1.16%	Fertility rate (per woman)	2.6
Pop. under 15	29.9%	Urban population	76.9%
Pop. over 60	8.7%		per 1,000 pop.
No. of men per 100 women	100.5	Crude birth rate	21.3
Human Development Index	80.6	Crude death rate	5.5

The economy

GDP	New Soles 378bn	GDP per head	$4,480
GDP	$129bn	GDP per head in purchasing	
Av. ann. growth in real		power parity (USA=100)	18.4
GDP 2003–08	7.6%	Economic freedom index	67.6

Origins of GDP		Components of GDP	
	% of total		% of total
Agriculture	7	Private consumption	64
Industry, of which:	36	Public consumption	9
manufacturing	16	Investment	26
Services	57	Exports	27
		Imports	-26

Structure of employment

	% of total		% of labour force
Agriculture	1	Unemployed 2007	7.0
Industry	24	Av. ann. rate 1996–2007	8.6
Services	75		

Energy

	m TOE		
Total output	12.2	Net energy imports as %	
Total consumption	14.1	of energy use	13
Consumption per head,			
kg oil equivalent	494		

Inflation and finance

Consumer price		av. ann. increase 2003–08	
inflation 2009	2.9%	Narrow money (M1)	17.9%
Av. ann. inflation 2004–09	2.8%	Broad money	15.3%
Money market rate, 2009	1.24%		

Exchange rates

	end 2009		December 2009
New Soles per $	2.89	Effective rates	2005 = 100
New Soles per SDR	4.53	– nominal	...
New Soles per €	4.16	– real	...

Trade

Principal exports		Principal imports	
	$bn fob		$bn fob
Copper	7.7	Intermediate goods	14.6
Gold	5.6	Capital goods	9.2
Fishmeal	1.8	Consumer goods	4.5
Zinc	1.5	Other goods	0.1
Total incl. others	**31.5**	Total incl. others	**28.4**

Main export destinations		Main origins of imports	
	% of total		% of total
United States	17.7	United States	23.9
China	13.5	China	10.7
Canada	7.3	Brazil	8.9
Japan	6.1	Ecuador	6.6

Balance of payments, reserves and debt, $bn

Visible exports fob	31.5	Change in reserves	3.5
Visible imports fob	-28.4	Level of reserves	
Trade balance	3.1	end Dec.	31.2
Invisibles inflows	5.5	No. months of import cover	8.5
Invisibles outflows	-15.5	Official gold holdings, m oz	1.1
Net transfers	2.8	Foreign debt	28.6
Current account balance	-4.2	– as % of GDP	24
– as % of GDP	-3.2	– as % of total exports	81
Capital balance	7.6	Debt service ratio	13
Overall balance	3.5		

Health and education

Health spending, % of GDP	4.3	Education spending, % of GDP	2.9
Doctors per 1,000 pop.	1.2	Enrolment, %: primary	119
Hospital beds per 1,000 pop.	1.5	secondary	98
Improved-water source access,		tertiary	34
% of pop.	82		

Society

No. of households	6.9m	Colour TVs per 100 households	54.7
Av. no. per household	4.1	Telephone lines per 100 pop.	10.0
Marriages per 1,000 pop.	2.8	Mobile telephone subscribers	
Divorces per 1,000 pop.	...	per 100 pop.	72.7
Cost of living, Feb. 2010		Computers per 100 pop.	10.3
New York = 100	67	Internet hosts per 1,000 pop.	9.5

PHILIPPINES

Area	300,000 sq km	Capital	Manila
Arable as % of total land	17	Currency	Philippine peso (P)

People

Population	89.7m	Life expectancy: men	70.7 yrs
Pop. per sq km	299.0	women	75.2 yrs
Av. ann. growth		Adult literacy	93.6%
in pop. 2010–15	1.82%	Fertility rate (per woman)	3.1
Pop. under 15	33.5%	Urban population	48.9%
Pop. over 60	6.7%		per 1,000 pop.
No. of men per 100 women	101.5	Crude birth rate	25.0
Human Development Index	75.1	Crude death rate	4.7

The economy

GDP	P7,423bn	GDP per head	$1,850
GDP	$167bn	GDP per head in purchasing	
Av. ann. growth in real		power parity (USA=100)	7.6
GDP 2003–08	5.5%	Economic freedom index	56.3

Origins of GDP		Components of GDP	
	% of total		% of total
Agriculture	15	Private consumption	77
Industry, of which:	32	Public consumption	10
manufacturing	22	Investment	15
Services	53	Exports	37
		Imports	-39

Structure of employment

	% of total		% of labour force
Agriculture	37	Unemployed 2008	7.4
Industry	14	Av. ann. rate 1995–2008	8.8
Services	47		

Energy

	m TOE		
Total output	22.4	Net energy imports as %	
Total consumption	40.0	of energy use	44
Consumption per head,			
kg oil equivalent	451		

Inflation and finance

Consumer price			av. ann. increase 2003–07
inflation 2009	3.3%	Narrow money (M1)	13.5%
Av. ann. inflation 2004–09	5.8%	Broad money	12.4%
Money market rate, 2009	4.54%		

Exchange rates

	end 2009		December 2009
P per $	46.36	Effective rates	2005 = 100
P per SDR	72.67	– nominal	109.1
P per €	66.78	– real	127.2

Trade

Principal exports		Principal imports	
	$bn fob		*$bn fob*
Electrical & electronic		Capital goods	15.7
equipment	28.5	Mineral fuels	12.3
Clothing	1.9	Chemicals	4.8
Petroleum products	1.2	Manufactured goods	4.3
Coconut oil	1.0		
Total incl. others	**49.2**	**Total incl. others**	**60.2**

Main export destinations		Main origins of imports	
	% of total		*% of total*
United States	16.7	United States	12.9
Japan	15.7	Japan	11.8
China	11.1	Singapore	10.3
Hong Kong	10.1	Saudi Arabia	8.6
Netherlands	7.5	China	7.6

Balance of payments, reserves and debt, $bn

Visible exports fob	48.3	Change in reserves	3.8
Visible imports fob	-61.1	Level of reserves	
Trade balance	-12.9	end Dec.	37.5
Invisibles inflows	16.2	No. months of import cover	5.9
Invisibles outflows	-14.6	Official gold holdings, m oz	4.9
Net transfers	15.2	Foreign debt	64.9
Current account balance	3.9	– as % of GDP	35
– as % of GDP	2.3	– as % of total exports	77
Capital balance	-1.9	Debt service ratio	16
Overall balance	0.1		

Health and education

Health spending, % of GDP	3.9	Education spending, % of GDP	3.2
Doctors per 1,000 pop.	...	Enrolment, %: primary	108
Hospital beds per 1,000 pop.	1.1	secondary	81
Improved-water source access,		tertiary	28
% of pop.	91		

Society

No. of households	18.6m	Colour TVs per 100 households	88.4
Av. no. per household	4.8	Telephone lines per 100 pop.	4.5
Marriages per 1,000 pop.	6.4	Mobile telephone subscribers	
Divorces per 1,000 pop.	...	per 100 pop.	75.4
Cost of living, Feb. 2010		Computers per 100 pop.	7.2
New York = 100	52	Internet hosts per 1,000 pop.	4.3

POLAND

Area	312,683 sq km	Capital	Warsaw
Arable as % of total land	41	Currency	Zloty (Zl)

People

Population	38.0m	Life expectancy: men		72.3 yrs
Pop. per sq km	121.5	women		80.4 yrs
Av. ann. growth		Adult literacy		99.5
in pop. 2010–15	-0.08%	Fertility rate (per woman)		1.3
Pop. under 15	14.8%	Urban population		61.0%
Pop. over 60	19.4%			per 1,000 pop.
No. of men per 100 women	93.1	Crude birth rate		9.8
Human Development Index	88.0	Crude death rate		10.5

The economy

GDP	Zl1,272bn	GDP per head	$13,850
GDP	$528bn	GDP per head in purchasing	
Av. ann. growth in real		power parity (USA=100)	37.3
GDP 2003–08	5.4%	Economic freedom index	63.2

Origins of GDP		**Components of GDP**	
	% of total		% of total
Agriculture	5	Private consumption	60
Industry, of which:	31	Public consumption	19
manufacturing	17	Investment	24
Services	65	Exports	40
		Imports	-43

Structure of employment

	% of total		% of labour force
Agriculture	15	Unemployed 2008	7.1
Industry	29	Av. ann. rate 1995–2008	14.4
Services	56		

Energy

	m TOE		
Total output	72.6	Net energy imports as %	
Total consumption	97.1	of energy use	25
Consumption per head,			
kg oil equivalent	2,547		

Inflation and finance

Consumer price		av. ann. increase 2003–08	
inflation 2009	3.9%	Narrow money (M1)	16.5%
Av. ann. inflation 2004–09	2.8%	Broad money	14.1%
Money market rate, 2009	3.18%	Household saving rate, 2009	7.9%

Exchange rates

	end 2009		December 2009
Zl per $	2.85	Effective rates	2005 = 100
Zl per SDR	4.47	– nominal	101.2
Zl per €	4.11	– real	103.7

Trade

Principal exports		Principal imports	
	$bn fob		*$bn cif*
Machinery &		Machinery &	
transport equipment	70.8	transport equipment	73.7
Manufactured goods	58.9	Manufactured goods	57.9
Foodstuffs & live animals	14.4	Chemicals & products	27.2
Total incl. others	**170.6**	**Total incl. others**	**207.6**

Main export destinations		Main origins of imports	
	% of total		*% of total*
Germany	25.1	Germany	28.8
France	6.2	Russia	9.7
Italy	6.0	Italy	6.4
United Kingdom	5.8	China	5.4
EU27	77.8	EU27	71.9

Balance of payments, reserves and debt, $bn

Visible exports fob	178.4	Change in reserves	-3.5
Visible imports fob	-204.4	Level of reserves	
Trade balance	-26.0	end Dec.	62.2
Invisibles inflows	45.7	No. months of import cover	2.9
Invisibles outflows	-54.9	Official gold holdings, m oz	3.3
Net transfers	8.3	Foreign debt	218.0
Current account balance	-26.9	– as % of GDP	42
– as % of GDP	-5.1	– as % of total exports	103
Capital balance	46.5	Debt service ratio	25
Overall balance	-2.0	Aid given	0.37
		% of GDP	0.07

Health and education

Health spending, % of GDP	6.4	Education spending, % of GDP	5.6
Doctors per 1,000 pop.	2.0	Enrolment, %: primary	97
Hospital beds per 1,000 pop.	5.2	secondary	100
Improved-water source access,		tertiary	67
% of pop.	100		

Society

No. of households	14.3m	Colour TVs per 100 households	97.5
Av. no. per household	2.7	Telephone lines per 100 pop.	25.5
Marriages per 1,000 pop.	5.2	Mobile telephone subscribers	
Divorces per 1,000 pop.	1.6	per 100 pop.	115.3
Cost of living, Feb. 2010		Computers per 100 pop.	16.9
New York = 100	85	Internet hosts per 1,000 pop.	269.7

PORTUGAL

Area	88,940 sq km	Capital	Lisbon
Arable as % of total land	12	Currency	Euro (€)

People

Population	10.7m	Life expectancy: men	76.1 yrs
Pop. per sq km	120.3	women	82.6 yrs
Av. ann. growth		Adult literacy	94.6%
in pop. 2010–15	0.35%	Fertility rate (per woman)	1.4
Pop. under 15	15.2%	Urban population	60.7%
Pop. over 60	23.6%		per 1,000 pop.
No. of men per 100 women	93.9	Crude birth rate	9.9
Human Development Index	90.9	Crude death rate	10.5

The economy

GDP	€166bn	GDP per head	$22,920
GDP	$243bn	GDP per head in purchasing	
Av. ann. growth in real		power parity (USA=100)	50.2
GDP 2003–08	1.1%	Economic freedom index	64.4

Origins of GDP		**Components of GDP**	
	% of total		% of total
Agriculture	2	Private consumption	67
Industry, of which:	24	Public consumption	21
manufacturing	14	Investment	22
Services	74	Exports	33
		Imports	-42

Structure of employment

	% of total		% of labour force
Agriculture	12	Unemployed 2008	7.6
Industry	29	Av. ann. rate 1995–2008	6.3
Services	59		

Energy

	m TOE		
Total output	4.6	Net energy imports as %	
Total consumption	25.1	of energy use	82
Consumption per head,			
kg oil equivalent	2,363		

Inflation and finance

Consumer price		av. ann. increase 2003–08	
inflation 2009	-0.8%	Euro area:	
Av. ann. inflation 2004–09	1.9%	Narrow money (M1)	8.2%
Deposit rate, h'holds, 2009	2.57%	Broad money	8.8%
		Household saving rate[a], 2009	9.6%

Exchange rates

	end 2009		December 2009
€ per $	0.69	Effective rates	2005 = 100
€ per SDR	1.09	– nominal	104.1
		– real	102.9

Trade

Principal exports		Principal imports	
	$bn fob		*$bn cif*
Machinery & transport equip.	17.0	Machinery & transport equip.	26.8
Food, drink & tobacco	5.1	Mineral fuels & lubricants	15.0
Chemicals & related products	4.0	Food, drink & tobacco	9.8
Raw materials	3.2	Chemicals & related products	9.7
Total incl. others	**55.8**	Total incl. others	**88.9**

Main export destinations		Main origins of imports	
	% of total		*% of total*
Spain	25.8	Spain	29.0
Germany	12.7	Germany	11.6
France	11.2	France	8.0
Angola	5.9	Italy	4.9
United Kingdom	5.3	Netherlands	4.4
EU27	73.8	EU27	73.5

Balance of payments, reserves and debt, $bn

Visible exports fob	56.4	Overall balance	0.1
Visible imports fob	-87.8	Change in reserves	0.5
Trade balance	-31.4	Level of reserves	
Invisibles inflows	44.4	end Dec.	12.0
Invisibles outflows	-46.2	No. months of import cover	1.1
Net transfers	3.6	Official gold holdings, m oz	12.3
Current account balance	-29.6	Aid given	0.62
– as % of GDP	-12.2	– as % of GDP	0.25
Capital balance	30.8		

Health and education

Health spending, % of GDP	10.0	Education spending, % of GDP	5.9
Doctors per 1,000 pop.	3.4	Enrolment, %: primary	115
Hospital beds per 1,000 pop.	3.5	secondary[b]	101
Improved-water source access,		tertiary	57
% of pop.	99		

Society

No. of households	4.1m	Colour TVs per 100 households	99.1
Av. no. per household	2.6	Telephone lines per 100 pop.	38.5
Marriages per 1,000 pop.	4.9	Mobile telephone subscribers	
Divorces per 1,000 pop.	2.4	per 100 pop.	139.6
Cost of living, Feb. 2010		Computers per 100 pop.	18.2
New York = 100	93	Internet hosts per 1,000 pop.	293.7

a Gross.
b Includes training for unemployed.

ROMANIA

Area	237,500 sq km	Capital	Bucharest
Arable as % of total land	37	Currency	Leu (RON)

People

Population	21.3m	Life expectancy:	men	70.3 yrs
Pop. per sq km	89.7		women	77.2 yrs
Av. ann. growth		Adult literacy		97.6%
in pop. 2010–15	-0.42%	Fertility rate (per woman)		1.3
Pop. under 15	15.2%	Urban population		57.5%
Pop. over 60	20.3%			per 1,000 pop.
No. of men per 100 women	94.5	Crude birth rate		10.0
Human Development Index	83.7	Crude death rate		12.6

The economy

GDP	RON504bn	GDP per head	$9,300
GDP	$200bn	GDP per head in purchasing	
Av. ann. growth in real		power parity (USA=100)	29.0
GDP 2003–08	6.8%	Economic freedom index	64.2

Origins of GDP		**Components of GDP**	
	% of total		% of total
Agriculture	7	Private consumption	64
Industry, of which:	25	Public consumption	16
manufacturing	21	Investment	31
Services	68	Exports	30
		Imports	-40

Structure of employment

	% of total		% of labour force
Agriculture	29	Unemployed 2008	5.8
Industry	31	Av. ann. rate 1995–2008	7.0
Services	40		

Energy

	m TOE		
Total output	27.6	Net energy imports as %	
Total consumption	38.9	of energy use	29
Consumption per head,			
kg oil equivalent	1,806		

Inflation and finance

Consumer price		av. ann. increase 2003–08	
inflation 2009	5.6%	Narrow money (M1)	52.2%
Av. ann. inflation 2004–09	6.7%	Broad money	33.8%
Money market rate, 2009	10.92%		

Exchange rates

	end 2009		December 2009
RON per $	2.94	Effective rates	2005 = 100
RON per SDR	4.60	– nominal	89.4
RON per €	4.24	– real	104.8

Trade

Principal exports		Principal imports	
	$bn fob		*$bn cif*
Machinery & equipment		Machinery & equipment	
(incl. transport)	17.8	(incl. transport)	29.7
Basic metals & products	5.9	Textiles & products	10.4
Textiles & apparel	5.2	Chemical products	9.0
Minerals, fuels & lubricants	4.5	Minerals, fuels & lubricants	3.6
Total incl. others	**49.5**	Total incl. others	**83.0**

Main export destinations		Main origins of imports	
	% of total		*% of total*
Germany	16.4	Germany	16.7
Italy	15.7	Italy	11.8
France	7.4	Hungary	7.6
Turkey	6.6	Russia	6.0
EU27	70.5	EU27	69.7

Balance of payments, reserves and debt, $bn

Visible exports fob	49.8	Change in reserves	-0.2
Visible imports fob	-77.9	Level of reserves	
Trade balance	-28.2	end Dec.	39.8
Invisibles inflows	16.2	No. months of import cover	4.8
Invisibles outflows	-20.6	Official gold holdings, m oz	3.3
Net transfers	8.9	Foreign debt	104.9
Current account balance	-23.7	– as % of GDP	55
– as % of GDP	-11.9	– as % of total exports	149
Capital balance	25.9	Debt service ratio	25
Overall balance	0.2		

Health and education

Health spending, % of GDP	4.7	Education spending, % of GDP	3.3
Doctors per 1,000 pop.	1.9	Enrolment, %: primary	105
Hospital beds per 1,000 pop.	6.5	secondary	87
Improved-water source access,		tertiary	58
% of pop.	57		

Society

No. of households	7.4m	Colour TVs per 100 households	92.6
Av. no. per household	2.9	Telephone lines per 100 pop.	23.6
Marriages per 1,000 pop.	6.4	Mobile telephone subscribers	
Divorces per 1,000 pop.	1.8	per 100 pop.	114.5
Cost of living, Feb. 2010		Computers per 100 pop.	19.2
New York = 100	64	Internet hosts per 1,000 pop.	116.6

RUSSIA

Area	17,075,400 sq km	Capital	Moscow
Arable as % of total land	7	Currency	Rouble (Rb)

People

Population	141.8m	Life expectancy: men	61.9 yrs
Pop. per sq km	8.3	women	74.1 yrs
Av. ann. growth		Adult literacy	99.5%
in pop. 2010–15	-0.40%	Fertility rate (per woman)	1.4
Pop. under 15	15.0%	Urban population	73.2%
Pop. over 60	18.1%		per 1,000 pop.
No. of men per 100 women	85.8	Crude birth rate	10.8
Human Development Index	81.7	Crude death rate	15.1

The economy

GDP	Rb41,668bn	GDP per head	$11,830
GDP	$1,679bn	GDP per head in purchasing	
Av. ann. growth in real		power parity (USA=100)	34.4
GDP 2003–08	7.0%	Economic freedom index	50.3

Origins of GDP		**Components of GDP**	
	% of total		% of total
Agriculture	5	Private consumption	48
Industry, of which:	37	Public consumption	17
manufacturing	18	Investment	26
Services	58	Exports	31
		Imports	-22

Structure of employment

	% of total		% of labour force
Agriculture	10	Unemployed 2008	6.2
Industry	28	Av. ann. rate 1995–2008	9.1
Services	62		

Energy

	m TOE		
Total output	1,230.6	Net energy imports as %	
Total consumption	672.1	of energy use	-83
Consumption per head,			
kg oil equivalent	4,730		

Inflation and finance

Consumer price		av. ann. increase 2003–08	
inflation 2009	11.7%	Narrow money (M1)	27.0%
Av. ann. inflation 2004–09	11.4%	Broad money	33.5%
Money market rate, 2009	7.78%		

Exchange rates

	end 2009		December 2009
Rb per $	30.24	Effective rates	2005 = 100
Rb per SDR	47.41	– nominal	91.2
Rb per 7	43.56	– real	118.9

Trade

Principal exports		Principal imports	
	$bn fob		*$bn fob*
Fuels	323.5	Machinery & equipment	153.8
Metals	55.2	Food & agricultural products	38.5
Chemicals	30.7	Chemicals	38.2
Machinery & equipment	23.1	Metals	20.1
Total incl. others	**471.6**	Total incl. others	**291.9**

Main export destinations		Main origins of imports	
	% of total		*% of total*
Germany	12.1	Germany	11.9
Netherlands	8.9	China	11.7
Turkey	6.9	Japan	6.4
Italy	5.8	Ukraine	5.6

Balance of payments, reserves and debt, $bn

Visible exports fob	471.6	Change in reserves	-49.4
Visible imports fob	-291.9	Level of reserves	
Trade balance	179.7	end Dec.	427.1
Invisibles inflows	110.3	No. months of import cover	10.8
Invisibles outflows	-184.5	Official gold holdings, m oz	16.7
Net transfers	-3.1	Foreign debt	402.5
Current account balance	102.4	– as % of GDP	26
– as % of GDP	6.1	– as % of total exports	81
Capital balance	-135.8	Debt service ratio	12
Overall balance	-45.3		

Health and education

Health spending, % of GDP	5.4	Education spending, % of GDP	3.1
Doctors per 1,000 pop.	4.3	Enrolment, %: primary	97
Hospital beds per 1,000 pop.	9.7	secondary	84
Improved-water source access,		tertiary	75
% of pop.	96		

Society

No. of households	52.9m	Colour TVs per 100 households	96.1
Av. no. per household	2.7	Telephone lines per 100 pop.	31.8
Marriages per 1,000 pop.	7.9	Mobile telephone subscribers	
Divorces per 1,000 pop.	3.9	per 100 pop.	141.1
Cost of living, Feb. 2010		Computers per 100 pop.	13.3
New York = 100	94	Internet hosts per 1,000 pop.	71.6

SAUDI ARABIA

Area	2,200,000 sq km	Capital	Riyadh
Arable as % of total land	2	Currency	Riyal (SR)

People

Population	25.3m	Life expectancy: men	71.9 yrs
Pop. per sq km	11.5	women	76.3 yrs
Av. ann. growth		Adult literacy	85.5%
in pop. 2010–15	2.12%	Fertility rate (per woman)	3.2
Pop. under 15	31.9%	Urban population	82.1%
Pop. over 60	4.6%		per 1,000 pop.
No. of men per 100 women	120.7	Crude birth rate	23.6
Human Development Index	84.3	Crude death rate	3.6

The economy

GDP	SR1,758bn	GDP per head	$19,020
GDP	$469bn	GDP per head in purchasing	
Av. ann. growth in real		power parity (USA=100)	51.8
GDP 2003–08	4.1%	Economic freedom index	64.1

Origins of GDP		**Components of GDP**	
	% of total		% of total
Agriculture	2	Private consumption	27
Industry, of which:	70	Public consumption	20
manufacturing	8	Investment	21
Services	27	Exports	69
		Imports	-38

Structure of employment

	% of total		% of labour force
Agriculture	4	Unemployed 2007	5.6
Industry	22	Av. ann. rate 1995–2007	4.7
Services	74		

Energy

	m TOE		
Total output	551.3	Net energy imports as %	
Total consumption	150.3	of energy use	-267
Consumption per head,			
kg oil equivalent	6,223		

Inflation and finance

Consumer price		av. ann. increase 2003–08	
inflation 2009	5.1%	Narrow money (M1)	13.8%
Av. ann. inflation 2004–09	4.4%	Broad money	17.8%
Deposit rate, 2009	1.22%		

Exchange rates

	end 2009		December 2009
SR per $	3.75	Effective rates	2005 = 100
SR per SDR	5.88	– nominal	92.4
SRE per €	5.40	– real	102.9

Trade

Principal exports		Principal imports	
	$bn fob		*$bn cif*
Crude oil	247.1	Machinery & transport equip.	52.1
Refined petroleum products	33.9	Foodstuffs	16.6
		Chemicals & metal products	8.7
Total incl. others	**313.5**	Total incl. others	**115.1**

Main export destinations		Main origins of imports	
	% of total		*% of total*
United States	17.2	United States	12.0
Japan	15.3	China	10.4
South Korea	10.2	Japan	7.6
China	9.4	Germany	7.3

Balance of payments, reserves and aid, $bn

Visible exports fob	313.4	Overall balance	143.5
Visible imports fob	-101.5	Change in reserves	137.2
Trade balance	212.0	Level of reserves	
Invisibles inflows	31.1	end Dec.	446.6
Invisibles outflows	-86.1	No. months of import cover	28.6
Net transfers	-23.0	Official gold holdings, m oz	4.6
Current account balance	134.0	Aid given	5.56
– as % of GDP	28.6	– as % of GDP	1.19
Capital balance	24.9		

Health and education

Health spending, % of GDP	3.4	Education spending, % of GDP	8.3
Doctors per 1,000 pop.	1.6	Enrolment, %: primary	98
Hospital beds per 1,000 pop.	2.2	secondary	95
Improved-water source access,		tertiary	30
% of pop.	96		

Society

No. of households	4.6m	Colour TVs per 100 households	97.9
Av. no. per household	5.5	Telephone lines per 100 pop.	16.3
Marriages per 1,000 pop.	4.5	Mobile telephone subscribers	
Divorces per 1,000 pop.	1.0	per 100 pop.	142.9
Cost of living, Feb. 2010		Computers per 100 pop.	69.8
New York = 100	66	Internet hosts per 1,000 pop.	19.1

SINGAPORE

Area	639 sq km	Capital	Singapore
Arable as % of total land	1	Currency	Singapore dollar (S$)

People

Population	4.5m	Life expectancy: men	78.5 yrs
Pop. per sq km	7,042.2	women	83.4 yrs
Av. ann. growth		Adult literacy	94.5%
in pop. 2010–15	2.51%	Fertility rate (per woman)	1.3
Pop. under 15	15.6%	Urban population	100.0%
Pop. over 60	16.0%		per 1,000 pop.
No. of men per 100 women	100.9	Crude birth rate	8.2
Human Development Index	94.4	Crude death rate	6.0

The economy

GDP	S$257bn	GDP per head	$37,600
GDP	$182bn	GDP per head in purchasing	
Av. ann. growth in real		power parity (USA=100)	106.4
GDP 2003–08	7.0%	Economic freedom index	86.1

Origins of GDP		Components of GDP	
	% of total		% of total
Agriculture	0	Private consumption	39
Industry, of which:	28	Public consumption	11
manufacturing	21	Investment	31
Services	72	Exports	234
		Imports	-215

Structure of employment

	% of total		% of labour force
Agriculture	0	Unemployed 2008	3.2
Industry	30	Av. ann. rate 1995–2008	4.0
Services	70		

Energy

	m TOE		
Total output	0.0	Net energy imports as %	
Total consumption	26.8	of energy use	100
Consumption per head,			
kg oil equivalent	5,831		

Inflation and finance

		av. ann. increase 2003–08	
Consumer price			
inflation 2009	0.2%	Narrow money (M1)	14.3%
Av. ann. inflation 2004–09	2.0%	Broad money	11.3%
Money market rate, 2009	0.69%		

Exchange rates

	end 2009		December 2009
S$ per $	1.40	Effective rates	2005 = 100
S$ per SDR	2.20	– nominal	110.1
S$ per 7	2.02	– real	109.4

Trade

Principal exports		**Principal imports**	
	$bn fob		*$bn cif*
Mineral fuels	81.6	Machinery & transport equip.	148.6
Electronic components & parts	73.7	Mineral fuels	90.8
Chemicals & products	34.1	Manufactured products	24.7
Manufactured products	21.1	Misc. manufacture articles	20.6
Total incl. others	**338.1**	Total incl. others	**319.8**

Main export destinations		**Main origins of imports**	
	% of total		*% of total*
Malaysia	12.1	Malaysia	11.9
Hong Kong	10.4	United States	11.7
China	9.2	China	10.5
United States	7.0	Japan	8.1
Japan	4.9	Taiwan	5.1
Australia	4.1	Saudi Arabia	4.6
Thailand	3.9	Thailand	3.5

Balance of payments, reserves and debt, $bn

Visible exports fob	344.4	Change in reserves	11.2
Visible imports fob	-313.5	Level of reserves	
Trade balance	30.9	end Dec.	174.2
Invisibles inflows	140.3	No. months of import cover	4.6
Invisibles outflows	-141.3	Official gold holdings, m oz	...
Net transfers	-2.8	Foreign debt	25.5
Current account balance	27.2	– as % of GDP	14
– as % of GDP	14.9	– as % of total exports	5
Capital balance	-11.5	Debt service ratio	1
Overall balance	13.1		

Health and education

Health spending, % of GDP	3.1	Education spending, % of GDP	...
Doctors per 1,000 pop.	1.6	Enrolment, %: primary	...
Hospital beds per 1,000 pop.	3.2	secondary	...
Improved-water source access,		tertiary	...
% of pop.	100		

Society

No. of households	1.0m	Colour TVs per 100 households	99.4
Av. no. per household	4.3	Telephone lines per 100 pop.	40.2
Marriages per 1,000 pop.	5.1	Mobile telephone subscribers	
Divorces per 1,000 pop.	1.7	per 100 pop.	138.2
Cost of living, Feb. 2010		Computers per 100 pop.	74.3
New York = 100	120	Internet hosts per 1,000 pop.	220.5

SLOVAKIA

Area	49,035 sq km	Capital	Bratislava
Arable as % of total land	29	Currency	Euro (€)

People

Population	5.4m	Life expectancy: men	71.8 yrs
Pop. per sq km	110.1	women	79.3 yrs
Av. ann. growth		Adult literacy	...
in pop. 2010–15	0.10%	Fertility rate (per woman)	1.3
Pop. under 15	15.2%	Urban population	55.0%
Pop. over 60	17.7%		per 1,000 pop.
No. of men per 100 women	94.2	Crude birth rate	10.2
Human Development Index	88.0	Crude death rate	10.1

The economy

GDP	€67.2bn	GDP per head	$18,210
GDP	$98.5bn	GDP per head in purchasing	
Av. ann. growth in real		power parity (USA=100)	47.8
GDP 2003–08	7.4%	Economic freedom index	69.7

Origins of GDP		**Components of GDP**	
	% of total		% of total
Agriculture	4	Private consumption	56
Industry, of which:	41	Public consumption	17
Manufacturing	22	Investment	29
Services	55	Exports	83
		Imports	-85

Structure of employment

	% of total		% of labour force
Agriculture	4	Unemployed 2008	9.5
Industry	40	Av. ann. rate 1995–2008	14.8
Services	56		

Energy

	m TOE		
Total output	6.0	Net energy imports as %	
Total consumption	17.8	of energy use	67
Consumption per head,			
kg oil equivalent	3,307		

Inflation and finance

Consumer price		av. ann. increase 2003–08	
inflation 2009	1.6%	Narrow money	10.2%
Av. ann. inflation 2004–09	3.2%	Broad money	20.6%
Deposit rate, h'holds, 2009	2.20%	Household saving rate, 2009	4.7%

Exchange rates

	end 2009		December 2009
€ per $	0.69	Effective rates	2005 = 100
€ per SDR	1.09	– nominal	118.4
		– real	123.9

Trade

Principal exports	$bn fob
Machinery & transport equipment	39.3
Semi-manufactures	15.0
Other manufactured goods	6.7
Chemicals	3.5
Total incl. others	**73.0**

Principal imports	$bn fob
Machinery & transport equipment	32.3
Semi-manufactures	12.5
Fuels	9.6
Chemicals	6.4
Total incl. others	**74.8**

Main export destinations	% of total
Germany	19.5
Czech Republic	12.8
France	6.5
Poland	6.4
EU27	85.4

Main origins of imports	% of total
Germany	19.6
Czech Republic	17.4
Russia	10.4
Hungary	6.8
EU27	73.1

Balance of payments, reserves and debt, $bn

Visible exports fob	70.3	Change in reserves	-0.1
Visible imports fob	-71.2	Level of reserves	
Trade balance	-0.9	end Dec.	18.8
Invisibles inflows	11.9	No. months of import cover	2.6
Invisibles outflows	-15.9	Official gold holdings, m oz	1.1
Net transfers	-1.3	Foreign debt	46.0
Current account balance	-6.2	– as % of GDP	48
– as % of GDP	-6.3	– as % of total exports	54
Capital balance	8.3	Debt service ratio	10
Overall balance	-0.1	Aid given	0.09
		% of GDP	0.09

Health and education

Health spending, % of GDP	7.7	Education spending, % of GDP	4.1
Doctors per 1,000 pop.	3.1	Enrolment, %: primary	102
Hospital beds per 1,000 pop.	6.8	secondary	93
Improved-water source access, % of pop.	100	tertiary	50

Society

No. of households	2.2m	Colour TVs per 100 households	99.0
Av. no. per household	2.5	Telephone lines per 100 pop.	20.3
Marriages per 1,000 pop.	5.1	Mobile telephone subscribers	
Divorces per 1,000 pop.	2.3	per 100 pop.	102.2
Cost of living, Feb. 2010		Computers per 100 pop.	58.1
New York = 100	...	Internet hosts per 1,000 pop.	199.6

SLOVENIA

Area	20,253 sq km	Capital	Ljubljana
Arable as % of total land	9	Currency	Euro (€)

People

Population	2.0m	Life expectancy: men	75.4 yrs
Pop. per sq km	98.8	women	82.6 yrs
Av. ann. growth		Adult literacy	99.7%
in pop. 2010–15	0.24%	Fertility rate (per woman)	1.4
Pop. under 15	13.8%	Urban population	49.5%
Pop. over 60	22.4%		per 1,000 pop.
No. of men per 100 women	95.5	Crude birth rate	9.6
Human Development Index	92.9	Crude death rate	10.2

The economy

GDP	€37.1bn	GDP per head	$27,020
GDP	$54.6bn	GDP per head in purchasing	
Av. ann. growth in real		power parity (USA=100)	60.1
GDP 2003–08	5.0%	Economic freedom index	64.7

Origins of GDP		Components of GDP	
	% of total		% of total
Agriculture	2	Private consumption	52
Industry, of which:	34	Public consumption	18
manufacturing	23	Investment	31
Services	63	Exports	70
		Imports	-71

Structure of employment

	% of total		% of labour force
Agriculture	10	Unemployed 2008	4.4
Industry	36	Av. ann. rate 1995–2008	6.4
Services	54		

Energy

	m TOE		
Total output	3.5	Net energy imports as %	
Total consumption	7.3	of energy use	53
Consumption per head,			
kg oil equivalent	3,632		

Inflation and finance

Consumer price		av. ann. increase 2003–08	
inflation 2009	0.9%	Euro area:	
Av. ann. inflation 2004–09	3.0%	Narrow money (M1)	8.2%
Deposit rate, h'holds, 2009	3.48%	Broad money	8.8%

Exchange rates

	end 2009		December 2009
€ per $	0.69	Effective rates	2005 = 100
€ per SDR	1.09	– nominal	...
		– real	...

Trade

Principal exports		**Principal imports**	
	$bn fob		*$bn fob*
Machinery & transport equip.	11.7	Machinery & transport equip.	11.4
Manufactures	7.0	Manufactures	6.9
Chemicals	4.2	Chemicals	4.0
Miscellaneous manufactures	3.6	Miscellaneous manufactures	3.2
Total incl. others	**29.3**	Total incl. others	**34.0**

Main export destinations		**Main origins of imports**	
	% of total		*% of total*
Germany	21.9	Germany	18.7
Italy	13.7	Italy	18.1
Croatia	9.7	Austria	12.2
Austria	8.8	France	5.1
France	6.6	Croatia	4.5
Russia	5.6	Hungary	3.9
EU27	68.1	EU27	71.3

Balance of payments, reserves and debt, $bn

Visible exports fob	29.6	Change in reserves	-0.1
Visible imports fob	-33.5	Level of reserves	
Trade balance	-3.9	end Dec.	1.0
Invisibles inflows	9.3	No. months of import cover	0.3
Invisibles outflows	-8.4	Official gold holdings, m oz	0.1
Net transfers	-0.3	Foreign debt[a]	21.4
Current account balance	-3.3	– as % of GDP[a]	55
– as % of GDP	-6.1	– as % of total exports[a]	80
Capital balance	3.5	Debt service ratio[a]	19
Overall balance	-0.0		

Health and education

Health spending, % of GDP	7.8	Education spending, % of GDP	5.2
Doctors per 1,000 pop.	2.4	Enrolment, %: primary	103
Hospital beds per 1,000 pop.	4.7	secondary	94
Improved-water source access,		tertiary	85
% of pop.	99		

Society

No. of households	0.7m	Colour TVs per 100 households	97.1
Av. no. per household	2.7	Telephone lines per 100 pop.	50.1
Marriages per 1,000 pop.	3.2	Mobile telephone subscribers	
Divorces per 1,000 pop.	1.2	per 100 pop.	102.0
Cost of living, Feb. 2010		Computers per 100 pop.	42.5
New York = 100	...	Internet hosts per 1,000 pop.	54.2

a 2006

SOUTH AFRICA

Area	1,225,815 sq km	Capital	Pretoria
Arable as % of total land	12	Currency	Rand (R)

People

Population	48.8m	Life expectancy: men	51.8 yrs
Pop. per sq km	39.1	women	53.8 yrs
Av. ann. growth		Adult literacy	89.0%
in pop. 2010–15	0.98%	Fertility rate (per woman)	2.6
Pop. under 15	30.3%	Urban population	61.7%
Pop. over 60	7.3%		per 1,000 pop.
No. of men per 100 women	97.3	Crude birth rate	22.1
Human Development Index	68.3	Crude death rate	15.1

The economy

GDP	R2,284bn	GDP per head	$5,680
GDP	$276bn	GDP per head in purchasing	
Av. ann. growth in real		power parity (USA=100)	21.8
GDP 2003–08	4.9%	Economic freedom index	62.8

Origins of GDP		**Components of GDP**	
	% of total		% of total
Agriculture	3	Private consumption	60
Industry, of which:	34	Public consumption	20
manufacturing	19	Investment	23
Services	63	Exports	35
		Imports	-38

Structure of employment

	% of total		% of labour force
Agriculture	8	Unemployed 2008	22.9
Industry	25	Av. ann. rate 1995–2008	24.2
Services	67		

Energy

	m TOE		
Total output	159.6	Net energy imports as %	
Total consumption	134.3	of energy use	-19
Consumption per head,			
kg oil equivalent	2,807		

Inflation and finance

Consumer price		av. ann. increase 2003–08	
inflation 2009	7.1%	Narrow money (M1)	13.6%
Av. ann. inflation 2004–09	6.7%	Broad money	19.0%
Money market rate, 2009	8.15%		

Exchange rates

	end 2009		December 2009
R per $	7.38	Effective rates	2005 = 100
R per SDR	11.57	– nominal	78.6
R per €	10.63	– real	99.7

Trade

Principal exports		Principal imports	
	$bn fob		*$bn cif*
Platinum	9.7	Petrochemicals	15.0
Ferro-alloys	6.3	Motor vehicle components	5.8
Gold	5.5	Petroleum oils & other	3.3
Coal	4.7	Cars & other vehicles	2.8
Cars & other components	4.5	Telecoms components	2.7
Total incl. others	**77.5**	Total incl. others	**90.4**

Main export destinations		Main origins of imports	
	% of total		*% of total*
Japan	10.0	Germany	12.5
United States	10.0	China	12.4
Germany	7.2	United States	8.8
United Kingdom	6.1	Saudi Arabia	7.0

Balance of payments, reserves and debt, $bn

Visible exports fob	86.1	Change in reserves	1.1
Visible imports fob	-90.6	Level of reserves	
Trade balance	-4.4	end Dec.	34.1
Invisibles inflows	18.3	No. months of import cover	3.3
Invisibles outflows	-32.1	Official gold holdings, m oz	4.0
Net transfers	-3.0	Foreign debt	41.9
Current account balance	-21.0	– as % of GDP	16
– as % of GDP	-7.6	– as % of total exports	46
Capital balance	12.5	Debt service ratio	4
Overall balance	2.2		

Health and education

Health spending, % of GDP	8.6	Education spending, % of GDP	5.7
Doctors per 1,000 pop.	0.8	Enrolment, %: primary	104
Hospital beds per 1,000 pop.	2.8	secondary	95
Improved-water source access,		tertiary	...
% of pop.	91		

Society

No. of households	13.4m	Colour TVs per 100 households	66.0
Av. no. per household	3.6	Telephone lines per 100 pop.	8.9
Marriages per 1,000 pop.	3.9	Mobile telephone subscribers	
Divorces per 1,000 pop.	1.0	per 100 pop.	90.6
Cost of living, Feb. 2010		Computers per 100 pop.	8.5
New York = 100	76	Internet hosts per 1,000 pop.	69.8

SOUTH KOREA

Area	99,274 sq km	Capital	Seoul
Arable as % of total land	16	Currency	Won (W)

People

Population	48.4m	Life expectancy: men	76.6 yrs
Pop. per sq km	487.5	women	83.2 yrs
Av. ann. growth		Adult literacy	...
in pop. 2010–15	0.39%	Fertility rate (per woman)	1.2
Pop. under 15	16.2%	Urban population	83.0%
Pop. over 60	15.6%		per 1,000 pop.
No. of men per 100 women	98.1	Crude birth rate	9.5
Human Development Index	93.7	Crude death rate	6.3

The economy

GDP	W1,024trn	GDP per head	$19,120
GDP	$929bn	GDP per head in purchasing	
Av. ann. growth in real		power parity (USA=100)	59.7
GDP 2003–08	4.2%	Economic freedom index	69.9

Origins of GDP		Components of GDP	
	% of total		% of total
Agriculture	3	Private consumption	55
Industry, of which:	37	Public consumption	15
manufacturing	28	Investment	31
Services	60	Exports	53
		Imports	-54

Structure of employment

	% of total		% of labour force
Agriculture	7	Unemployed 2008	3.2
Industry	27	Av. ann. rate 1995–2008	3.7
Services	66		

Energy

	m TOE		
Total output	42.5	Net energy imports as %	
Total consumption	222.2	of energy use	81
Consumption per head,			
kg oil equivalent	4,586		

Inflation and finance

		av. ann. increase 2003–08	
Consumer price			
inflation 2009	2.8%	Narrow money (M1)	7.1%
Av. ann. inflation 2004–09	3.0%	Broad money	4.5%
Money market rate, 2009	1.98%	Household saving rate, 2009	3.9%

Exchange rates

	end 2009		December 2009
W per $	1,165	Effective rates	2005 = 100
W per SDR	1,826	– nominal	...
W per €	1,677	– real	75.6

Trade

Principal exports		Principal imports	
	$bn fob		*$bn cif*
Information & communications		Crude petroleum	84.9
products	54.9	Machinery & equipment	48.8
Semiconductors	43.5	Chemicals	36.6
Chemicals	42.2	Semiconductors	34.8
Machinery & equipment	40.1		
Total incl. others	**422.0**	Total incl. others	**435.3**

Main export destinations		Main origins of imports	
	% of total		*% of total*
China	21.7	China	17.7
United States	11.0	Japan	14.0
Japan	6.7	United States	8.8
Hong Kong	4.7	Germany	3.4

Balance of payments, reserves and debt, $bn

Visible exports fob	433.4	Change in reserves	-61.0
Visible imports fob	-427.4	Level of reserves	
Trade balance	6.0	end Dec.	201.5
Invisibles inflows	98.7	No. months of import cover	4.5
Invisibles outflows	-110.3	Official gold holdings, m oz	0.5
Net transfers	-0.8	Foreign debt	382.3
Current account balance	-6.4	– as % of GDP	41
– as % of GDP	-0.7	– as % of total exports	71
Capital balance	-50.8	Debt service ratio	9
Overall balance	-56.4	Aid given	0.80
		% of GDP	0.09

Health and education

Health spending, % of GDP	6.3	Education spending, % of GDP	4.9
Doctors per 1,000 pop.	1.4	Enrolment, %: primary	104
Hospital beds per 1,000 pop.	7.1	secondary	97
Improved-water source access,		tertiary	96
% of pop.	98		

Society

No. of households	17.5m	Colour TVs per 100 households	99.4
Av. no. per household	2.8	Telephone lines per 100 pop.	44.3
Marriages per 1,000 pop.	7.1	Mobile telephone subscribers	
Divorces per 1,000 pop.	4.4	per 100 pop.	94.7
Cost of living, Feb. 2010		Computers per 100 pop.	57.6
New York = 100	92	Internet hosts per 1,000 pop.	6.1

SPAIN

Area	504,782 sq km	Capital	Madrid
Arable as % of total land	25	Currency	Euro (€)

People

Population	44.6m	Life expectancy: men	78.6 yrs
Pop. per sq km	88.3	women	84.7 yrs
Av. ann. growth		Adult literacy	97.9%
in pop. 2010–15	1.02%	Fertility rate (per woman)	1.4
Pop. under 15	14.9%	Urban population	77.4%
Pop. over 60	22.4%		per 1,000 pop.
No. of men per 100 women	97.4	Crude birth rate	11.0
Human Development Index	95.5	Crude death rate	8.9

The economy

GDP	€1,095bn	GDP per head	$35,220
GDP	$1,604bn	GDP per head in purchasing	
Av. ann. growth in real		power parity (USA=100)	68.3
GDP 2003–08	3.1%	Economic freedom index	69.6

Origins of GDP		Components of GDP	
	% of total		% of total
Agriculture	3	Private consumption	57
Industry, of which:	29	Public consumption	19
manufacturing	15	Investment	30
Services	68	Exports	26
		Imports	-32

Structure of employment

	% of total		% of labour force
Agriculture	4	Unemployed 2008	11.3
Industry	28	Av. ann. rate 1995–2008	14.2
Services	68		

Energy

	m TOE		
Total output	30.3	Net energy imports as %	
Total consumption	144.0	of energy use	79
Consumption per head,			
kg oil equivalent	3,208		

Inflation and finance

Consumer price		*av. ann. increase 2003–08*	
inflation 2009	-0.4%	Euro area:	
Av. ann. inflation 2004–09	2.7%	Narrow money (M1)	8.2%
Money market rate, 2009	0.68%	Broad money	8.8%
		Household saving rate[a], 2009	17.8%

Exchange rates

	end 2009		December 2009
€ per $	0.69	Effective rates	2005 = 100
€ per SDR	1.09	– nominal	104.4
		– real	107.3

Trade

Principal exports		Principal imports	
	$bn fob		*$bn cif*
Machinery & transport equip.	99.6	Machinery & transport equip.	135.2
Food, drink & tobacco	36.0	Mineral fuels & lubricants	80.2
Chemicals & related products	36.0	Chemicals & related products	49.8
Mineral fuels & lubricants	20.8	Food, drink & tobacco	34.5
Total incl. others	**277.5**	Total incl. others	**416.7**

Main export destinations		Main origins of imports	
	% of total		*% of total*
France	18.7	Germany	14.9
Germany	10.7	France	12.1
Portugal	9.2	Italy	8.1
EU27	69.6	EU27	59.3

Balance of payments, reserves and aid, $bn

Visible exports fob	285.9	Overall balance	0.7
Visible imports fob	-415.5	Change in reserves	1.3
Trade balance	-129.6	Level of reserves	
Invisibles inflows	233.2	end Dec.	20.3
Invisibles outflows	-243.9	No. months of import cover	0.4
Net transfers	-13.8	Official gold holdings, m oz	9.1
Current account balance	-154.1	Aid given	6.87
– as % of GDP	-9.6	– as % of GDP	0.43
Capital balance	150.7		

Health and education

Health spending, % of GDP	8.5	Education spending, % of GDP	4.4
Doctors per 1,000 pop.	3.8	Enrolment, %: primary	105
Hospital beds per 1,000 pop.	3.4	secondary	119
Improved-water source access,		tertiary	68
% of pop.	100		

Society

No. of households	17.1m	Colour TVs per 100 households	99.4
Av. no. per household	2.6	Telephone lines per 100 pop.	45.4
Marriages per 1,000 pop.	4.8	Mobile telephone subscribers	
Divorces per 1,000 pop.	1.1	per 100 pop.	111.7
Cost of living, Feb. 2010		Computers per 100 pop.	39.3
New York = 100	116	Internet hosts per 1,000 pop.	85.1

a Gross.

SWEDEN

Area	449,964 sq km	Capital	Stockholm
Arable as % of total land	6	Currency	Swedish krona (Skr)

People

Population	9.2m	Life expectancy: men	79.6 yrs
Pop. per sq km	20.4	women	83.6 yrs
Av. ann. growth		Adult literacy	...
In pop. 2010–15	0.49%	Fertility rate (per woman)	1.9
Pop. under 15	16.5%	Urban population	84.7%
Pop. over 60	25.0%		per 1,000 pop.
No. of men per 100 women	98.6	Crude birth rate	11.7
Human Development Index	96.3	Crude death rate	9.8

The economy

GDP	Skr3,157bn	GDP per head	$51,950
GDP	$479bn	GDP per head in purchasing	
Av. ann. growth in real		power parity (USA=100)	79.7
GDP 2003–08	2.8%	Economic freedom index	72.4

Origins of GDP		**Components of GDP**	
	% of total		% of total
Agriculture	2	Private consumption	46
Industry, of which:	28	Public consumption	26
manufacturing	20	Investment	20
Services	70	Exports	54
		Imports	-47

Structure of employment

	% of total		% of labour force
Agriculture	2	Unemployed 2008	6.2
Industry	22	Av. ann. rate 1995–2008	6.3
Services	76		

Energy

	m TOE		
Total output	33.6	Net energy imports as %	
Total consumption	50.4	of energy use	33
Consumption per head,			
kg oil equivalent	5,512		

Inflation and finance

			av. ann. increase 2003–08
Consumer price			
inflation 2009	-0.3%	Narrow money	10.4%
Av. ann. inflation 2004–09	1.4%	Broad money	11.6%
Repurchase rate, end 2009	0.25%	Household saving rate, 2009	14.5%

Exchange rates

	end 2009		December 2009
Skr per $	7.12	Effective rates	2005 = 100
Skr per SDR	11.16	– nominal	94.1
Skr per €	10.26	– real	92.8

Trade

Principal exports		**Principal imports**	
	$bn fob		*$bn cif*
Machinery & transport equipment	76.3	Machinery & transport equipment	60.2
Chemicals & related products	19.9	Fuels & lubricants	24.2
Mineral fuels & lubricants	14.4	Chemicals & related products	18.6
Raw materials	11.1	Food, drink & tobacco	12.5
Total incl. others	**183.9**	Total incl. others	**169.0**

Main export destinations		**Main origins of imports**	
	% of total		*% of total*
Germany	10.4	Germany	17.4
Norway	9.5	Denmark	9.3
United States	6.6	Norway	8.5
Denmark	7.4	United Kingdom	6.2
United Kingdom	7.4	Finland	5.7
EU27	60.1	EU27	68.9

Balance of payments, reserves and aid, $bn

Visible exports fob	185.9	Overall balance	1.3
Visible imports fob	-167.8	Change in reserves	-1.3
Trade balance	18.1	Level of reserves	
Invisibles inflows	146.4	end Dec.	29.7
Invisibles outflows	-117.8	No. months of import cover	1.2
Net transfers	-6.3	Official gold holdings, m oz	4.4
Current account balance	40.3	Aid given	4.73
– as % of GDP	8.4	– as % of GDP	0.99
Capital balance	6.9		

Health and education

Health spending, % of GDP	9.1	Education spending, % of GDP	7.6
Doctors per 1,000 pop.	3.6	Enrolment, %: primary	94
Hospital beds per 1,000 pop.	...	secondary	103
Improved-water source access,		tertiary	75
% of pop.	100		

Society

No. of households	4.5m	Colour TVs per 100 households	97.7
Av. no. per household	2.0	Telephone lines per 100 pop.	57.8
Marriages per 1,000 pop.	5.0	Mobile telephone subscribers	
Divorces per 1,000 pop.	2.1	per 100 pop.	118.3
Cost of living, Feb. 2010		Computers per 100 pop.	88.1
New York = 100	104	Internet hosts per 1,000 pop.	464.9

SWITZERLAND

Area	41,293 sq km	Capital	Berne
Arable as % of total land	10	Currency	Swiss franc (SFr)

People

Population	7.5m	Life expectancy: men	80.2 yrs
Pop. per sq km	181.6	women	84.7 yrs
Av. ann. growth		Adult literacy	...
in pop. 2010–15	0.41%	Fertility rate (per woman)	1.5
Pop. under 15	15.2%	Urban population	73.6%
Pop. over 60	23.3%		per 1,000 pop.
No. of men per 100 women	95.4	Crude birth rate	9.7
Human Development Index	96.0	Crude death rate	8.5

The economy

GDP	SFr533bn	GDP per head	$64,330
GDP	$492bn	GDP per head in purchasing	
Av. ann. growth in real		power parity (USA=100)	91.5
GDP 2003–08	2.8%	Economic freedom index	81.1

Origins of GDP		**Components of GDP**	
	% of total		% of total
Agriculture	1	Private consumption	58
Industry, of which:	28	Public consumption	11
manufacturing	20	Investment	22
Services	71	Exports	56
		Imports	-47

Structure of employment

	% of total		% of labour force
Agriculture	4	Unemployed 2008	3.4
Industry	22	Av. ann. rate 1995–2008	3.6
Services	74		

Energy

	m TOE		
Total output	12.6	Net energy imports as %	
Total consumption	25.7	of energy use	51
Consumption per head,			
kg oil equivalent	3,406		

Inflation and finance

Consumer price		av. ann. increase 2003–08	
inflation 2009	-0.5%	Narrow money (M1)	4.2%
Av. ann. inflation 2004–09	1.0%	Broad money	4.2%
Money market rate, 2009	0.05%	Household saving rate, 2009	14.3%

Exchange rates

	end 2009		December 2009
SFr per $	1.03	Effective rates	2005 = 100
SFr per SDR	1.62	– nominal	108.3
SFr per €	1.48	– real	104.1

Trade

Principal exports		Principal imports	
	$bn		*$bn*
Chemicals	66.4	Chemicals	35.3
Machinery , equipment & electronics	40.4	Machinery, equipment & electronics	32.9
Watches & jewellery	35.1	Metals	16.7
Metals & metal manufactures	14.1	Motor vehicles	16.1
Total incl. others	**191.4**	Total incl. others	**173.3**

Main export destinations		Main origins of imports	
	% of total		*% of total*
Germany	20.6	Germany	35.2
United States	10.0	Italy	11.6
Italy	9.1	France	10.0
France	9.0	United States	6.1
United Kingdom	5.4	Netherlands	4.8
Spain	3.6	Austria	4.2
Japan	3.4	United Kingdom	3.9
EU27	61.0	EU27	78.8

Balance of payments, reserves and aid, $bn

Visible exports fob	241.2	Overall balance	3.2
Visible imports fob	-227.7	Change in reserves	-1.0
Trade balance	13.5	Level of reserves	
Invisibles inflows	162.6	end Dec.	74.1
Invisibles outflows	-156.5	No. months of import cover	2.3
Net transfers	-12.7	Official gold holdings, m oz	33.4
Current account balance	6.9	Aid given	2.04
– as % of GDP	1.4	– as % of GDP	0.41
Capital balance	-18.5		

Health and education

Health spending, % of GDP	10.8	Education spending, % of GDP	5.6
Doctors per 1,000 pop.	4.0	Enrolment, %: primary	102
Hospital beds per 1,000 pop.	5.5	secondary	96
Improved-water source access, % of pop.	100	tertiary	47

Society

No. of households	3.4m	Colour TVs per 100 households	94.6
Av. no. per household	2.2	Telephone lines per 100 pop.	64.1
Marriages per 1,000 pop.	5.1	Mobile telephone subscribers	
Divorces per 1,000 pop.	2.7	per 100 pop.	118.0
Cost of living, Feb. 2010		Computers per 100 pop.	96.2
New York = 100	124	Internet hosts per 1,000 pop.	612.9

TAIWAN

Area	36,179 sq km	Capital	Taipei
Arable as % of total land	25	Currency	Taiwan dollar (T$)

People

Population	22.9m	Life expectancy:[a] men	75.1 yrs
Pop. per sq km	633.0	women	81.1 yrs
Av. ann. growth		Adult literacy	96.1%
in pop. 2010–15	0.10%	Fertility rate (per woman)	1.10
Pop. under 15	16.7%	Urban population	...
Pop. over 60	14.5%		per 1,000 pop.
No. of men per 100 women	101	Crude birth rate	9.0
Human Development Index	...	Crude death rate[a]	6.8

The economy

GDP	T$12,341bn	GDP per head	$17,050
GDP	$403bn	GDP per head in purchasing	
Av. ann. growth in real		power parity (USA=100)	64.3
GDP 2003–08	4.6%	Economic freedom index	70.4

Origins of GDP		Components of GDP	
	% of total		% of total
Agriculture	2	Private consumption	60
Industry, of which:	25	Public consumption	12
manufacturing	21	Investment	23
Services	71	Exports	73
		Imports	-68

Structure of employment

	% of total		% of labour force
Agriculture	5	Unemployed 2008	5.1
Industry	37	Av. ann. rate 1995–2008	3.4
Services	59		

Energy

	m TOE		
Total output	...	Net energy imports as %	
Total consumption	...	of energy use	...
Consumption per head,			
kg oil equivalent	...		

Inflation and finance

		av. ann. increase 2003–08	
Consumer price			
inflation 2009	-0.9%	Narrow money (M1)	4.5%
Av. ann. inflation 2004–09	1.5%	Broad money	5.4%
Interbank rate, 2009	0.12%		

Exchange rates

	end 2009		December 2009
T$ per $	32.24	Effective rates	2005 = 100
T$ per SDR	50.71	– nominal	...
T$ per €	46.44	– real	...

Trade

Principal exports		**Principal imports**	
	$bn fob		*$bn cif*
Electronic products	42.1	Intermediate goods	189.9
Base metals	28.2	Capital goods	32.7
Information & communications		Consumer goods	16.9
products	22.0		
Textiles & clothing	10.9		
Total incl. others	**243.8**	Total incl. others	**239.5**

Main export destinations		**Main origins of imports**	
	% of total		*% of total*
China	27.4	Japan	19.4
Hong Kong	13.4	China	13.1
United States	12.6	United States	11.0
Japan	7.2	South Korea	5.5

Balance of payments, reserves and debt, $bn

Visible exports fob	254.9	Change in reserves	21.4
Visible imports fob	-236.8	Level of reserves	
Trade balance	18.2	end Dec.	291.7
Invisibles inflows	57.7	No. months of import cover	12.3
Invisibles outflows	-47.9	Official gold holdings, m oz	0.0
Net transfers	-3.0	Foreign debt	90.4
Current account balance	25.0	– as % of GDP	22
– as % of GDP	6.4	– as % of total exports	29
Capital balance	-2.1	Debt service ratio	3
Overall balance	26.3	Aid given	0.44
		% of GDP	0.11

Health and education

Health spending, % of GDP	...	Education spending, % of GDP	...
Doctors per 1,000 pop.	...	Enrolment, %: primary	...
Hospital beds per 1,000 pop.	...	secondary	...
Improved-water source access,		tertiary	...
% of pop.	...		

Society

No. of households	7.5m	Colour TVs per 100 households	99.4
Av. no. per household	3.1	Telephone lines per 100 pop.	62.0
Marriages per 1,000 pop.	7.4	Mobile telephone subscribers	
Divorces per 1,000 pop.	3.5	per 100 pop.	110.3
Cost of living, Feb. 2010		Computers per 100 pop.	...
New York = 100	83	Internet hosts per 1,000 pop.	272.0

a 2002 estimate.

THAILAND

Area	513,115 sq km	Capital	Bangkok
Arable as % of total land	30	Currency	Baht (Bt)

People

Population	64.3m	Life expectancy: men	67.1 yrs
Pop. per sq km	125.3	women	72.8 yrs
Av. ann. growth		Adult literacy	93.5%
in pop. 2010–15	0.65%	Fertility rate (per woman)	1.8
Pop. under 15	21.5%	Urban population	34.0%
Pop. over 60	11.7%		per 1,000 pop.
No. of men per 100 women	96.7	Crude birth rate	14.6
Human Development Index	78.3	Crude death rate	9.1

The economy

GDP	Bt9,075bn	GDP per head	$4,040
GDP	$272bn	GDP per head in purchasing	
Av. ann. growth in real		power parity (USA=100)	17.4
GDP 2003–08	4.7%	Economic freedom index	64.1

Origins of GDP		Components of GDP	
	% of total		% of total
Agriculture	12	Private consumption	56
Industry, of which:	44	Public consumption	12
manufacturing	35	Investment	29
Services	44	Exports	77
		Imports	-74

Structure of employment

	% of total		% of labour force
Agriculture	42	Unemployed 2008	1.4
Industry	20	Av. ann. rate 1995–2008	1.8
Services	38		

Energy

	m TOE		
Total output	59.4	Net energy imports as %	
Total consumption	104.0	of energy use	43
Consumption per head,			
kg oil equivalent	1,553		

Inflation and finance

Consumer price		av. ann. increase 2003–08	
inflation 2009	-0.8%	Narrow money (M1)	6.8%
Av. ann. inflation 2004–09	3.2%	Broad money	7.0%
Money market rate, 2009	1.21%		

Exchange rates

	end 2009		December 2009
Bt per $	33.32	Effective rates	2005 = 100
Bt per SDR	52.24	– nominal	...
Bt per €	48.00	– real	...

Trade

Principal exports		Principal imports	
	$bn fob		$bn cif
Machinery & mech. appliances	25.3	Fuel & lubricants	37.1
Vehicle parts & accessories	16.7	Minerals & metal products	26.8
Integrated circuits & parts	15.5	Electronic parts	15.2
Electrical appliances	12.0	Industry machinery,	
		tools & parts	11.6
Total incl. others	**175.9**	Total incl. others	**178.7**

Main export destinations		Main origins of imports	
	% of total		% of total
Japan	11.2	Japan	18.8
United States	11.2	China	11.2
China	9.1	United States	6.4
Singapore	5.6	United Arab Emirates	6.0

Balance of payments, reserves and debt, $bn

Visible exports fob	175.3	Change in reserves	23.5
Visible imports fob	-157.3	Level of reserves	
Trade balance	17.9	end Dec.	111.0
Invisibles inflows	40.7	No. months of import cover	6.0
Invisibles outflows	-63.5	Official gold holdings, m oz	2.7
Net transfers	4.8	Foreign debt	64.8
Current account balance	-0.1	– as % of GDP	32
– as % of GDP	-0.0	– as % of total exports	32
Capital balance	12.6	Debt service ratio	8
Overall balance	24.4	Aid given	0.18
		– as % of GDP	0.07

Health and education

Health spending, % of GDP	3.7	Education spending, % of GDP	5.2
Doctors per 1,000 pop.	...	Enrolment, %: primary	77
Hospital beds per 1,000 pop.	...	secondary	83
Improved-water source access,		tertiary	46
% of pop.	98		

Society

No. of households	18.0m	Colour TVs per 100 households	96.1
Av. no. per household	3.6	Telephone lines per 100 pop.	10.4
Marriages per 1,000 pop.	4.4	Mobile telephone subscribers	
Divorces per 1,000 pop.	1.1	per 100 pop.	92.0
Cost of living, Feb. 2010		Computers per 100 pop.	7.0
New York = 100	79	Internet hosts per 1,000 pop.	19.9

TURKEY

Area	779,452 sq km	Capital	Ankara
Arable as % of total land	28	Currency	Turkish Lira (YTL)

People

Population	75.8m	Life expectancy: men	70.3 yrs
Pop. per sq km	97.2	women	75.2 yrs
Av. ann. growth		Adult literacy	88.7%
in pop. 2010–15	1.24%	Fertility rate (per woman)	2.1
Pop. under 15	26.4%	Urban population	69.6%
Pop. over 60	9.0%		per 1,000 pop.
No. of men per 100 women	100.9	Crude birth rate	18.4
Human Development Index	80.6	Crude death rate	6.1

The economy

GDP	YTL950bn	GDP per head	$9,940
GDP	$735bn	GDP per head in purchasing	
Av. ann. growth in real		power parity (USA=100)	28.9
GDP 2003–08	6.0%	Economic freedom index	63.8

Origins of GDP		**Components of GDP**	
	% of total		% of total
Agriculture	9	Private consumption	70
Industry, of which:	28	Public consumption	13
manufacturing	18	Investment	22
Services	64	Exports	24
		Imports	-28

Structure of employment

	% of total		% of labour force
Agriculture	26	Unemployed 2008	9.4
Industry	26	Av. ann. rate 1995–2008	8.6
Services	48		

Energy

	m TOE		
Total output	27.3	Net energy imports as %	
Total consumption	100.0	of energy use	73
Consumption per head,			
kg oil equivalent	1,370		

Inflation and finance

			av. ann. increase 2003–08
Consumer price			
inflation 2009	6.3%	Narrow money (M1)	30.0%
Av. ann. inflation 2004–09	9.2%	Broad money	23.6%
Money market rate, 2009	9.24%		

Exchange rates

	end 2009		December 2009
YTL per $	1.49	Effective rates	2005 = 100
YTL per SDR	2.34	– nominal	...
YTL per €	2.15	– real	...

Trade

Principal exports		Principal imports	
	$bn fob		*$bn cif*
Textiles & clothing	23.0	Fuels	48.3
Transport equipment	20.9	Chemicals	25.5
Iron & steel	16.8	Mechanical machinery	21.0
Agricultural products	9.1	Transport equipment	15.2
Total incl. others	**132.0**	Total incl. others	**202.0**

Main export destinations		Main origins of imports	
	% of total		*% of total*
Germany	9.8	Russia	15.5
United Kingdom	6.2	Germany	9.3
United Arab Emirates	6.0	China	7.8
Italy	5.9	United States	5.9
France	5.0	Italy	5.5
EU27	48.2	EU27	37.3

Balance of payments, reserves and debt, $bn

Visible exports fob	141.0	Change in reserves	-2.8
Visible imports fob	-193.8	Level of reserves	
Trade balance	-52.8	end Dec.	73.7
Invisibles inflows	41.9	No. months of import cover	3.9
Invisibles outflows	-32.3	Official gold holdings, m oz	3.7
Net transfers	2.0	Foreign debt	277.3
Current account balance	-41.3	– as % of GDP	35
– as % of GDP	-5.6	– as % of total exports	170
Capital balance	33.4	Debt service ratio	30
Overall balance	-2.8	Aid given	0.78
		% of GDP	0.11

Health and education

Health spending, % of GDP	5.0	Education spending, % of GDP	3.7
Doctors per 1,000 pop.	1.5	Enrolment, %: primary	98
Hospital beds per 1,000 pop.	2.8	secondary	82
Improved-water source access,		tertiary	37
% of pop.	99		

Society

No. of households	17.8m	Colour TVs per 100 households	92.8
Av. no. per household	4.3	Telephone lines per 100 pop.	23.7
Marriages per 1,000 pop.	6.4	Mobile telephone subscribers	
Divorces per 1,000 pop.	0.8	per 100 pop.	89.1
Cost of living, Feb. 2010		Computers per 100 pop.	6.1
New York = 100	98	Internet hosts per 1,000 pop.	39.9

UKRAINE

Area	603,700 sq km	Capital	Kiev
Arable as % of total land	56	Currency	Hryvnya (UAH)

People

Population	45.9m	Life expectancy: men		63.9 yrs
Pop. per sq km	76.0		women	74.3 yrs
Av. ann. growth		Adult literacy		99.7%
in pop. 2010–15	-0.65%	Fertility rate (per woman)		1.3
Pop. under 15	13.9%	Urban population		68.8%
Pop. over 60	20.9%			per 1,000 pop.
No. of men per 100 women	85.5	Crude birth rate		9.9
Human Development Index	79.6	Crude death rate		16.1

The economy

GDP	UAH950bn	GDP per head	$3,900
GDP	$180bn	GDP per head in purchasing	
Av. ann. growth in real		power parity (USA=100)	15.7
GDP 2003–08	6.4%	Economic freedom index	46.4

Origins of GDP		Components of GDP	
	% of total		% of total
Agriculture	8	Private consumption	64
Industry, of which:	37	Public consumption	17
manufacturing	23	Investment	25
Services	55	Exports	42
		Imports	-48

Structure of employment

	% of total		% of labour force
Agriculture	17	Unemployed 2008	6.4
Industry	24	Av. ann. rate 1995–2008	8.8
Services	59		

Energy

	m TOE		
Total output	81.6	Net energy imports as %	
Total consumption	137.3	of energy use	41
Consumption per head,			
kg oil equivalent	2,953		

Inflation and finance

		av. ann. increase 2003–08	
Consumer price			
inflation 2009	15.9%	Narrow money (M1)	34.3%
Av. ann. inflation 2004–09	15.2%	Broad money	40.2%
Money market rate, 2009	12.64%		

Exchange rates

	end 2009		December 2009
			2005 = 100
UAH per $	7.99	Effective rates	
UAH per SDR	12.52	– nominal	61.0
UAH per €	11.51	– real	92.9

Trade

Principal exports		Principal imports	
	$bn fob		$bn cif
Metals	27.6	Machinery & equipment	26.7
Machinery & equipment	10.9	Fuels, mineral products	25.4
Food & agricultural produce	10.8	Chemicals	7.0
Fuels & mineral products	7.0	Food & agricultural produce	6.5
Chemicals	5.0		
Total incl. others	**67.0**	Total incl. others	**85.5**

Main export destinations		Main origins of imports	
	% of total		% of total
Russia	23.5	Russia	23.2
Turkey	6.9	Germany	8.5
Italy	4.4	Turkmenistan	6.7
Poland	3.5	China	5.1

Balance of payments, reserves and debt, $bn

Visible exports fob	67.7	Change in reserves	-0.9
Visible imports fob	-83.8	Level of reserves	
Trade balance	-16.1	end Dec.	31.5
Invisibles inflows	23.3	No. months of import cover	3.5
Invisibles outflows	-23.2	Official gold holdings, m oz	0.9
Net transfers	3.1	Foreign debt	92.5
Current account balance	-12.8	– as % of GDP	52
– as % of GDP	-7.1	– as % of total exports	124
Capital balance	9.2	Debt service ratio	19
Overall balance	-3.0		

Health and education

Health spending, % of GDP	6.9	Education spending, % of GDP	4.2
Doctors per 1,000 pop.	3.1	Enrolment, %: primary	98
Hospital beds per 1,000 pop.	8.7	secondary	94
Improved-water source access,		tertiary	79
% of pop.	98		

Society

No. of households	20.0m	Colour TVs per 100 households	92.7
Av. no. per household	2.3	Telephone lines per 100 pop.	28.7
Marriages per 1,000 pop.	5.7	Mobile telephone subscribers	
Divorces per 1,000 pop.	3.5	per 100 pop.	121.1
Cost of living, Feb. 2010		Computers per 100 pop.	4.5
New York = 100	58	Internet hosts per 1,000 pop.	22.4

UNITED ARAB EMIRATES

Area	83,600 sq km	Capital	Abu Dhabi
Arable as % of total land	1	Currency	Dirham (AED)

People

Population	4.5m	Life expectancy: men	77.3 yrs
Pop. per sq km	53.8	women	79.5 yrs
Av. ann. growth		Adult literacy	90.0%
in pop. 2010–15	2.82%	Fertility rate (per woman)	1.9
Pop. under 15	19.1%	Urban population	84.1%
Pop. over 60	2.0%		per 1,000 pop.
No. of men per 100 women	203.6	Crude birth rate	14.0
Human Development Index	90.3	Crude death rate	1.5

The economy

GDP	AED1,054bn	GDP per head	$63,970
GDP	$287bn	GDP per head in purchasing	
Av. ann. growth in real		power parity (USA=100)[a]	122.1
GDP 2003–08	7.5%	Economic freedom index	67.3

Origins of GDP		Components of GDP	
	% of total		% of total
Agriculture	2	Private consumption	44
Industry, of which:	61	Public consumption	10
manufacturing	12	Investment	21
Services	38	Exports	91
		Imports	-67

Structure of employment

	% of total		% of labour force
Agriculture	8	Unemployed 2005	3.1
Industry	22	Av. ann. rate 1995–2005	2.4
Services	70		

Energy

			m TOE
Total output	178.4	Net energy imports as %	
Total consumption	51.6	of energy use	-245
Consumption per head,			
kg oil equivalent	11,832		

Inflation and finance

Consumer price		av. ann. increase 2003-08	
inflation 2009	1.6%	Narrow money (M1)	29.0%
Av. ann. inflation 2004–09	8.0%	Broad money	27.4%
Interbank rate, end 2009	1.89%		

Exchange rates

	end 2009		December 2009
AED per $	3.67	Effective rates	2005 = 100
AED per SDR	5.76	– nominal	95.3
AED per €	5.29	– real	...

Trade

Principal exports

	$bn fob
Re-exports	94.2
Crude oil	85.4
Gas	9.3
Total incl. others	**239.2**

Principal imports[a]

	$bn cif
Machinery & electrical equip.	36.2
Precious stones & metals	28.6
Transport equipment	20.0
Total incl. others	**200.3**

Main export destinations

	% of total
Japan	22.7
South Korea	9.3
Thailand	9.1
India	6.4

Main origins of imports

	% of total
China	12.9
India	12.0
United States	8.7
Germany	6.4

Balance of payments, reserves and debt, $bn

Visible exports fob	239.8	Change in reserves	-45.5
Visible imports fob	-176.3	Level of reserves	
Trade balance	63.5	end Dec.	31.7
Invisibles, net	-30.7	No. months of import cover	1.7
Net transfers	-10.6	Official gold holdings, m oz	0.0
Current account balance	22.2	Foreign debt	134.7
– as % of GDP	7.7	– as % of GDP	53
Capital balance	-55.3	– as % of total exports	51
Overall balance	-46.9	Debt service ratio	3
		Aid given	0.09
		% of GDP	0.03

Health and education

Health spending, % of GDP	2.7	Education spending, % of GDP	1.9
Doctors per 1,000 pop.	1.5	Enrolment, %: primary	108
Hospital beds per 1,000 pop.	1.9	secondary	94
Improved-water source access,		tertiary	25
% of pop.	100		

Society

No. of households	0.7m	Colour TVs per 100 households	99.8
Av. no. per household	6.3	Telephone lines per 100 pop.	33.6
Marriages per 1,000 pop.	3.6	Mobile telephone subscribers	
Divorces per 1,000 pop.	1.0	per 100 pop.	208.7
Cost of living, Feb. 2010		Computers per 100 pop.	33.1
New York = 100	75	Internet hosts per 1,000 pop.	84.3

a 2007

UNITED KINGDOM

Area	242,534 sq km	Capital	London
Arable as % of total land	25	Currency	Pound (£)

People

Population	61.0m	Life expectancy:	men	77.8 yrs
Pop. per sq km	251.5		women	82.3 yrs
Av. ann. growth		Adult literacy		...
in pop. 2010–15	0.54%	Fertility rate (per woman)		1.8
Pop. under 15	17.4%	Urban population		79.6%
Pop. over 60	22.7%			per 1,000 pop.
No. of men per 100 women	96.4	Crude birth rate		12.2
Human Development Index	94.7	Crude death rate		9.8

The economy

GDP	£1,443bn	GDP per head	$43,540
GDP	$2,674bn	GDP per head in purchasing	
Av. ann. growth in real		power parity (USA=100)	76.5
GDP 2003–08	2.2%	Economic freedom index	76.5

Origins of GDP		**Components of GDP**	
	% of total		% of total
Agriculture	1	Private consumption	64
Industry, of which:	24	Public consumption	22
manufacturing	...	Investment	17
Services	76	Exports	29
		Imports	-32

Structure of employment

	% of total		% of labour force
Agriculture	1	Unemployed 2008	5.6
Industry	21	Av. ann. rate 1995–2008	5.9
Services	78		

Energy

	m TOE		
Total output	176.2	Net energy imports as %	
Total consumption	211.3	of energy use	17
Consumption per head,			
kg oil equivalent	3,464		

Inflation and finance

Consumer price		av. ann. increase 2003–08	
inflation 2009	-0.6%	Narrow money	...
Av. ann. inflation 2004–09	2.7%	Broad money (M4)	12.4%
Money market rate, 2009	0.63%	Household saving rate[a], 2009	5.3%

Exchange rates

	end 2009		December 2009
£ per $	0.62	Effective rates	2005 = 100
£ per SDR	0.97	– nominal	79.1
£ per €	0.89	– real	82.8

Trade

Principal exports	$bn fob
Machinery & transport equip.	147.8
Chemicals & related products	80.1
Mineral fuels & lubricants	62.6
Food, drink & tobacco	24.9
Total incl. others	**462.6**

Principal imports	$bn fob
Machinery & transport equip.	200.8
Chemicals & related products	81.4
Mineral fuels & lubricants	70.9
Food, drink & tobacco	55.8
Total incl. others	**634.3**

Main export destinations	% of total
United States	13.8
Germany	11.4
Netherlands	7.8
France	7.5
Ireland	7.5
EU27	57.0

Main origins of imports	% of total
Germany	13.1
United States	8.7
China	7.5
Netherlands	7.4
France	6.8
EU27	53.3

Balance of payments, reserves and aid, $bn

Visible exports fob	466.8	Overall balance	-3.1
Visible imports fob	-640.9	Change in reserves	-4.3
Trade balance	-174.1	Level of reserves	
Invisibles inflows	788.1	end Dec.	53.0
Invisibles outflows	-632.8	No. months of import cover	0.5
Net transfers	-35.9	Official gold holdings, m oz	10.0
Current account balance	-44.7	Aid given	11.50
– as % of GDP	-1.7	– as % of GDP	0.43
Capital balance	56.0		

Health and education

Health spending, % of GDP	8.4	Education spending, % of GDP	4.8
Doctors per 1,000 pop.	2.1	Enrolment, %: primary	104
Hospital beds per 1,000 pop.	3.9	secondary	97
Improved-water source access,		tertiary	59
% of pop.	100		

Society

No. of households	27.0m	Colour TVs per 100 households	99.0
Av. no. per household	2.3	Telephone lines per 100 pop.	54.2
Marriages per 1,000 pop.	5.1	Mobile telephone subscribers	
Divorces per 1,000 pop.	2.9	per 100 pop.	126.3
Cost of living, Feb. 2010		Computers per 100 pop.	80.2
New York = 100	118	Internet hosts per 1,000 pop.	119.7

a Gross.

UNITED STATES

Area	9,372,610 sq km	Capital	Washington DC
Arable as % of total land	19	Currency	US dollar ($)

People

Population	308.8m	Life expectancy: men	77.7 yrs
Pop. per sq km	32.9	women	82.1 yrs
Av. ann. growth		Adult literacy	...
in pop. 2010–15	0.96%	Fertility rate (per woman)	2.1
Pop. under 15	20.2%	Urban population	82.3%
Pop. over 60	18.2%		per 1,000 pop.
No. of men per 100 women	97.5	Crude birth rate	14.2
Human Development Index	95.6	Crude death rate	7.8

The economy

GDP	$14,093bn	GDP per head	$46,350
Av. ann. growth in real		GDP per head in purchasing	
GDP 2003–08	2.4%	power parity (USA=100)	100
		Economic freedom index	78.0

Origins of GDP		**Components of GDP**	
	% of total		% of total
Agriculture	1	Private consumption	71
Industry, of which:	22	Public consumption	16
manufacturing	14	Non-government investment	18
Services[a]	77	Exports	12
		Imports	-17

Structure of employment

	% of total		% of labour force
Agriculture	2	Unemployed 2008	5.8
Industry	22	Av. ann. rate 1995–2008	5.1
Services	76		

Energy

	m TOE		
Total output	1,665.2	Net energy imports as %	
Total consumption	2,339.9	of energy use	29
Consumption per head,			
kg oil equivalent	7,766		

Inflation and finance

Consumer price		av. ann. increase 2003–08	
inflation 2009	-0.4%	Narrow money	4.0%
Av. ann. inflation 2004–09	2.6%	Broad money	8.6%
Fed funds rate, 2009	0.16%	Household saving rate, 2009	3.9%

Exchange rates

	end 2009		December 2009
$ per SDR	1.57	Effective rates	2005 = 100
$ per €	1.44	– nominal	91.3
		– real	92.8

Trade

Principal exports		Principal imports	
	$bn fob		*$bn fob*
Capital goods, excl. vehicles	457.7	Industrial supplies	779.5
Industrial supplies	388.0	Consumer goods, excl. vehicles	481.6
Consumer goods, excl. vehicles	161.3	Capital goods, excl. vehicles	453.7
Vehicles & products	121.5	Vehicles & products	233.8
Total incl. others	**1,287.4**	Total incl. others	**2,103.6**

Main export destinations		Main origins of imports	
	% of total		*% of total*
Canada	20.3	China	16.9
Mexico	11.8	Canada	16.1
China	5.6	Mexico	10.4
Japan	5.2	Japan	6.8
Germany	4.3	Germany	4.7
United Kingdom	4.2	United Kingdom	2.8
EU27	21.2	EU27	17.4

Balance of payments, reserves and aid, $bn

Visible exports fob	1,281.0	Overall balance	4.8
Visible imports fob	-2,117.3	Change in reserves	16.5
Trade balance	-836.3	Level of reserves	
Invisibles inflows	1,310.2	end Dec.	294.1
Invisibles outflows	-1,051.7	No. months of import cover	1.1
Net transfers	-128.4	Official gold holdings, m oz	261.5
Current account balance	-706.1	Aid given	26.84
– as % of GDP	-5.0	– as % of GDP	0.19
Capital balance	510.9		

Health and education

Health spending, % of GDP	15.7	Education spending, % of GDP	5.7
Doctors per 1,000 pop.	2.7	Enrolment, %: primary	98
Hospital beds per 1,000 pop.	3.1	secondary	94
Improved-water source access,		tertiary	82
% of pop.	99		

Society

No. of households	117.3m	Colour TVs per 100 households	98.9
Av. no. per household	2.6	Telephone lines per 100 pop.	49.6
Marriages per 1,000 pop.	7.7	Mobile telephone subscribers	
Divorces per 1,000 pop.	3.3	per 100 pop.	86.8
Cost of living, Feb. 2010		Computers per 100 pop.	80.6
New York = 100	100	Internet hosts per 1,000 pop.[b]	1,346.3

a Including utilities.
b Includes all hosts ending ".com", ".net" and ".org" which exaggerates the numbers.

VENEZUELA

Area	912,050 sq km	Capital	Caracas
Arable as % of total land	3	Currency	Bolivar (Bs)

People

Population	28.1m	Life expectancy:	men	71.8 yrs
Pop. per sq km	30.8		women	77.7 yrs
Av. ann. growth		Adult literacy		95.2%
in pop. 2010–15	1.66%	Fertility rate (per woman)		2.5
Pop. under 15	29.5%	Urban population		93.4%
Pop. over 60	8.6%			per 1,000 pop.
No. of men per 100 women	100.7	Crude birth rate		21.4
Human Development Index	84.4	Crude death rate		5.2

The economy

GDP	Bs674bn	GDP per head	$11,250
GDP	$314bn	GDP per head in purchasing	
Av. ann. growth in real		power parity (USA=100)	27.7
GDP 2003–08	10.2%	Economic freedom index	37.1

Origins of GDP		Components of GDP	
	% of total		% of total
Agriculture	4	Private consumption	54
Industry, of which:	37	Public consumption	11
manufacturing	16	Investment	25
Services	59	Exports	30
		Imports	-20

Structure of employment

	% of total		% of labour force
Agriculture	9	Unemployed 2008	7.4
Industry	21	Av. ann. rate 1995–2008	12.2
Services	70		

Energy

	m TOE		
Total output	183.8	Net energy imports as %	
Total consumption	63.7	of energy use	-188
Consumption per head,			
kg oil equivalent	2,319		

Inflation and finance

			av. ann. increase 2003–08
Consumer price			
inflation 2009	28.6%	Narrow money	52.3%
Av. ann. inflation 2004–09	21.5%	Broad money	43.5%
Money market rate, 2009	10.03%		

Exchange rates

	end 2009		December 2009
		Effective rates	2005 = 100
Bs per $	2.15		
Bs per SDR	3.36	– nominal	91.7
Bs per €	3.10	– real	204.2

Trade

Principal exports		Principal imports	
	$bn fob		*$bn fob*
Oil	89.1	Intermediate goods	23.4
Non-oil	6.0	Consumer goods	13.4
		Capital goods	11.1
Total incl. others	**95.1**	Total incl. others	**49.6**

Main export destinations		Main origins of imports	
	% of total		*% of total*
United States	50.3	United States	27.9
Netherlands Antilles	9.6	Colombia	13.5
China	5.9	Brazil	11.4
Spain	3.6	Mexico	7.4

Balance of payments, reserves and debt, $bn

Visible exports fob	95.1	Change in reserves	9.3
Visible imports fob	-49.5	Level of reserves	
Trade balance	45.7	end Dec.	43.1
Invisibles inflows	10.2	No. months of import cover	7.7
Invisibles outflows	-17.9	Official gold holdings, m oz	11.5
Net transfers	-0.6	Foreign debt	50.2
Current account balance	37.4	– as % of GDP	16
– as % of GDP	11.9	– as % of total exports	58
Capital balance	-24.6	Debt service ratio	6
Overall balance	9.5		

Health and education

Health spending, % of GDP	5.8	Education spending, % of GDP	3.7
Doctors per 1,000 pop.	1.4	Enrolment, %: primary	103
Hospital beds per 1,000 pop.	1.3	secondary	81
Improved-water source access,		tertiary	78
% of pop.	83		

Society

No. of households	6.2m	Colour TVs per 100 households	91.7
Av. no. per household	4.5	Telephone lines per 100 pop.	22.4
Marriages per 1,000 pop.	2.6	Mobile telephone subscribers	
Divorces per 1,000 pop.	0.9	per 100 pop.	96.3
Cost of living, Feb. 2010		Computers per 100 pop.	9.3
New York = 100	125	Internet hosts per 1,000 pop.	6.8

VIETNAM

Area	331,114 sq km	Capital	Hanoi
Arable as % of total land	20	Currency	Dong (D)

People

Population	88.5m	Life expectancy: men	73.3 yrs
Pop. per sq km	267.3	women	77.4 yrs
Av. ann. growth		Adult literacy	92.5%
in pop. 2010–15	1.15%	Fertility rate (per woman)	2.1
Pop. under 15	25.1%	Urban population	30.4%
Pop. over 60	6.7%		per 1,000 pop.
No. of men per 100 women	97.8	Crude birth rate	17.3
Human Development Index	72.5	Crude death rate	5.5

The economy

GDP	D1,478trn	GDP per head	$1,050
GDP	$90.6bn	GDP per head in purchasing	
Av. ann. growth in real		power parity (USA=100)	6.0
GDP 2003–08	7.8%	Economic freedom index	49.8

Origins of GDP		Components of GDP	
	% of total		% of total
Agriculture	22	Private consumption	69
Industry, of which:	40	Public consumption	6
manufacturing	21	Investment	41
Services	38	Exports	78
		Imports	-95

Structure of employment

	% of total		% of labour force
Agriculture	52	Unemployed 2004	2.1
Industry	18	Av. ann. rate 2003–2004	2.2
Services	30		

Energy

	m TOE		
Total output	73.9	Net energy imports as %	
Total consumption	55.8	of energy use	-33
Consumption per head,			
kg oil equivalent	655		

Inflation and finance

Consumer price		av. ann. increase 2003–08	
inflation 2009	7.0%	Narrow money (M1)	22.5
Av. ann. inflation 2004–09	10.7%	Broad money	32.0
Treasury bill rate, Q1 2009	6.79%		

Exchange rates

	end 2009		December 2009
D per $	17,941	Effective rates	2005 = 100
D per SDR	28,126	– nominal	...
D per €	25,844	– real	...

Trade

Principal exports		Principal imports	
	$bn fob		*$bn cif*
Crude oil	10.2	Machinery & equipment	13.5
Textiles & garments	9.3	Petroleum products	10.0
Footwear	4.7	Steel	6.4
Fisheries products	4.5	Textiles	2.3
Total incl. others	**61.2**	Total incl. others	**77.5**

Main export destinations		Main origins of imports	
	% of total		*% of total*
United States	19.4	China	20.2
Japan	14.0	Singapore	12.1
China	7.4	South Korea	9.1
Australia	6.9	Thailand	6.3
Singapore	4.4	Hong Kong	3.4
Germany	3.4	United States	3.4
Malaysia	3.2	Malaysia	3.3

Balance of payments, reserves and debt, $bn

Visible exports fob	62.7	Change in reserves	0.3
Visible imports fob	-75.5	Level of reserves	
Trade balance	-12.8	end Dec.	24.2
Invisibles inflows	8.5	No. months of import cover	3.3
Invisibles outflows	-13.7	Official gold holdings, m oz	0.0
Net transfers	7.3	Foreign debt	26.2
Current account balance	-10.7	– as % of GDP	30
– as % of GDP	-11.8	– as % of total exports	36
Capital balance	12.3	Debt service ratio	2
Overall balance	0.5		

Health and education

Health spending, % of GDP	7.1	Education spending, % of GDP	...
Doctors per 1,000 pop.	0.7	Enrolment, %: primary	...
Hospital beds per 1,000 pop.	2.7	secondary	...
Improved-water source access,		tertiary	...
% of pop.	94		

Society

No. of households	19.5m	Colour TVs per 100 households	83.8
Av. no. per household	4.5	Telephone lines per 100 pop.	34.0
Marriages per 1,000 pop.	5.6	Mobile telephone subscribers	
Divorces per 1,000 pop.	0.2	per 100 pop.	80.4
Cost of living, Feb. 2010		Computers per 100 pop.	9.6
New York = 100	65	Internet hosts per 1,000 pop.	1.4

ZIMBABWE

Area	390,759 sq km	Capital	Harare
Arable as % of total land	8	Currency	Zimbabwe dollar (Z$)

People

Population	13.5m	Life expectancy: men	50.4 yrs
Pop. per sq km	34.5	women	49.8 yrs
Av. ann. growth		Adult literacy	91.4%
in pop. 2010–15	0.27%	Fertility rate (per woman)	3.5
Pop. under 15	39.5%	Urban population	38.3%
Pop. over 60	5.8%		per 1,000 pop.
No. of men per 100 women	93.7	Crude birth rate	30.0
Human Development Index	...	Crude death rate	12.9

The economy

GDP[a]	$3.9bn	GDP per head[a]	$310
Av. ann. growth in real		GDP per head in purchasing	
GDP 2005–08	-7.4%	power parity (USA=100)	0.4
		Economic freedom index	21.4

Origins of GDP[b]		**Components of GDP**[b]	
	% of total		% of total
Agriculture	19	Private consumption	72
Industry, of which:	24	Public consumption	27
manufacturing	14	Investment	17
Services	57	Exports	57
		Imports	-73

Structure of employment

	% of total		% of labour force
Agriculture	...	Unemployed 2004	4.2
Industry	...	Av. ann. rate 1997–2004	6.3
Services	...		

Energy

	m TOE		
Total output	8.7	Net energy imports as %	
Total consumption	9.4	of energy use	8
Consumption per head,			
kg oil equivalent	759		

Inflation and finance

		av. ann. increase 2003–08	
Consumer price			
inflation 2007	24,411%	Narrow money (M1)	1,053%
Av. ann. inflation 2004–07	2,176%	Broad money	1,044%
Treasury bill rate, 2007	248.8%		

Exchange rates

	end 2009		December 2009
Z$ per $	...	Effective rates	2005 = 100
Z$ per SDR	...	– nominal	...
Z$ per €	...	– real	...

Trade

Principal exports[ab]		Principal imports[ab]	
	$m fob		$m cif
Gold	237	Machinery & transport equip.	455
Ferro-alloys	215	Fuels	405
Tobacco	190	Manufactured products	255
Platinum	167	Chemicals	235
Total incl. others	**1,555**	Total incl. others	**2,054**

Main export destinations		Main origins of imports	
	% of total		% of total
South Africa	32.3	South Africa	59.6
Congo-Kinshasa	9.8	China	4.2
Botswana	8.7	Botswana	3.7
China	5.6	United States	3.0
Zambia	4.8	Zambia	3.0

Balance of payments, reserves and debt, $bn

Visible exports fob	1.6	Change in reserves	-0.1
Visible imports fob	-2.6	Level of reserves	
Trade balance	-1.0	end Dec.	0.0
Invisibles, net	...	No. months of import cover	0.0
Net transfers	...	Official gold holdings, m oz	0.0
Current account balance	-0.9	Foreign debt	6.0
– as % of GDP	-23.2	– as % of GDP	380
Capital balance[c]	...	– as % of total exports	302
Overall balance[c]	-0.6	Debt service ratio[a]	94

Health and education

Health spending, % of GDP	8.9	Education spending, % of GDP	4.7
Doctors per 1,000 pop.	0.2	Enrolment, %: primary	104
Hospital beds per 1,000 pop.	3.0	secondary	41
Improved-water source access,		tertiary	...
% of pop.	82		

Society

No. of households	3.4m	Colour TVs per 100 households	...
Av. no. per household	4.0	Telephone lines per 100 pop.	2.8
Marriages per 1,000 pop.	...	Mobile telephone subscribers	
Divorces per 1,000 pop.	...	per 100 pop.	13.3
Cost of living, Feb. 2010		Computers per 100 pop.	7.6
New York = 100	...	Internet hosts per 1,000 pop.	2.2

a Estimates.
b 2007
c 2001 estimates.

EURO AREA[a]

| Area | 2,573,704 sq km | Capital | – |
| Arable as % of total land | 25 | Currency | Euro (€) |

People

Population	318.6m	Life expectancy: men	76.9 yrs
Pop. per sq km	125.9	women	82.7 yrs
Av. ann. growth		Adult literacy	...
in pop. 2010–15	0.10%	Fertility rate (per woman)	1.5
Pop. under 15	15.4%	Urban population	72.8%
Pop. over 60	23.8%		per 1,000 pop.
No. of men per 100 women	95.6	Crude birth rate	10.1
Human Development Index	95.0	Crude death rate	9.7

The economy

GDP	€9,272bn	GDP per head	$41,650
GDP	$13,582bn	GDP per head in purchasing	
Av. ann. growth in real		power parity (USA=100)	72.2
GDP 2003–08	2.0%	Economic freedom index	67.8

Origins of GDP		Components of GDP	
	% of total		% of total
Agriculture	2	Private consumption	57
Industry, of which:	27	Public consumption	20
manufacturing	18	Investment	22
Services	72	Exports	41
		Imports	-39

Structure of employment

	% of total		% of labour force
Agriculture	3.7	Unemployed 2008	7.5
Industry	26.8	Av. ann. rate 1995–2008	9.1
Services	68.0		

Energy

	m TOE		
Total output	459.9	Net energy imports as %	
Total consumption	1,229.2	of energy use	63
Consumption per head,			
kg oil equivalent	3,789		

Inflation and finance

Consumer price		av. ann. increase 2003–08	
inflation 2009	0.3%	Narrow money (M1)	8.2%
Av. ann. inflation 2004–09	2.0%	Broad money	8.8%
Money market rate, 2009	1.00%	Household saving rate, 2009	12.5%

Exchange rates

	end 2009		December 2009
€ per $	0.69	Effective rates	2005 = 100
€ per SDR	1.09	– nominal	111.9
		– real	108.7

Trade[b]

Principal exports		Principal imports	
	$bn fob		*$bn cif*
Machinery & transport equip.	836.6	Machinery & transport equip.	763.8
Manufactures	465.3	Manufactures	608.3
Chemicals	301.6	Mineral fuels & lubricants	550.2
Mineral fuels & lubricants	166.3	Chemicals	186.4
Food, drink & tobacco	100.4	Food, drink & tobacco	117.7
Total incl. others	**1,924.2**	Total incl. others	**2,278.9**

Main export destinations		Main origins of imports	
	% of total		*% of total*
United States	19.1	China	16.0
Russia	8.0	United States	12.0
Switzerland	7.5	Russia	11.2
China	6.0	Norway	5.9
Turkey	4.1	Switzerland	5.2
Japan	3.2	Japan	4.8

Balance of payments, reserves and aid, $bn

Visible exports fob	2,320	Overall balance	6
Visible imports fob	-2,329	Change in reserves	12.0
Trade balance	-9	Level of reserves	
Invisibles inflows	1,521	end Dec.	522.4
Invisibles outflows	1,630	No. months of import cover	1.6
Net transfers	-142	Official gold holdings, m oz	349.2
Current account balance	-201	Aid given[c]	51.9
– as % of GDP	-1.5	– as % of GDP[c]	0.39
Capital balance	252		

Health and education

Health spending, % of GDP	9.7	Education spending, % of GDP	5.3
Doctors per 1,000 pop.	3.6	Enrolment, %: primary	...
Hospital beds per 1,000 pop.	6.0	secondary	...
Improved-water source access,		tertiary	...
% of pop.	100		

Society

No. of households	130.5	Colour TVs per 100 households	97.6
Av. no. per household	2.39	Telephone lines per 100 pop.	45.5
Marriages per 1,000 pop.	4.5	Mobile telephone subscribers	
Divorces per 1,000 pop.	1.9	per 100 pop.	122.7
Cost of living, Feb. 2010		Computers per 100 pop.	50.4
New York = 100	...	Internet hosts per 1,000 pop.	270.8

---

a Data generally refer to the 15 EU members that had adopted the euro before
   December 31 2008: Austria, Belgium, Cyprus, Finland, France, Germany, Greece,
   Ireland, Italy, Luxembourg, Malta, Netherlands, Portugal, Slovenia and Spain.
b EU27, excluding intra-trade.
c Excluding Cyprus, Malta and Slovenia.

WORLD

| Area | 148,698,382 sq km | Capital | ... |
| Arable as % of total land | 11 | Currency | ... |

People

Population	6,749.7m	Life expectancy: men	66.7 yrs
Pop. per sq km	45.4	women	71.1 yrs
Av. ann. growth		Adult literacy	82.4%
in pop. 2010–15	1.20%	Fertility rate (per woman)	2.54
Pop. under 15	26.9%	Urban population	50.4%
Pop. over 60	11.0%		per 1,000 pop.
No. of men per 100 women	101.7	Crude birth rate	20.0
Human Development Index	75.3	Crude death rate	8.3

The economy

GDP	$60.6trn	GDP per head	$9,040
Av. ann. growth in real		GDP per head in purchasing	
GDP 2003–08	3.4%	power parity (USA=100)	22.4
		Economic freedom index	56.6

Origins of GDP

	% of total
Agriculture	3
Industry, of which:	28
manufacturing	18
Services	69

Components of GDP

	% of total
Private consumption	61
Public consumption	17
Investment	22
Exports	28
Imports	-28

Structure of employment[a]

	% of total		% of labour force
Agriculture	...	Unemployed 2008	5.9
Industry	...	Av. ann. rate 1995–2008	6.6
Services	...		

Energy

	m TOE		
Total output	11,926.4	Net energy imports as %	
Total consumption	11,664.3	of energy use	-2
Consumption per head,			
kg oil equivalent	1,819		

Inflation and finance

		av. ann. increase 2003–08	
Consumer price			
inflation 2009	2.2%	Narrow money (M1)[a]	6.2%
Av. ann. inflation 2004–09	3.9%	Broad money[a]	7.6%
LIBOR $ rate, 3-month, 2009	0.69%	Household saving rate, 2009[a]	6.9%

Trade

World exports

	$bn fob		$bn fob
Manufactures	11,291	Ores & metals	645
Fuels	1,936	Agricultural raw materials	323
Food	1,290		
		Total incl. others	**16,130**

Main export destinations

	% of total
United States	12.7
Germany	7.2
China	6.2
France	4.5
Japan	4.3
United Kingdom	4.2

Main origins of imports

	% of total
China	10.3
Germany	8.8
United States	8.1
Japan	5.0
France	3.8
United Kingdom	2.9

Balance of payments, reserves and aid, $bn

Visible exports fob	16,015	Overall balance	0
Visible imports fob	15,858	Change in reserves	544
Trade balance	157	Level of reserves	
Invisibles inflows	7,906	end Dec.	7,808
Invisibles outflows	-7,796	No. months of import cover	4
Net transfers	31	Official gold holdings, m oz	955
Current account balance	298	Aid given[b]	130.6
– as % of GDP	0.5	– as % of GDP[b]	0.30
Capital balance	-333		

Health and education

Health spending, % of GDP	9.7	Education spending, % of GDP	4.6
Doctors per 1,000 pop.	1.5	Enrolment, %: primary	106
Hospital beds per 1,000 pop.	...	secondary	65
Improved-water source access,		tertiary	24
% of pop.	83		

Society

No. of households	...	TVs per 100 households	...
Av. no. per household	...	Telephone lines per 100 pop.	18.5
Marriages per 1,000 pop.	...	Mobile telephone subscribers	
Divorces per 1,000 pop.	...	per 100 pop.	59.7
Cost of living, Feb. 2010		Computers per 100 pop.	15.3
New York = 100	...	Internet hosts per 1,000 pop.	153.5

a OECD countries.
b OECD, non-OECD Europe and Middle East countries.

Glossary

Balance of payments The record of a country's transactions with the rest of the world. The **current account** of the balance of payments consists of: visible trade (goods); "invisible" trade (services and income); private transfer payments (eg, remittances from those working abroad); official transfers (eg, payments to international organisations, famine relief). Visible imports and exports are normally compiled on rather different definitions to those used in the trade statistics (shown in principal imports and exports) and therefore the statistics do not match. The **capital account** consists of long- and short-term transactions relating to a country's assets and liabilities (eg, loans and borrowings). The current account and the capital account, plus an errors and omissions item, make up the **overall balance**. In the country pages of this book this item is included in the overall balance. **Changes in reserves** include gold at market prices and are shown without the practice often followed in balance of payments presentations of reversing the sign.

Big Mac index A light-hearted way of looking at exchange rates. If the dollar price of a burger at McDonald's in any country is higher than the price in the United States, converting at market exchange rates, then that country's currency could be thought to be over-valued against the dollar and vice versa.

Body-mass index A measure for assessing obesity – weight in kilograms divided by height in metres squared. An index of 30 or more is regarded as an indicator of obesity; 25 to 29.9 as over-weight. Guidelines vary for men and for women and may be adjusted for age.

CFA Communauté Financière Africaine. Its members, most of the francophone African nations, share a common currency, the CFA franc, which used to be pegged to the French franc but is now pegged to the euro.

Cif/fob Measures of the value of merchandise trade. Imports include the cost of "carriage, insurance and freight" (cif) from the exporting country to the importing. The value of exports does not include these elements and is recorded "free on board" (fob). Balance of payments statistics are generally adjusted so that both exports and imports are shown fob; the cif elements are included in invisibles.

Crude birth rate The number of live births in a year per 1,000 population. The crude rate will automatically be relatively high if a large proportion of the population is of childbearing age.

Crude death rate The number of deaths in a year per 1,000 population. Also affected by the population's age structure.

Debt, foreign Financial obligations owed by a country to the rest of the world and repayable in foreign currency. **The debt service ratio** is debt service (principal repayments plus interest payments) expressed as a percentage of the country's earnings from exports of goods and services.

EU European Union. Members are: Austria, Belgium, Denmark, Finland, France, Germany, Greece, Ireland, Italy, Luxembourg, Netherlands, Portugal, Spain, Sweden and the United Kingdom and, as of May 1 2004, Cyprus, Czech Republic, Estonia, Hungary, Latvia, Lithuania, Malta, Poland, Slovakia and Slovenia and, as of January 1 2007, Bulgaria and Romania.

Effective exchange rate The nominal index measures a currency's depreciation (figures below 100) or appreciation (figures over 100) from a base date against a trade-weighted basket of the currencies of the country's main trading partners. The real effective exchange rate reflects adjustments for relative movements in prices or costs.

Euro area The 16 euro area members of the EU are Austria, Belgium, Finland, France, Germany, Greece, Ireland, Italy, Luxembourg, Netherlands, Portugal and Spain and, from January 1 2007,

Slovenia. Cyprus and Malta joined on January 1 2008. Slovakia joined on January 1 2009. Their common currency is the euro, which came into circulation on January 1 2002.

Fertility rate The average number of children born to a woman who completes her childbearing years.

G7 Group of seven countries: United States, Japan, Germany, United Kingdom, France, Italy and Canada.

GDP Gross domestic product. The sum of all output produced by economic activity within a country. GNP (gross national product) and GNI (gross national income) include net income from abroad eg, rent, profits.

Household saving rate Household savings as % of disposable household income.

Import cover The number of months of imports covered by reserves ie, reserves ÷ $\frac{1}{12}$ annual imports (visibles and invisibles).

Inflation The annual rate at which prices are increasing. The most common measure and the one shown here is the increase in the consumer price index.

Internet hosts Websites and other computers that sit permanently on the internet.

Life expectancy The average length of time a baby born today can expect to live.

Literacy is defined by UNESCO as the ability to read and write a simple sentence, but definitions can vary from country to country.

Median age Divides the age distribution into two halves. Half of the population is above and half below the median age.

Money supply A measure of the "money" available to buy goods and services. Various definitions exist. The measures shown here are based on definitions used by the IMF and may differ from measures used nationally. Narrow money (M1) consists of cash in circulation and demand deposits (bank deposits that can be withdrawn on demand). "Quasi-money" (time, savings and foreign currency deposits) is added to this to create broad money.

OECD Organisation for Economic Co-operation and Development. The "rich countries" club was established in 1961 to promote economic growth and the expansion of world trade. It is based in Paris and now has 31 members.

Opec Organisation of Petroleum Exporting Countries. Set up in 1960 and based in Vienna, Opec is mainly concerned with oil pricing and production issues. Members are: Algeria, Indonesia, Iran, Iraq, Kuwait, Libya, Nigeria, Qatar, Saudi Arabia, United Arab Emirates and Venezuela.

PPP Purchasing power parity. PPP statistics adjust for cost of living differences by replacing normal exchange rates with rates designed to equalise the prices of a standard "basket"of goods and services. These are used to obtain PPP estimates of GDP per head. PPP estimates are shown on an index, taking the United States as 100.

Real terms Figures adjusted to exclude the effect of inflation.

Reserves The stock of gold and foreign currency held by a country to finance any calls that may be made for the settlement of foreign debt.

SDR Special drawing right. The reserve currency, introduced by the IMF in 1970, was intended to replace gold and national currencies in settling international transactions. The IMF uses SDRs for book-keeping purposes and issues them to member countries. Their value is based on a basket of the US dollar (with a weight of 44%), the euro (34%), the Japanese yen (11%) and the pound sterling (11%).

List of countries

Wherever data is available, the world rankings consider 193 countries: all those which had (in 2008) or have recently had a population of at least 1m or a GDP of at least $1bn. Here is a list of them.

	Population	GDP	GDP per head	Area '000 sq	Median age
	m, 2008	$bn, 2008	$PPP, 2008	km	yrs, 2009
Afghanistan	28.2	10.6	1,100	652	16.9
Albania	3.2	12.3	7,290	29	30.0
Algeria	34.4	166.5	8,040	2,382	26.2
Andorra	0.1	3.7	44,900[c]	0.4	39.9
Angola	17.5	84.9	5,820	1,247	17.4
Antigua & Barbuda	0.1	1.2	20,970	0.1	29.5
Argentina	39.9	328.5	14,310	2,767	30.4
Armenia	3.0	11.9	6,080	30	32.0
Aruba	0.1	2.7	21,800[ac]	0.2	38.7
Australia	21.0	1,015.2	38,780	7,682	37.8
Austria	8.4	413.5	37,910	84	41.8
Azerbaijan	8.5	46.1	8,770	87	28.4
Bahamas	0.3	7.5	29,800[c]	14	29.7
Bahrain	0.8	21.9	34,900	1	28.1
Bangladesh	161.3	79.6	1,340	144	24.5
Barbados	0.3	3.7	18,500[c]	0.4	37.8
Belarus	9.6	60.3	12,280	208	38.2
Belgium	10.5	504.2	35,240	31	41.3
Belize	0.3	1.4	6,740	23	22.3
Benin	9.3	6.7	1,470	113	18.4
Bermuda	0.1	6.4	69,900[ac]	0.1	41.6
Bhutan	0.7	1.3	4,760	47	24.2
Bolivia	9.7	16.7	4,280	1,099	21.9
Bosnia	3.9	18.5	8,100	51	39.3
Botswana	1.9	13.4	13,570	581	22.8
Brazil	194.2	1,575.2	10,300	8,512	29.0
British Virgin Islands	0.0	1.1	38,500[ac]	0.01	32.6
Brunei	0.4	14.5	50,820[a]	6	27.8
Bulgaria	7.6	49.9	11,790	111	41.7
Burkina Faso	15.2	7.9	1,160	274	16.7
Burundi	8.9	1.2	380	28	20.3
Cambodia	14.7	10.4	1,950	181	22.3
Cameroon	18.9	23.4	2,200	475	19.2
Canada	33.2	1,501.3	39,080	9,971	39.9
Cape Verde	0.5	1.6	3,200	4	21.3
Cayman Islands	0.1	2.8	43,800[ac]	0.3	38.4
Central African Rep	4.4	2.0	740	622	19.5
Chad	11.1	8.4	1,340	1,284	17.1
Channel Islands	0.2	11.5[a]	49,790[a]	0.2	42.2
Chile	16.8	169.5	14,440	757	32.1
China	1,336.3	4,327.0	5,970	9,561	34.2
Colombia	46.7	243.8	8,800	1,142	26.8

	Population	GDP	GDP per head	Area '000 sq	Median age
	m, 2008	$bn, 2008	$PPP, 2008	km	yrs, 2009
Congo-Brazzaville	3.8	10.7	3,950	342	19.5
Congo-Kinshasa	64.7	11.7	310	2,345	16.6
Costa Rica	4.5	29.7	11,230	51	28.2
Côte d'Ivoire	19.6	23.4	1,650	322	19.5
Croatia	4.6	69.3	17,660	57	41.6
Cuba	11.3	62.7	9,700	111	38.3
Cyprus	0.9	24.9	26,920	9	36.5
Czech Republic	10.2	215.5	24,640	79	39.6
Denmark	5.5	341.3	36,850	43	40.8
Dominican Republic	9.9	45.5	8,130	48	25.0
Ecuador	13.5	54.7	8,010	272	25.4
Egypt	76.8	162.3	5,430	1,000	23.9
El Salvador	7.0	22.1	6,800	21	23.9
Equatorial Guinea	0.5	18.5	33,900	28	19.3
Eritrea	5.0	1.7	640	117	19.1
Estonia	1.3	23.4	20,650	45	39.6
Ethiopia	85.2	25.6	870	1,134	18.0
Faroe Islands	0.1	2.5	48,200[c]	1	37.1
Fiji	0.8	3.6	4,360	18	25.0
Finland	5.3	272.7	36,200	338	42.0
France	61.9	2,856.6[b]	33,060	544	40.1
French Guiana	0.2	4.0[a]	14,810[a]	90	24.0
French Polynesia	0.3	6.1[a]	18,000[ac]	3	28.5
Gabon	1.4	14.5	14,580	268	21.6
Gambia, The	1.8	0.8	1,360	11	18.8
Georgia	4.4	12.8	4,970	70	37.6
Germany	82.5	3,649.5	35,370	358	44.3
Ghana	23.9	16.7	1,460	239	20.6
Greece	11.2	355.9	29,360	132	41.6
Greenland	0.1	1.7	35,400[ac]	2,176	25.0
Guadeloupe	0.5	11.5[a]	23,270[a]	2	36.6
Guam	0.2	2.5[ac]	15,000[ac]	1	29.2
Guatemala	0.8	39.0	4,760	109	18.8
Guinea	13.7	3.8	1,060	246	18.5
Guinea-Bissau	9.6	0.4	540	36	18.7
Guyana	1.7	1.2	3,060	215	27.4
Haiti	9.8	7.2	1,120	28	21.6
Honduras	7.2	13.3	3,930	112	20.9
Hong Kong	7.3	215.4	43,960	1	41.9
Hungary	10.0	154.7	19,790	93	39.8
Iceland	0.3	16.7	36,900	103	35.1
India	1,186.2	1,159.2	2,950	3,287	25.0
Indonesia	234.3	510.7	3,990	1,904	28.2
Iran	72.2	346.6	10,970[a]	1,648	26.8
Iraq	29.5	23.7	3,600[ac]	438	19.3
Ireland	4.4	267.6	41,850	70	34.6
Israel	7.0	202.1	27,910	21	29.7

	Population	GDP	GDP per head	Area '000 sq	Median age
	m, 2008	$bn, 2008	$PPP, 2008	km	yrs, 2009
Italy	58.9	2,303.1	31,280	301	43.3
Jamaica	2.7	14.6	7,720	11	26.3
Japan	127.9	4,910.8	34,130	378	44.7
Jordan	6.1	21.2	5,470	89	22.8
Kazakhstan	15.5	133.4	11,320	2,717	29.4
Kenya	38.6	30.4	1,550	583	18.4
Kosovo	1.8	5.4	2,500ac	11	26.3
Kuwait	2.9	148.0	48,270a	18	30.6
Kyrgyzstan	5.4	5.1	2,190	199	25.1
Laos	6.0	5.5	2,120	237	20.6
Latvia	2.3	33.8	16,360	64	40.0
Lebanon	4.1	29.3	11,780	10	29.2
Lesotho	2.0	1.6	1,560	30	19.8
Liberia	3.9	0.8	390	111	18.5
Libya	6.3	93.2	16,210	1,760	26.2
Lithuania	3.4	47.3	17,750	65	39.8
Luxembourg	0.5	53.7	78,920	3	39.3
Macau	0.6	21.8	59,480	0.02	38.3
Macedonia	2.0	9.5	9,340	26	36.0
Madagascar	20.2	9.5	1,050	587	18.4
Malawi	14.3	4.3	810	118	16.8
Malaysia	27.0	221.8	14,220	333	26.3
Maldives	0.4	1.3	5,600	0.3	24.4
Mali	12.7	8.7	1,130	1,240	17.6
Malta	0.4	8.3	21,140a	0.3	39.0
Martinique	0.4	11.2a	22,910a	1	38.7
Mauritania	3.2	2.9	1,920a	1,031	20.1
Mauritius	1.3	9.3	12,360	2	32.6
Mexico	107.8	1,088.1	14,570	1,973	27.6
Moldova	3.8	6.0	2,980	34	35.2
Mongolia	2.7	5.3	3,560	1,565	26.3
Montenegro	0.6	4.9	13,390	14	35.9
Morocco	31.6	88.9	4,260	447	26.2
Mozambique	21.8	9.8	840	799	17.9
Myanmar	49.2	28.7	1,100ac	677	27.9
Namibia	2.1	8.8	6,400	824	21.1
Nepal	28.8	12.6	1,100	147	21.6
Netherlands	16.5	871.0	40,960	42	40.8
Netherlands Antilles	0.2	3.8	16,000ac	1	38.4
New Caledonia	0.3	9.3	15,000ac	19	30.3
New Zealand	4.2	129.9	27,260	271	36.6
Nicaragua	5.7	6.6	2,690	130	22.0
Niger	14.7	5.4	680	1,267	15.0
Nigeria	151.5	207.1	2,100	924	18.6
North Korea	23.9	13.3	1,900ac	121	34.0
Norway	4.7	451.8	58,710	324	38.9
Oman	2.7	52.6	22,700a	310	24.3

	Population	GDP	GDP per head	Area '000 sq	Median age
	m, 2008	$bn, 2008	$PPP, 2008	km	yrs, 2009
Pakistan	167.0	164.5	2,540	804	21.3
Panama	3.4	23.1	12,500	77	27.3
Papua New Guinea	6.5	8.2	2,180	463	20.0
Paraguay	6.2	16.0	4,700	407	23.1
Peru	28.2	129.1	8,510	1,285	25.6
Philippines	89.7	166.9	3,510	300	23.2
Poland	38.0	527.9	17,280	313	38.2
Portugal	10.7	243.5	23,250	89	41.0
Puerto Rico	4.0	97.5	17,200[c]	9	36.0
Qatar	0.9	114.0	121,700[c]	11	30.1
Réunion	0.8	18.7[a]	19,110[a]	3	30.2
Romania	21.3	200.1	13,450	238	38.5
Russia	141.8	1,679.5	15,920	17,075	38.1
Rwanda	10.0	4.5	1,030	26	18.7
St. Lucia	0.2	1.0	9,840	0.6	27.5
Saudi Arabia	25.3	468.8	23,990	2,200	24.6
Senegal	12.7	13.3	1,790	197	18.0
Serbia	9.9	50.1	10,550	88	37.6
Sierra Leone	6.0	2.0	780	72	18.2
Singapore	4.5	181.9	49,320	1	40.6
Slovakia	5.4	98.5	22,140	49	37.2
Slovenia	2.0	54.6	27,870	20	41.7
Somalia	9.0	2.7	600[ac]	638	17.6
South Africa	48.8	276.4	10,120	1,226	24.9
South Korea	48.4	929.1	27,660	99	37.9
Spain	44.6	1,604.2	31,670	505	40.2
Sri Lanka	19.4	40.6	4,560	66	30.6
Sudan	39.4	55.9	2,160	2,506	20.3
Suriname	0.5	3.0	7,400	164	27.6
Swaziland	1.1	2.8	4,930	17	19.3
Sweden	9.2	479.0	36,960	450	40.9
Switzerland	7.5	491.9	42,420	41	41.9
Syria	20.4	55.2	4,580	185	22.5
Taiwan	22.9	391.2	29,800	36	37.0
Tajikistan	6.8	5.1	1,910	143	20.7
Tanzania	41.5	20.5	1,300	945	17.5
Thailand	64.3	272.4	8,090	513	33.2
Timor-Leste	1.2	0.5	800	15	17.4
Togo	6.8	2.9	830	57	19.8
Trinidad and Tobago	1.3	24.1	25,170	5	30.8
Tunisia	10.4	40.3	7,960	164	29.1
Turkey	75.8	734.9	13,420	779	28.3
Turkmenistan	5.0	15.3	6,630	488	24.7
Uganda	31.9	14.3	1,170	241	15.6
Ukraine	45.9	180.4	7,280	604	39.5
United Arab Emirates	4.5	286.9	56,580[a]	84	31.7
United Kingdom	61.0	2,674.1	35,470	243	39.9

	Population	GDP	GDP per head	Area '000 sq	Median age
	m, 2008	$bn, 2008	$PPP, 2008	km	yrs, 2009
United States	308.8	14,093.3	46,350	9,373	36.6
Uruguay	3.4	32.2	12,740	176	33.7
Uzbekistan	27.8	27.9	2,660	447	24.5
Venezuela	28.1	314.2	12,820	912	26.1
Vietnam	88.5	90.6	2,790	331	28.5
Virgin Islands (US)	0.1	1.6[ac]	14,500[ac]	0.4	38.5
West Bank and Gaza	4.1	6.2	2,900[ac]	6	17.6
Yemen	23.1	26.6	2,420	528	17.8
Zambia	12.2	14.3	1,360	753	16.8
Zimbabwe	13.5	3.9	200[ac]	391	19.0
Euro area (15)	318.6	13,581.6	33,450	2,497	41.8
World	6,749.7	60,557.0	10,390	148,698	29.1

a Latest available year.
b Including French Guiana, Guadeloupe, Martinique and Réunion.
c Estimate.

Sources

Academy of Motion Picture Arts and Sciences

AFM Research

Airports Council International, *Worldwide Airport Traffic Report*

Bloomberg

BP, *Statistical Review of World Energy*

Business Software Alliance

CB Richard Ellis, *Global MarketView Office Occupancy Costs*

Central Bank Directory

Central banks

Central Intelligence Agency, *The World Factbook*

CIRFS, *International Rayon and Synthetic Fibres Committee*

Corporate Resources Group, *Quality of Living Report*

The Economist
www.economist.com

Economist Intelligence Unit, *Cost of Living Survey*; *Country Forecasts*; *Country Reports*; *E-readiness rankings*; *Global Outlook – Business Environment Rankings*

ERC Statistics International, *World Cigarette Report*

Euromonitor, *International Marketing Data and Statistics*; *European Marketing Data and Statistics*

Eurostat, *Statistics in Focus*

Food and Agriculture Organisation

The Heritage Foundation, *Index of Economic Freedom*

IFPI

IMD International, World Competitive Centre, www.imd.ch/wcc

IMF, *International Financial Statistics; World Economic Outlook*

International Centre for Prison Studies, *World Prison Brief*

International Cocoa Organisation, *Quarterly Bulletin of Cocoa Statistics*

International Coffee Organisation

International Cotton Advisory Committee, *Bulletin*

International Diabetes Federation, *Diabetes Atlas*

International Grains Council

International Institute for Strategic Studies, *Military Balance*

International Labour Organisation

International Obesity Task Force

International Rubber Study Group, *Rubber Statistical Bulletin*

International Sugar Organisation, *Statistical Bulletin*

International Tea Committee, *Annual Bulletin of Statistics*

International Telecommunication Union, *ITU Indicators*

International Union of Railways

Johnson Matthey

Mercer, *Quality of Living Survey*

National statistics offices

Network Wizards

Nobel Foundation

OECD, *Development Assistance Committee Report; Economic Outlook; Environmental Data; Revenue Statistics*

www.olympic.org

Population Reference Bureau

Reporters Without Borders, *Press Freedom Index*
Reuters Thomson

Space.com
Standard & Poor's *Emerging Stock Markets Factbook*

Taiwan Statistical Data Book
The Times, *Atlas of the World*
Transparency International

UN, *Demographic Yearbook*; *Global Refugee Trends*; *Review of Maritime Transport*; *State of World Population Report*; *Survey on Crime Trends*; *World Contraceptive Use*; *World Population Database*; *World Population Prospects*; *World Urbanisation Prospects*
UNAIDS, *Report on the Global AIDS Epidemic*
UNCTAD, *Review of Maritime Transport*; *World Investment Report*
UNCTAD/WTO International Trade Centre
UN Development Programme, *Human Development Report*

UNESCO, Institute for Statistics
Unicef, *Child Poverty in Perspective*
Union Internationale des Chemins de Fer, *Statistiques Internationales des Chemins de Fer*
US Census Bureau
US Department of Agriculture
University of Michigan, Windows to the Universe website

WHO, *Global Tuberculosis Report*; *Immunisation Summary*; *World Health Statistics Annual*
World Bank, *Doing Business*; *Global Development Finance*; *World Development Indicators*; *World Development Report*
World Bureau of Metal Statistics, *World Metal Statistics*
World Economic Forum/Harvard University, *Global Competitiveness Report*
World Resources Institute, *World Resources*
World Tourism Organisation, *Yearbook of Tourism Statistics*
World Trade Organisation, *Annual Report*